The Virginia Landscape

The Virginia Landscape

A CULTURAL HISTORY

James C. Kelly and William M. S. Rasmussen

HOWELL PRESS

Charlottesville, Virginia

Designed by Carolyn Weary Brandt

Publisher's Cataloging-in-Publication
(Provided by Quality Books, Inc.)

Kelly, James C., 1949-
    The Virginia landscape : a cultural history /
James C. Kelly and William M. S. Rasmussen. — 1st
ed.
        p. cm.
    Includes bibliographical references and index.
    ISBN: 1-57427-110-5 (hbk.)
    ISBN: 1-57427-115-6 (pbk.)

    1. Landscape drawing, American—Virginia—
History. 2. Virginia—In art—History.
I. Rasmussen, William M. S. (William Meade Stith),
1946-   II. Title.
N8214.5.V8K45 2000   704.9436′755
                        QBI00-341

Printed in China

09 08 07 06 05 04 03 02 01 00   10 9 8 7 6 5 4 3 2 1

Published by Howell Press, Inc.
1713-2D Allied Lane
Charlottesville, VA 22903
(804) 977-4006
http://www.howellpress.com

Cover:
David Johnson, **Natural Bridge**, 1860, oil on canvas, 30 x 24 in.
(Courtesy of C. Kevin Landry)

Back cover:
Rockwell Kent, **Child Under Tree, Virginia**, 1956, oil on canvas, 28 x 34 in.
(Virginia Historical Society, Lora Robins Collection of Virginia Art)

This book is dedicated to

Lora Robins

With affection and gratitude for her vision to establish

The Lora Robins Collection of Virginia Art

CONTENTS

FOREWORD

The Virginia Historical Society is known for its distinguished collection of portraits, now numbering nearly a thousand, acquired since 1831, almost always by gift. When I became director, however, there were fewer than a dozen landscapes, of varying quality, and none at all of such landmarks as Natural Bridge. To fill this gap, the Society would need access to the rapidly escalating market in landscape art. Yet, we lacked the means. Then a remarkable woman stepped forward with a vision of her own that generously enabled us to fulfill our dream. That person is Lora Robins. Over the past five years, she has purchased for us nearly one hundred history paintings and landscapes, many of the latter reproduced in this volume.

Indeed, she is largely responsible for this book, because it always was conceived as a companion to an exhibition of Virginia landscapes. That exhibition never would have been undertaken, at least not by the Virginia Historical Society, without the core collection of landscape paintings that now constitute the Lora Robins Collection of Virginia Art. Accordingly, this book is dedicated to her.

The Virginia landscape is exceptionally beautiful and diverse, comprehending some of the fairest portions of the continent—seashore, tidal land and waters, piedmont, valley, mountains, and every gradation among them. In the 1800s this embarrassment of visual riches defined the commonwealth in the public consciousness, both inside and outside its borders, as much as did Virginia's already rich historical associations.

As the authors James C. Kelly and William M. S. Rasmussen make clear, however, landscape pictures are no foolproof guide to Virginia history. They are selective and unrepresentative in what they depict. Some things are depicted often, others never. But, besides being works of art, landscapes are historical documents that, carefully scrutinized, yield historical insights as much as written materials or archaeological evidence. The Virginia Historical Society prides itself on the comprehensiveness of its holdings, so it is fitting that landscapes should now take their place alongside portraits, history paintings, books, manuscripts, maps, sheet music, museum objects, advertising, political memorabilia, and all the other categories of material we hold for study and display.

At first glance, this may appear to be an art book and, indeed, some pictures are analyzed for their artistic proper-

ties. The real subject, however, is the landscape itself and Virginians' and visitors' perceptions of it through time. It is not a full monographic treatment. For that we await a book in progress by Professor Stephen Adams of the University of Minnesota. Instead, what the reader will find here is an extended, and I think entertaining, essay, an introduction to a vast, complex, and rewarding subject. I offer my sincere appreciation to Drs. Kelly and Rasmussen for conceiving this splendid exhibition and for once again demonstrating their abilities as first-rate scholars and curators.

There is no substitute for seeing these works of art in person at the exhibition at the Virginia Historical Society (13 July–13 November 2000) or later at the Art Museum of Western Virginia in Roanoke, but for those unable to do so this handsome volume will enable you, vicariously, to partake of these significant works and to experience something of the natural beauty they represent.

Charles F. Bryan, Jr.
Director
Virginia Historical Society

ACKNOWLEDGMENTS

Our greatest debt is to Lora Robins. Her vision and generosity have made possible the society's collection of Virginia art that is named for her. Her paintings form the core around which this exhibition is formed.

We thank our principal advisers for this project, Robert Mayo and Dr. R. Lewis Wright. Bob Mayo has observed the art scene in Virginia for decades; R. Lewis Wright is author of *Artists in Virginia before 1900* as well as several articles about Virginia artists. David Meschutt pointed us to landscapes and their locations. Stephen Adams of the University of Minnesota at Duluth generously shared with us his research on literature and art about the Virginia landscape. Daniel J. Philippon provided us with copies of the catalogue for an exhibition that he curated at the University of Virginia Library in 1997. That show was based on his work with Michael P. Branch that was published in 1998 as *The Height of Our Mountains: Nature Writing from Virginia's Blue Ridge Mountains and Shenandoah Valley*, a publication that we refer to often. Beverley W. Reynolds of Reynolds Gallery helped us to locate a number of works by contemporary Virginia artists.

This exhibition was underwritten by generous grants from the National Endowment for the Arts, the E. Rhodes and Leona B. Carpenter Foundation, the Robins Foundation, and the Virginia Commission for the Arts.

At the Virginia Historical Society, Dr. Nelson D. Lankford edited this book. AnnMarie Price gathered the illustrations for it and arranged the shipping for the exhibition. E. Lee Shepard, Robert F. Strohm, Frances Pollard, and Janet Schwarz located significant books and manuscripts in the society's collection. E. Lee Shepard also shared his research on the Virginia springs. In the Reading Room, Tom Illmensee and Michelle McClintick pulled a large volume of material for us in a short amount of time. Bryan Green answered our questions about the art of photography and arranged for needed in-house photography. Ron Jennings took many of the photographs for this book. Canan Boomer translated German for us. Stacy Gibford-Rusch conserved works on paper. Dale Kostelny installed the exhibition. We also thank Pamela R. Seay, the society's director of development, and Patricia Morris, formerly its grants officer, for securing the needed funding. Maribeth Cowan, director of public affairs, and William B. Obrochta, director of educational services, also contributed.

We especially want to thank our director, Dr. Charles F. Bryan, Jr., for his unswerving support of the project and his confidence in us.

We also have been aided by the staff at many museums, galleries, libraries, and institutions. We are particularly indebted to Parker Agelasto, Eva Ahladas, Linda Ayres, Kenneth W. Barnes, Carrie Rebora Barratt, Barbara Batson, Mary Lynn Bayliss, Graham W. J. Beal, David S. Berreth, Nanine Bilski, Lynne Bjarnesen, Richard Born, Lorraine Brevig, Lisa Browar, Louise T. Brownell, Ronald J. Burch, Linda M. Cagney, Edward D. C. Campbell, Jr., Julie A. Campbell, Sarah Cash, Joanna D. Catron, Melanie Christian, Louise Keith Claussen, Malinda Collier, Robert S. Conte, Jack Cowart, Barbara Crawford, David Curry, John A. Cuthbert, Nancy Davis, Stuart P. Feld, Genevieve Fisher, Sherry French, Jay Gates, Elizabeth M. Gushee, Jonathan P. Harding, William J. Hennessey, Robert M. Hicklin, Jr., Jenni Holder, Raymond E. Holland, Julian D. Hudson, Joseph Jacobs, Brock Jobe, Audrey C. Johnson, Carol Marie Johnson, Denise J. H. Johnson, Michael Kammen, Ray Kass, Peter M. Kenny, Ted J. Kleisner, Carol Lawson, Thomas J. Litzenburg, Barbara Luck, Linda Merrill, Sarah Bevan Meschutt, Lewis N. Miller, Jr., Donald Moomaw, Roddy Moore, Leslie A. Morris, Cleo Mullins, Libby Myers, William Myzk, Michelle S. Peplin, Earl A. Powell, III, Sue Rainey, Bradford L. Rauschenberg, Sue Welsh Reed, William S. Reese, Theresa Roane, Barbara Rothermel, Gail Serfaty, Pamela H. Simpson, Peter Tatistcheff, Kimberly Terbush, James Tottis, Saul Viener, Richard Waller, Catherine Jordan Wass, Debra G. Wieder, Jeanne Willoz-Egnor, and Jon Zachman. We also thank the chairmen of the art departments at the state's colleges and universities for advising us concerning the landscape artists active in the second half of the twentieth century. We should also mention that for every contemporary artist mentioned here, there are two or three others whom we did not have space to include.

At Howell Press, we wish to thank Ross Howell for taking on this ambitious project, which is tied to a tight schedule, and Carolyn Brandt for her design of the book.

James C. Kelly
William M. S. Rasmussen

Their rype corne

Their greene corne.

Corne newly sprong.

Their sitting at meate

the place of solemne prayer.

The howse wherin the Tombe of their Herounds standeth

SECOTON.

A Ceremony in their prayers with strange iesturs and songs dansing abowt posts carued on the topps lyke mens faces.

1.1 John White, *Indian Village of Secoton*, 1585–86, watercolor, 12 ¾ x 7 ¾ in. (Courtesy of the British Museum)

I

LAND WITHOUT LANDSCAPE: COLONIAL VIRGINIA

"Landscapes are . . . constructs of the imagination projected onto wood and water and rock."
　　　　—Simon Schama, *Landscape and Memory*

While the land may be eternal, or nearly so, landscape requires a human observer. When one thinks about it, nature is but a random display of rocks, trees, and grasses. We compose these into landscapes in our minds, using prevailing aesthetic ideas.[1] Accordingly, the eons that passed before mankind were eras of land without landscape. The coming of man brought landscape into being, but it did not necessarily result in the creation of landscape art. The English artist John Constable said that "there has never been an age, however rude or uncultivated, in which the love of landscape has not in some way been manifested."[2] If so, this love often was *not* expressed as landscape art. As Kenneth Clark has noted, "People who have given the matter no thought are apt to assume that the appreciation of natural beauty and the painting of landscape is a normal and enduring part of our spiritual activity. But the truth is that in times when the human spirit seems to have burned most brightly the painting of landscape for its own sake did not exist and was unthinkable."[3]

In Virginia, ninety-nine percent of the history of *human* habitation is without any landscape art. From its first coming perhaps sixteen thousand years ago until the arrival of Europeans, the indigenous population apparently created no landscape art. The first Europeans neither encountered any such works, nor did the native people ever claim to have had any. Of course, they drew maps that reflected their geographical understanding, but these merely recorded the *location* of places, not their *appearance.*

The absence of landscape art hardly signified indifference to the land. Indeed, identifying with the spirits of plants and animals and even inanimate objects, the Indians lacked the detachment from nature that seems to have been among the preconditions for recording it. They saw themselves as part of nature, not apart from it, and certainly not above it.

Contrary to myth, the Indians often had intervened in the environment, but they lacked the Europeans' sense of a divine mandate to subdue nature.

More surprising than the lack of aboriginal landscape art is its absence during fully half of Virginia's European history. The first English colonists were evolving into that secular, detached, scientific, yet possessive culture that would develop landscape art, but they were not there yet. True, John White, artist of the Roanoke colony from 1585 to 1586, did produce a watercolor of the Algonquin town of Secoton that is a landscape (fig. 1.1). This setting is in what we now call North Carolina, but which then was called Virginia. In its own day this watercolor was not conceived as a work of art, and it is both more and less than a landscape. The Indian village has been tidied up in keeping with European pictorial conventions and also, perhaps, to attract support to the colony. It is ordered and essentially symmetrical, more so than any European town. The engravers made White's scene even more appealing—to investors—by adding a patch of tobacco. Within a small space one sees not only the Indians' architecture, but also their horticultural and spiritual activities. The corn is shown in three stages— newly planted, green, and ripe. Unlike the first settlements the English would build, Secoton seems to have no palisade wall sharply dividing it from the adjoining countryside. But the Indians themselves, not the landscape, were White's principal subjects. Renaissance man that he was, the proper study of mankind was man.

In the early 1600s, Theodor de Bry published engravings of events in Virginia, such as "Pocahontas Visited by Her Brothers," but the landscape is merely suggested in a very schematic and totally inaccurate way (fig. 1.2). The incident with Pocahontas took place along the Pamunkey River, where it narrows to virtually a channel and the forest grows close to its banks; this landscape was unknown to the artist, who never set foot in the colony. De Bry's 1618 scene of hawking and hunting in Virginia is more detailed and perhaps was based on verbal descriptions by those who had

1.2 Unknown artist, ***Pocahontas Visited by Her Brothers***, c. 1634, engraving, 5⅝ x 7½ in., published in the de Bry family, *America*. (Virginia Historical Society)

been to the New World, but essentially it is an imaginative backdrop to the human action in the print (see fig. 4.14 below). Likewise, a 1675 engraving of the killing of the Jesuits in Virginia in 1571 merely depicts a generic setting—a dark, forested, threatening scene appropriate for the brutal action.[4]

During the ninety-two years that Jamestown was Virginia's capital (1607–99), there is no image of it or any other place in the colony. Even more surprising is that during the eighty-one years that Williamsburg was the capital (1699–1780), there is no image of it. A Swiss traveler did crude sketches of a few of the buildings in 1701, and the so-called Bodleian plate of thirty years later likewise records elevations of specific buildings, but none of these show the structures' surroundings. Why? The aesthetic appreciation of the land for its own sake had not yet developed. In all the propagandist literature describing Virginia as "earth's only paradise" there is not a single graphic depiction of the place. As Samuel Eliot Morison wrote, the English were more interested in the bounties than the beauties of nature.[5] Theirs was a paradigm of utility. Ralph Hamor and John Rolfe *did* catalog the natural resources of the new Eden. Where we see trees they saw lumber. Where we see mountains they saw minerals. They saw a warehouse of commodities, not an ecosystem. The first Virginia is remembered as the Roanoke colony, and it is worth noting that in Algonquin "roanoke" means "money." The first account of Virginia, written by Thomas Hariot and published by Theodor de Bry, originally in French, was

entitled *Merveilleux and Étrange Rapport, Toutefois Fidèle, des Commoditez qui se Trouvent en Virginia (Marvelous and Strange Report, Completely Accurate, of the Commodities That Are Found in Virginia)*. Nature itself was of little interest; it was not valued unless it yielded natural resources, especially ones that England lacked and needed, which could be sold for profit. About these the literature was immense. But of emotional responses to the environment there were none.

To give credit where it is due, the Chinese were the first people among whom landscape developed as a proper subject for art. In western civilization, landscape painting emerged during the Renaissance, and Pieter Bruegel the Elder in the 1560s was perhaps the first to make it a major branch of painting. The word landscape first appeared in print in English in 1584. The Dutch, Flemings, and Italians developed the genre in the 1600s. The former specialized in scenes of bourgeois serenity that later would be considered picturesque. Claude Lorrain, a Frenchman working in Rome (and hereafter referred to as Claude), developed another kind of picturesque view when he composed classical scenes of the pastoral or Arcadian ideal. The Italian Salvator Rosa produced landscapes of erupting volcanoes and tempests that later would be called sublime; Dutch artists did the same with comparable mountain scenery and with views of storm-tossed seas.

During the 1600s landscape art came to be appreciated in England. A third of Charles I's famous collection of paintings were landscapes. Later in the century, after the Restoration of 1660, and particularly after the Glorious Revolution of 1688, which augmented the power of the aristocracy and gentry, there developed a self-confidence and pride in land ownership that promoted the popularity of

English landscape painting. The constant enlargement of geographical knowledge, and the exposure of Englishmen to foreign lands and landscape art, also contributed.

But the appreciation of rural scenery that exploded in England in the 1700s depended on a knowledge of painting. It was a sophisticated taste. Scenery was admired for its resemblance to paintings rather than the other way around. A view was called a landscape because it resembled what the Dutch first called a "landschap" picture (which the English colloquialized at first as "landskip"). A view was "picturesque" because it was like a picture by Claude. To us today, the cart was indeed before the horse.

Although no landscapes were drawn in Virginia in the 1600s, neither were any done of Quebec, Florida, or the Mississippi territories being explored by Robert, Sieur de la Salle. Inventories taken at death reveal that some Virginia homes of that time had "pictures," but whether these were paintings or prints, and whether any were landscapes, is unknown. Most no doubt were prints, the subjects of which were wide ranging, from views of English scenery and cities to episodes from mythology and, by the eighteenth century, genre by William Hogarth. In 1649 William Moseley of lower Norfolk County, who before his emigration from England had traded with Rotterdam, brought twenty-two pictures to Virginia; many were portraits of family, and four were said to be by Anthony van Dyck, but a few could have been landscapes. In 1669 John Brewer of Isle of Wight County had "12 small pictures." Thomas Madestard of Lancaster in 1675 was also an owner of pictures. In 1692 Edward Digges of York had "6 pictures." David Fox of Lancaster, at his death in 1690, had "3 pictures in the parlor and 25 Pictures of the Sences in the hall"; these must have been prints.[6]

John Swann of Lancaster County in 1711 left "a prospect of the City of London." Capt. William Rogers of Yorktown in 1739 had "a Dutch picture in a gilt frame," seven "cartoons," four "glass pictures," and three "small pictures." Alexander Spotswood, the former lieutenant governor, in 1740 had "26 prints Overton's Theatrum Passion," as well as sixty-two "prints with glasses." Col. John Tayloe of Richmond County in 1747 had "a sett of Rubens Gallery of Lusenburgh." Maj. Harry Turner of King George in 1751 had sixty-nine pictures "in gilt frames." In 1757 George Washington of Fairfax ordered from London "1 neat Landskip," an oil painting in the tradition of Claude that is still at Mount Vernon. Col. John Tabb of Elizabeth City in 1762 owned one dozen prints in frames. John Pleasants of Cumberland in 1765 owned "The Ten Seasons" and "a prospect of Philadelphia." In 1767 George Johnston of Fairfax left six Hogarth prints; Adam Menzies of Northumberland County left seven engravings of Raphael's tapestry cartoons, four large prints in gilt frames, and one small print. In 1775 Professor Henley of the College of William and Mary advertised for sale "a portfolio of engravings, etchings and Mezzotints—all fine impressions and many of them proofs by [after] the most celebrated Masters." William Hunter of Williamsburg had on the eve of the Revolution a "sea piece," a landscape, a large picture of the "Ruins of Rome," nineteen prints, and two small pictures. This evidence is fragmentary and sometimes cryptic but clear enough: many of the "prints" inventoried in colonial Virginia were not even landscapes, and nearly all of the imagery that hung on the walls in colonial Virginia houses was made in the Old World and pictured Old World subjects. The Virginia landscape was not the subject of the day.[7]

1.3 Unknown artist, ***Imaginary Landscape***, painted overmantle from Morattico, Richmond County, c. 1720s, oil on board. (Courtesy of the Henry Francis du Pont Winterthur Museum)

1.4 Attributed to John Hesselius, **_James Gordon_**, c. 1750, oil on canvas, 48 1/8 x 38 1/4 in. (Virginia Historical Society)

We do know from a 1731 inventory that Robert Dowsing of York County had "8 pictures on landskips."[8] These, too, may have been prints, although the inventory also lists "sixteen painting boards covered with canvas," indicating that Dowsing was a painter. In 1751 John Keeff advertised in Williamsburg's _Virginia Gazette_ as a landscape painter who also painted heraldry. Henry Warren, however, advertised there in 1769 that he would paint almost anything, "landscapes excepted." In 1773, Charles Tinsley advertised that his servant painted landscapes. A year later Thomas Campbell touted himself, like Keeff, as a painter of both landscapes and heraldry.[9] What landscape commissions these men received, if any, probably were for imagined, ideal views like those that decorated the paneling of Marmion, a mid-eighteenth-century house in King George County, now preserved in part at the Metropolitan Museum of Art in New York City.[10] At Morattico, a Virginia house of the 1720s, the overmantel featured an imaginary landscape with mansion, garden walls and gates, hunters

departing, and clearly delineated portions of tamed and untamed land that reflected the English mind-set (fig. 1.3).[11] Ideal landscapes also found their way into Virginia portraits. One of the best known is that of George Booth of Gloucester, c. 1748–50, in which an idealized and rigidly formal garden appears as the background. It must have been invented, because the imagery is even more fanciful than any mezzotint source that would have provided the artist a point of departure.[12] In all likelihood, the background in the portrait of James Gordon, attributed to John Hesselius c. 1750, is borrowed from a London engraving (fig. 1.4). Both subject and artist were far more interested in projecting an affinity to Old World gentility than with the New World environment.

From an early date, then, Virginia gentlemen would have been familiar with landscape art through prints, as well as through their travel to England. Among the many prints listed in the early Virginia inventories must have been a number of the popular engravings of the seats of the English noblemen and gentlemen—works of topographical transcription that embodied ideals of ordered, hierarchical liberty, and of land at the service of man. Members of the Virginia gentry, although they shared those beliefs, do not seem to have commissioned any such pictures of their own residences. An intriguing hint of how such pictures would have appeared is given in an early map of Westover plantation showing geometric gardens that flanked an early house on the property at a cross-axis perpendicular to the James River (fig. 1.5). The plan is bold yet orderly and stands in

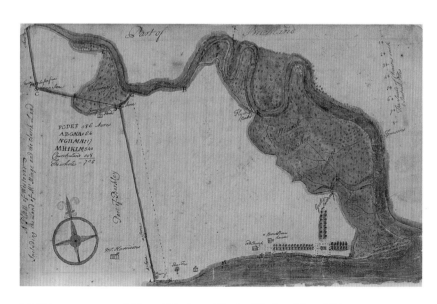

1.5 Unknown surveyor, **_A Plan of Westover_** (Charles City County), c. 1731, ink and wash. (Virginia Historical Society)

1.6 Capt. Thomas Davies, *A View of the Town of York Virginia from the River*, c. 1755, watercolor, 13 x 20 in. (Courtesy of The Mariners' Museum)

1.7 Capt. Thomas Davies, *A View of the Town of Gloucester York River Virginia*, c. 1755, watercolor, 13 x 20 in. (Courtesy of The Mariners' Museum)

contrast to the irregular lines of the natural terrain that in this map threaten to engulf what seems a tiny outpost of civilization in a vast wilderness.

By mid-century, several of the other American colonies already had true landscapes of local subjects. "A South Prospect of the Flourishing City of New York" was painted in 1717 and issued as an engraving in 1719 or 1720.[13] The first view of Philadelphia appeared about 1720.[14] More surprisingly, so did one of the French outpost at New Biloxi on the Gulf coast.[15] A prospect or panorama of New Orleans, another French colony, was done in 1726.[16] A year earlier the first landscape of Boston was executed, also issued as a print.[17] In 1726 the same artist drew "A Prospect of the Colledges [*sic*] in Cambridge in New England."[18] The first landscape of Charleston seems to

have been done between 1735 and 1739.[19]

Mostly, these panoramas of city skylines were promotional. "The South East Prospect of the City of Philadelphia," done about 1720, was designed to promote the city's commerce in London.[20] The "East Prospect of the City of Philadelphia," commissioned about 1750 by Thomas Penn, proprietor of Pennsylvania, aimed at increasing both investment and immigration.[21] William Burgis's "View of the Lighthouse" at Boston appeared in 1729 as a print dedicated to the merchants of Boston whose wares presumably were secured by erection of this first American beacon.[22] Bishop Roberts's "Prospect of Charles Town," South Carolina, was engraved in London and published with text extolling the prosperity and products of the port.[23]

Apparently, the first true landscapes of Virginia are

four views, produced about 1755, of the towns of York and Gloucester (figs. 1.6 and 1.7) and of Capes Henry and Charles. These were anomalies for the colony, the product of a fortuitous visit by an amateur artist of no small talent, Capt. Thomas Davies of the British army. The fact that views of Virginia came thirty or forty years after some other colonies probably is because, though no other colony then equaled Virginia in population, Virginia had no cities of the size of Philadelphia, New York, Boston, or Charleston. It would seem that Davies arrived in Virginia with the armada that brought Edward Braddock and his army to capture Fort Duquesne and thereby end the French and Indian War, because his four watercolors were bound in a manuscript entitled "Voyage of HMS *Success* and HMS *Norwich* to Nova Scotia and Virginia 1754–56"; the *Norwich* carried Braddock.[24] While waiting for Braddock's return, which of course never happened, Davies apparently had the opportunity to visit Yorktown and Gloucester. Trained at the Royal Military Academy at Woolwich as a topographical artist, this officer was exceptional in that he would soon develop from that rough beginning into a remarkably capable watercolorist. Davies served four tours of duty in North America, until 1790, commanding artillery troops against the rebellious colonists during the American Revolution and, during his free moments before and after the war, producing views of such natural wonders as Niagara Falls, the Falls of the Passaic, and the Chaudière Falls near Quebec. This work was of sufficient quality for it to be exhibited at the Royal Academy in London and to earn him election to the Royal Society in 1781 and to the Linnean Society.[25]

Davies no doubt was attracted to Yorktown and Gloucester because these two towns that flank the York River formed something of a trade center; at least here was as much of an urban commercial setting as was to be found in colonial Virginia, Norfolk excepted. In "A View of the Town of York Virginia from the River," Davies shows the expanse of the settlement and is able to suggest a sense of its prosperity, albeit by means of the somewhat naive style of a developing artist. A traveler to these towns in 1736 described this setting:

> We discovered the red clifts of York Town, and the opposite Town of Gloucester; and [to be] sure, nothing could form a more romantic sight. The

place being somewhat situated like Dover. . . . Yorktown . . . tho but stragglingly built, yet makes no inconsiderable figure. You perceive a great air of opulence amongst the inhabitants, who have some of them built themselves houses, equal in magnificence to many of our superb ones at St. James's; as those of Mr. Lightfoot, Nelson, etc. . . . Gloucester, Hampton and Norfolk are towns of near the same structure, there being little difference, save at the last mentioned place, a spirit of trade reigns, far surpassing that of any other part of Virginia.[26]

We have no indication as to whether Davies sketched Norfolk. At any rate, cities were what attracted the first landscapists, and the first travel writers, in colonial America; natural landmarks would wait their turn. It happened that Davies was also one of the first to do the latter, though not in Virginia.

The purpose of the early panoramas, those by Davies included, was primarily documentary, not aesthetic. At least in the colonies, landscape art was still primarily utilitarian. These works were first of all topographical transcriptions. As such, they ranked near the bottom of Sir Joshua Reynolds's hierarchy of paintings enumerated in his Third Discourse to the Royal Academy in December 1770. "A mere copier of nature," said Reynolds, "can never produce any thing great; can never raise and enlarge the conceptions, or warm the heart of the spectator."[27] Serious artists felt obliged to rearrange the topography for effect.

Most of the artists in early Virginia were not Virginians, or even Americans. We may effectively have achieved our political independence in 1781—the year a French soldier at Yorktown sketched that place, thereby producing the first souvenir art of Virginia—but our cultural independence was much longer in coming. After Yorktown, Virginians and their fellow Americans turned around in an intellectual sense and faced the interior of their own continent. Previously, we had spoken of our own hinterlands as the *back settlements*, the *back parts*, or the *back country*. The fact that they were seen as the back rather than the front tells us which way Virginians were facing. Where once we had identified with our origins, we came to identify with our destinations.[28] These were manifestations of a sense of American identity that took root after the Revolution and established the basis for an American artistic, and landscape, tradition.

It was a gradual process, however, and for nearly half a century after the Revolution English artists and travelers continued to be major actors in the story of Virginia's landscape art. Even by late in the nineteenth century a school of resident landscape artists had not formed. There were many reasons for this. There had been an agricultural depression that made the landscape of eastern Virginia seem less than Eden. There was a slave population on this land that in the same way negated the idyllic illusion. There were no urban centers peopled with wealthy merchants, as in New York, Philadelphia, or Baltimore, who would purchase scenes of the landscape that their urban environment denied them. Transportation remained difficult in the far reaches of the state. After the Civil War the editor of the *Southern Review* mused on why the beautiful South had so few artists while "stern, harsh, unlovely New England" had so many? He concluded that the South's relative poverty could not be the whole explanation because, before the war, there were many rich people in the South.[29] Much of their wealth, however, was tied up in land and slaves before the war and, afterward, the property in slaves was expropriated without compensation. It would be nearly the twentieth century before Virginia had a class of New South capitalists and entrepreneurs with ready cash to buy landscapes to cover the walls of their increasingly ostentatious homes. But even then they rarely bought any.

Nonetheless, the editor was correct in searching for causes apart from poverty. In Virginia at least, the reason that seems predominant is the overwhelmingly rural character of the state. In nineteenth-century America and through half of the twentieth century, the people who bought landscapes were city folk. Not until after World War I did Virginia have true metropolises, and it is only in such large cities that the infrastructure of museums, galleries, patrons, and other artists exists in which any branch of painting can thrive. Thus, until well into the 1900s, the story of landscape painting in Virginia will mostly concern visitors to the commonwealth who took their sketches back home to finish and sell.

Today there is a flourishing "Virginia School" of landscape artists, which was put into place largely by the state's colleges and universities when they established departments of art at mid-century. But earlier there was not, so that our survey will often reflect a national perspective of which Virginia may be seen as a microcosm. The Deep South may have been an "exotic other," an antithesis to the national norms with its swamps and bayous, but Virginia, apart from the ever-diminishing Great Dismal Swamp, was different. Yet, it was long a land with slaves, and that mattered. It was never northern, but not wholly southern. It was Virginian, and most of its people thought nothing could be better. Their attitude is well reflected in some doggerel ending in the verse:

> *And I believe that happy land*
> *The Lord's prepared for mortal man*
> *Is built exactly on the plan*
> *Of old Virginia.*[30]

2.17 William James Bennett after George Cooke, ***Richmond,
from the Hill above the Waterworks***, 1834, aquatint, 17 $^7/_8$ x
25 in. (Virginia Historical Society)

II

Methods of the Artists

"Taste . . . is far from a simple and determinate idea in the minds of most men."

—Edmund Burke, *Philosophical Enquiry into the Origins of Our Ideas of the Sublime and the Beautiful*, 1757

Early European Ideals: The Sublime and the Picturesque

*I*n the late eighteenth century, when artists first directed serious attention to the Virginia landscape, a revolutionary change was taking place in man's approach to the arts. For more than three hundred years the philosophy revived by Renaissance artists and architects had guided aesthetic thought; this was the viewpoint of the ancient Romans and Greeks that beauty could be defined in terms of qualities that are inherent in the object. A building, for example, was beautiful if it conformed to fixed rules, like those about symmetry, proportion, and the relationship of the parts to the whole that were put into writing by the Roman architect Vitruvius. In the eighteenth century the tables were turned, in that interest shifted from the object to the emotional response of the viewer. The term "romantic," which is often used to describe the period that followed, means in this context an appeal to the emotions.[1] The classical approach had attempted to bring order and symmetry to the landscape and to those works of architecture and art that were added to it; this no longer seemed adequate, or at least that philosophy now seemed restrictive and incomplete. New avenues of thought were opened. Man yearned to acknowledge the presence of those natural forces that he could not control, to look outside the classical canon of order to discover different beauties in nature and in art, and to reach for goals that lay beyond his immediate grasp. The pursuit of idealistic goals would be addressed in any number of art forms, including the music of Ludwig van Beethoven and the poetry of Lord Byron. The new approaches to the landscape, which would help to establish

this as the dominant genre of painting in the nineteenth century, were centered around ideals that were called the Sublime and the Picturesque. These quickly made their way to America.

Of the published explanations that explored these new ideas about the arts, the one that was the most influential was Edmund Burke's *Philosophical Enquiry into the Origins of Our Ideas of the Sublime and the Beautiful*, first issued in 1757 and then republished routinely for decades. The ideal of beauty, Burke argued, cannot be confined within classicist rules about symmetry, proportion, and harmony; beauty is found in any number of things small, smooth, varied in form, delicate, fragile, or clear and brightly colored that "induce in us a sense of affection and tenderness." The British statesman-to-be questioned whether beauty "be at all an idea belonging to proportion"; a swan, for example, is beautiful despite the disproportion of its neck and tail, as is a large rose that grows upon a small shrub. Burke placed under the complementary heading of the Sublime a different type of pleasure, the one that results from knowing of perils that pose no immediate threat to the viewer. "The passions which belong to self-preservation turn on pain and danger," Burke wrote, "they are delightful when we have an idea of pain and danger, without being actually in such circumstances . . . . Whatever excites this delight I call *sublime*. The passions belonging to self-preservation are the strongest of all the passions." Burke said that terror, obscurity, power, vastness, infinity, magnitude, light, darkness, sound, suddenness, and the cries of animals are all associated with the Sublime.[2] The Beautiful had little application for landscape painters, although a garden designer could devise a plan with rounded shapes and graceful curves akin to William Hogarth's nonclassical "line of beauty."[3] But the Sublime was encountered not infrequently in nature. This term could be evoked to help the artist or traveler come to grips intellectually with powerful forces, like a storm at sea, an avalanche, or a wild cataract; with extremes encountered in the landscape, like total stillness or total darkness, or the great size or height of a mountain; and with death and the passage of time. The cultural historian Kenneth Clark has identified a common ground for these phenomena; he defines the Sublime as relating to those savage incomprehensible powers of nature that make us aware of the futility of human arrangements.[4] Throughout the nineteenth century two landmarks in America, Niagara Falls and the Natural Bridge, were almost universally accepted as being truly sublime. But many travelers in Virginia were quick to also associate the Sublime with their experiences at other sites, including Harpers Ferry, the Great Falls of the Potomac, the Peaks of Otter, and several of the subterranean caves.

Burke did not address the ideal of the Picturesque, which was developed instead by his contemporaries. One of them, the Reverend William Gilpin, suggested that objects with rough surfaces and irregular outlines are distinct and of sufficient interest to form a subcategory of the Beautiful; he thought that such objects possessed "picturesque beauty." Although such a term would have effectively described the varied but gentle landscapes composed by Claude, as we will soon observe, the idea seemed confusing to Sir Uvedale Price, who suggested instead that a third principal category was needed for the channeling of aesthetic thought, that of the Picturesque. To Price, picturesque landscapes were rough, irregular, and characterized by sudden variation.[5] His readers accepted the term, which soon came to be used as an adjective with regard to landscapes, meaning "like or suitable for a picture," a picture with interesting elements that are well composed. The specific pictures that everyone had in mind were the landscapes of the Italian countryside that had been painted by Claude in the seventeenth century. Claude's work was surprisingly well known by those artists who carried the ideal of the Picturesque to America.

Perhaps ironically, these picturesque landscapes were rooted in the traditions of the Renaissance that seemed so inadequate to eighteenth-century connoisseurs. Renaissance aesthetes believed that every canvas, including landscapes, had to aspire to a high ideal, be it religious, historical, or poetic. For the latter type, which was the more difficult to conceive, they found inspiration in the writings of the Roman poet Virgil, who displayed a delicate sensitivity to nature and imbued the landscape with an enchanting myth, that of a rustic Golden Age of the past when man lived on the fruits of the earth in peaceful simplicity.[6] A few Renaissance artists, including Giorgione, were able to visualize the golden light and quiet harmony of such an Arcadia, but those painters produced few pure landscapes and their work was much less accessible than that of Claude, who not only perpetuated the myth of Arcadia but painted it many times during a long career.

Like all who appreciated Claude, Englishmen in Italy on the Grand Tour were attracted by the remarkable tonality of light in his canvases; this unifies all elements of the landscape and makes the artist's poetic vision of a Virgilian Golden Age seem almost convincing. They also were impressed by Claude's vision of how nature could be laid out like a park for the enjoyment of man, complete with architectural fragments that speak about the ancient civilizations that they saw as part of their heritage. The English tourist carried home both Claude's canvases and his perception of how to view nature. Although the essential features of the English or landscape garden, which replaced the axial Continental type, already were developed, the paintings by Claude at least inspired patrons and designers to continue in the same direction.[7] The paintings also provided the developing English school of landscape artists with a model to follow; in that way, and in turn, the model made its way to Virginia. Travelers, both in England and in America, began to search the landscape for views that seemed picturesque; they would critique nature as if it were a work of art.

Because the Claudian model underlies so many of the images that appeared in nineteenth-century Virginia, it is useful to define it here, if for no other reason than to measure the success of the followers. Claude routinely structured his canvas like a stage set that has coulisses on either side; these serve to lead the eye, gradually and gently, through planes of space. On one side is usually a large and dark tree, the shadow of which extends across and defines the foreground. The middle plane is established by the placement on the opposite side of a second coulisse, perhaps a group of trees. The eye is lured across water through two additional planes, the second of which is distant and luminous.[8] Because water was a key element in Claude's formula, he painted a number of seaport scenes for which his structure remained essentially the same; as for the coulisses, towering ships and great classical buildings replaced the trees.

2.1 Claude Joseph Vernet, *Entrée dans la Baye de Chesapeak dans l'Amerique*, after 1781, engraving, 7 x 8 $^{15}/_{16}$ in. (Virginia Historical Society)

Curiously, the most Claudian views of the Virginia landscape are two imaginary port scenes that were painted by an eighteenth-century French follower of Claude. "Entrée dans la Baye de Chesapeak" (fig. 2.1), by Claude Joseph Vernet, is a Claudian pastiche built up with the expected coulisses and distant view. Vernet imagined that Cape Henry, or perhaps Cape Charles, enjoyed a harbor guarded by medieval fortifications. His "Port de Fredericsbourg, Virginia," the other Virginia image in what was a series of American views conceived in France, is an even more obvious recasting of a Claudian scene. Vernet no doubt selected the first subject because at Yorktown a French fleet that controlled the capes forced the surrender of Lord Cornwallis to combined French and American forces under the command of George Washington. The residency of Washington's mother in Fredericksburg may be what made the port town of Fredericksburg of interest to the artist. Vernet's canvases were engraved to answer the curiosity of the French people to learn something about conditions in Virginia, even though the imagery contributed only fantasy.

The Sublime in Virginia

In his *Notes on the State of Virginia*, published in 1785, Thomas Jefferson brought to the attention of an international audience both the Natural Bridge and the idea of its sublimity. He had purchased the bridge from the king of England in 1774 in order to safeguard and make accessible to visitors what he recognized as a natural treasure; he knew this landscape well. A decade later, as he penned his *Notes*, which were a response to a French request for information about the state, Jefferson reasoned, no doubt correctly, that Virginia would receive the acclaim that was due to Natural Bridge only if he described it, as he did, as "the most sublime of nature's works." Stressing the idea of sublimity, he used terminology that would be understandable to the reader of Edmund Burke and that clearly was borrowed from that source:

> Few men have resolution to . . . look over into the abyss. You involuntarily fall on your hands and feet, creep to the parapet, and peep over it. Looking down from this height about a minute, gave me a violent head ach. If the view from the top is painful and intolerable, that from below is delightful in an equal extreme. It is impossible for the emotions, arising from the sublime, to be felt beyond what they are here: so beautiful an arch, so elevated, so light, and springing, as it were up to heaven, the rapture of the spectator is really indescribable![9]

This brief account was remarkably successful in establishing renown for the bridge, which it accomplished by luring others to the site who in turn wrote about it and sketched it, mimicking Jefferson's ideas about sublimity.

One of the first of many visitors from America and Europe who traveled to view Natural Bridge was the Marquis de Chastellux, who following the French victory at Yorktown arrived at the site predisposed to experience there the Sublime: "All this apparatus of rude and shapeless Nature . . . attacks at once the senses and the thoughts, and excites a gloomy and melancholy admiration," he wrote.[10] Two decades later William Roberts, a now obscure English painter, created a remarkable image of the bridge that exaggerates its sublimity in a way that conforms to Jefferson's account (fig. 2.2). The artist painted both Natural Bridge and Harpers Ferry on canvases (now lost) that he gave to the president; in 1808 he referred to Jefferson's "approbation of my design to have [the two scenes] engraved."[11] Roberts had allied himself to the president, and his print did much to promulgate the Jeffersonian interpretation of the bridge. It was copied in 1828 by the French scientist and artist Jacques Gérard Milbert in a lithograph that adds little to Roberts's view, only three small Indian figures who serve to suggest the element of extended time, which is itself a sublime idea. In Milbert's account of his

2.2 J. C. Stradler after William Roberts, ***Natural Bridge***, 1808, aquatint, 32 $\frac{1}{4}$ x 24 $\frac{1}{2}$ in. (Courtesy of the Museum of Early Southern Decorative Arts)

travels he wrote about the bridge in the manner that Jefferson did:

> To appreciate its true grandeur one must contemplate its gigantic proportions and savage majesty, the crown of superb trees on the summit, the curious accidents of the fracture, the green curtain stretching at the base. . . . The traveler is suddenly terrified to find himself on the edge of an apparently bottomless abyss.[12]

Milbert entered one additional thought that is sublime, that

the bridge will someday fall. In this way he came close to the modern explanation that Natural Bridge was formed when most of a limestone cavern collapsed.

Many artists recognized the Sublime at Natural Bridge. To cite another example, the Lexington photographer Michael Miley, in response to the type of imagery that was produced by the painters and draftsmen who were his competition, also chose to exaggerate the image of the bridge, in at least one of his many views of it (fig. 2.3). With

2.3 Michael Miley, *Natural Bridge*, c. 1880–90, carbon print, 13 $\frac{1}{2}$ x 10 in. (Virginia Historical Society)

light and shade Miley is able to suggest that the bridge tilts. He further manipulated his image by working the glass plate to give better visual evidence that the rock sides of it have been shaved away with the passage of time. To enhance the effect of mood in this image he used carbon printing, which gives this photograph its unusual tint. As with Roberts and Milbert, small figures serve to establish the massive scale of the bridge. It would appear that Miley was aware of the Roberts-Milbert image and deliberately set out to duplicate that type of exaggeration by means of the camera, because he also photographed the bridge in a more traditional way and printed those images in albumen to give a less obtrusive tint.

One of the more insightful interpretations of the sublimity of Natural Bridge was offered in 1816 by the accomplished author James Kirke Paulding, who under-stood Edmund Burke's emphasis on emotions instead of the objects that kindle them. Paulding complained that Jefferson had written "so inexcusably correct" a description of the bridge that "none can expect to rival him, and therefore the less I say about it the better"; he then went on

to match the president in a lengthy explanation as to how "my knees shook under me" when looking down and how from below "I was struck with a feeling of sublimity which no object I have ever seen had hitherto inspired." Echoing the English aesthetes of the eighteenth century, Paulding stressed that "we cannot measure the extent of our feelings of the sublime, by calculating the dimensions of any object; it is the effect, and not the cause, that furnishes the criterion of sublimity." He said that what evokes the Sublime at Natural Bridge is "a feeling independent of magnitude, and dimensions"; this emotion comes from a combination of causes—the admirable "simplicity" of the form of the bridge, its "unbroken" surface that suggests "duration," and its name that "quick as lightning" invites a comparison between "the lofty work of nature" and the works of man:

> All the views of the Natural Bridge that I have seen are utterly deficient in conveying a tolerable idea of the general aspect and expression of this admirable scene, which seems calculated to mortify the pride of man, by proving that neither his imagination or his art is capable of conveying even a remote idea of its majestic beauty.[13]

At Natural Bridge, then, man is aware of the futility of human arrangements.

Most who visited the bridge, at least in the early nineteenth century, reacted to its sublimity. According to an account of 1842 by Archibald Alexander, a minister: "Although I have conversed with many thousands who had seen the Natural Bridge; and although the liveliness of the emotion is very different in different persons; yet I never saw one, of any class, who did not view the object with considerable emotion." He described his own response as "sudden" and "entirely new" to him; it was the "animal sensation which accompanied the genuine emotion of the sublime."[14]

One of the sensations experienced at Natural Bridge that was not noted by Paulding or Alexander, but was recorded by others, was that of "peace and calm."[15] This agrees with Jefferson's mention of distant views there that are "delightful in an equal extreme." It conforms as well with an interpretation offered in 1870 that while Niagara Falls represents "the sublime as allied to the terrific," because of its sound and fury, Natural Bridge "associates the sublime with the pleasing and curious." At the bridge but not at the falls one enjoys "the grandeur and beneficence and variety of Nature."[16]

The visitor to Natural Bridge did not necessarily limit his thoughts to Edmund Burke's Sublime, with its emphasis on peril and delight; the grandeur of the bridge might also inspire him to consider the Divinity. The calmness of the surrounding landscape encouraged such an idea. When Chastellux looked for evidence as to how the bridge was created, he wrote, "it is to the labor only of the Creator that we owe the magnificent construction of the Natural Bridge." A visitor to the bridge in 1851, who previously "did not think it could be so sublime," was now "sure no one could view that splendid arch without a feeling of awe, and a thought of the wisdom of its Creator."[17]

Edmund Burke reluctantly offered at least a few thoughts about the Almighty. In the section of his book where he discusses power as a source of the Sublime, he links God with the emotion of terror. He wrote, "To be struck with his [God's] power, it is only necessary that we should open our eyes," but in the process "we shrink into the minuteness of our own nature, and are, in a manner annihilated before him."[18] When early Americans saw God in the landscape, even in its most powerful elements, they may have felt humility, but they were not rendered helpless as Burke said that they would be; they responded instead with reverence. James Kirke Paulding, who had described the Sublime at Natural Bridge perhaps better than Jefferson, explained the American's perspective: "The voice of nature, uttered amid rocks, and mountains, and roaring floods, is the voice of God, and as we listen to it, we become wiser and better."[19]

Paulding's remark was offered as he penned his observations about Harpers Ferry, another site that Thomas Jefferson introduced to an international audience through his *Notes* and that he evaluated in terms of the Sublime. For Jefferson this setting evokes the passions of self-preservation if the viewer is able to imagine its magnificent creation, at which time, as he argued in *Notes*, two rivers must have broken through a range of mountains:

> The passage of the Potowmac through the Blue ridge is perhaps one of the most stupendous scenes in nature. You stand on a very high point of land. On your right comes up the Shenandoah, having ranged along the foot of the mountain an hundred miles to

> seek a vent. On your left approaches the Potowmac, in quest of a passage also. In the moment of their junction they rush together against the mountain, rend it asunder, and pass off to the sea. The first glance of this scene hurries our senses into the opinion, that this earth has been created in time; that the mountains were formed first; that the rivers began to flow afterwards; that in this place particularly they have been dammed up by the Blue Ridge of mountains, and have formed an ocean which filled the whole valley; that, continuing to rise, they have at length broken over at this spot and have torn the mountain down from its summit to its base.[20]

Jefferson justified what would become his famous judgment that "this scene is worth a voyage across the Atlantic" by interpreting the elements of this landscape as "monuments of a war between rivers and mountains, which must have shaken the earth itself to its center." The thought of what would have been akin to a great flood or a tidal wave is of course sublime, as is the idea of the immense amount of time that would have been taken to create this landscape.

One artist who depicted Harpers Ferry as scenery that evokes the Sublime was the modern photographer Aubrey Bodine (fig. 2.4). Standing with his camera near the spot where Jefferson did, Bodine shows the convergence of the two rivers, while he introduces a new element, history, by picturing the town's cemetery; this had expanded considerably since the eighteenth century. Bodine matched Jefferson's vision when he imagined highly dramatic atmospheric conditions that he almost certainly never saw at Harpers Ferry; the artist is known to have pieced together scenery and skies that he photographed in different regions of the country.

Many who were drawn to Harpers Ferry by Jefferson's account were disappointed with what they found there. A foreign visitor, Count Carlo Vidua, could excuse the Sage of Monticello because he "never saw Switzerland or Italy"; he added that "Americans have a habit of exalting their own things."[21] William Gilmore Simms, a leading literary figure of the Old South, was critical of the "extravagance of admiration" that he had read in *Notes*. Jefferson, he said, was "no little of a humbug" for talking about "the sublimity and grandeur of a scene, which in no place rises above the picturesque." The rivers, Simms argued, "neither rive, nor rend, nor rage, nor roar among the rocks."[22] The

2.4 Aubrey Bodine, *Harpers Ferry*, c. 1950, gelatin silver print, 9 1/8 x 12 in. (Virginia Historical Society)

traveler Isaac Weld understood that Jefferson "had beheld the scene, not in its present state, but at the very moment when the disruption happened, and when every thing was in a state of tumult and confusion"; nonetheless, he was "far from thinking with Mr. Jefferson."[23]

Other visitors to Harpers Ferry, however, agreed with Jefferson's assessment of the sublimity of the site. James Kirke Paulding "was more than satisfied with the reality." He added that the "lofty barriers of solid rock" there are "both rugged, and of the full height of sublimity."[24] Another traveler wrote that "every body has been telling me . . . that I should be disappointed, that the scene was by no means as grand as [Jefferson] described it." He asked what other scenery could be "as wonderful or grand," adding, as Jefferson might have, that "you cannot see it without reflecting on the means by which it was caused."[25]

It is entirely possible that these widely varying impressions of Harpers Ferry were influenced in no small part by the time of year that each visitor was there, and by whether or not the rivers were at flood stage. William A. Blake, writing in his book *The Blue Ridge* (1977), explains that "with the passing seasons, the rivers and their effects on the land change in sometimes profound ways." The colors of the water vary, and fogs and mists come and go.

The amount and speed of the water varies even more:

> When the rivers are in flood, as they are each year, the quantity and power of their flow in this constricted place is nothing short of awesome. No flood-control dams impound either river, and when nature wills it, the floods passing through the Potomac Water Gap are just as ferocious as they always have been. . . . The increase of the Potomac's flow in flood is fantastic. At 11:30 P.M. on the night of June 23, 1972 (during Hurricane Agnes), the river was pouring 347,000 cubic feet of water per second through the Blue Ridge—roughly thirty-seven and a half times its normal average flow. On March 19, 1936, a maximum flow of 480,000 cubic feet per second (fifty-two times normal and the greatest since record keeping began) passed the same spot. Confined to roughly its normal channel by the cliffs of the Blue Ridge, the Potomac produced a tremendous surge. The ground seemed to tremble, the damp air reeked with the smell of mud, and the very sight of the river so suggested power that standing near it was somehow a matter of pure nerve.[26]

The passions of self-preservation are easily aroused by a river that surges so powerfully that it makes the viewer tremble, if not the ground as well.

The waters from Harpers Ferry form another excep-

2.5 William Russell Birch, *Falls of the Potomac*, c. 1800–10, pencil and watercolor, 6 x 8 ¹/₂ in. (Courtesy of Corcoran Gallery of Art)

2.6 Andrew J. Russell, *Great Falls, Potomac River, March 1864, General View, showing large quantities of Ice in foreground*, 1864, albumen print, 9 ¹/₂ x 15 ³/₄ in. (Virginia Historical Society)

tional landscape where they cross the fall line. Today the Great Falls of the Potomac attract little attention, but early travelers in Virginia found the setting sublime; no doubt many approached it with thoughts of Niagara on their minds. Jefferson said of the falls only that they are "of very great descent."[27] The Englishman William Birch, who had exhibited in London before relocating in Philadelphia in 1794, envisioned them as a wild cataract that would endanger the visitor (fig. 2.5). In 1803 the artist was in northern Virginia to sketch George Washington's home. There he would have seen George Beck's large oil painting of the Great Falls, which still hangs at Mount Vernon and must have inspired both Birch's visit to the falls and his romantic characterization of them.

In the account of his American travels Jacques

Milbert quoted an earlier visitor to the Great Falls who had discovered the significance of a seasonal viewing of the Potomac. There was only one time to see the full sublimity of these "savage and romantic" cataracts: "If [the traveler] happens to visit this area at the close of winter, the picture is even more terrifying and sublime, for enormous masses of ice dash on the rocks with a horrible din."[28] The Civil War photographer Andrew J. Russell, anxious to create an image that would effectively evoke sublimity, pictured these "large quantities of Ice," as he points out in his title (fig. 2.6). Russell peopled the scene with figures whose gestures serve to underscore the awesome nature of the spectacular rocks and crashing water of the falls, in case the artist's point might be missed. He struggled with the limitations of his medium; with aperture wide open, Russell tried to capture the movement of the water, and he did stop the action of a few of the smaller falls that trickle between rocks. But the camera failed to freeze the movement of most of the river, and the trade-off for the quick exposure is that large areas of composition beyond the foreground remain indistinct; there was too little time for the details in those areas to be recorded on the plate. Even if he was only moderately successful in replicating his vision of the falls, there can be no doubt as to how Russell perceived this landscape.

The Peaks of Otter, located in the Blue Ridge Mountains near where the James River crosses, attracted more than a few visitors who described their experience there in terms of the Sublime, not only because the view from its pinnacle is vast but also because simply standing there seemed to be fraught with the sort of dangers that Burke said excite delight. To reach the top of the steepest peak, the viewer had to scale great boulders that appeared to rest there precariously. This unusual setting, which seemed to elevate its climber into the heavens and isolate him there "over a tremendous abyss, into which we hardly dared to look," was illustrated by Thomas Moran for the readers of Edward King's *The Great South* (fig. 2.7). In King's account the passions of self-preservation were brought into play: "We could not help fancying that some of the masses of stone . . . might fall and crush us." "Under the great dome of the translucent sky we stood trembling, shut off from the lower world, and poised on a narrow pinnacle, from which we might at any moment, by an unwary step, be hurled down." The word sublime was used in this passage

2.7 Thomas Moran, *The Summit of the Peak of Otter, Virginia*, 1874, wood engraving, $4^{1}/_{2}$ x $3^{1}/_{8}$ in. (Virginia Historical Society)

to describe the sensation of "seeming suspension in mid-air."[29] A second visitor, also there in the 1870s, said that this "effect of sublimity [was] perhaps unequaled by any mountain view in the world":

> There are many mountains higher than where we stood; there are others, it may be, with more merit or interest in the surroundings; but none, we imagine, which produce so terribly sublime an emotion of suspension in the sky. . . . The traveler stands up in the great hollowness of the sky, alone, naked in the dead air. It is not the common intoxication of a pinnacle; it is the awful sublimity of an insecure suspension. . . .[30]

Atop that pinnacle the views were remarkable; they inspired thoughts of divinity in a place where ideas about the Sublime were not only compatible with religious faith, but almost mandated by the evangelical Protestantism that swept Virginia after the Second Great Awakening in the early 1800s. "Boundless space seemed spread out before me," wrote a traveler in 1851.[31] Another called the panoramic view "the finest in the world," adding that "besides magnificent distances, the Tourist often witnesses the thunder storm hundreds of feet below, shrouding the earth from the eye, and encircling the Mountain with its livid fire," and that the spectacles of sunrise and sunset were "soul-inspiring, and beyond doubt the grandest on which human eye is permitted to gaze!"[32] This was a place that inspired religion, as a different visitor recounted: "My enjoyment increased to the highest point of enthusiasm, as I communed with nature. . . . Soon the thoughts of the infinite majesty of the Creator of all I looked upon . . . entered my mind and overpowered me."[33] Yet another traveler carried this idea further:

> I was impressively reminded of the extreme littleness with which these things of earth would all appear, when the tie of life which binds us here, is broken, and we shall be able to look back, and down, upon them from another world. The scene and place are well calculated to excite such thoughts. It is said that the eccentric John Randolph once spent the night on these elevated rocks, attended by no one but his servant; and that when, in the morning, he witnessed the sun rising over the majestic scene, he turned to his servant, and impressively charged him, 'never to believe any one who said there was no God!'[34]

The anecdote about Randolph was repeated in several of the

2.8 David Hunter Strother, ***The Great Valley***, 1857, wood engraving, 6¼ x 4½ in. (Virginia Historical Society)

accounts that were written about the Peaks. In the event that the religiosity of the experience might be lost on some of his viewers, Thomas Moran posed his figure at the summit in the form of Christ on the cross.

In 1856 *Harper's Magazine* published a series of five articles by David Hunter Strother, under his nom de plume Porte Crayon, that are a fictional report of a trip that he had taken in the Valley, accompanied by three young women. Included on the itinerary were the Peaks of Otter. Strother not only provided the physical characteristics of this landmark (the location, estimated height, and appearance), but he also recreated for the reader the experience of a visit. With characteristic wit that made the author immensely popular and caused this series to be reissued in 1857 as *Virginia Illustrated*, Strother acknowledged the sublimity of the view from the Peaks while at the same time lampooning his countrymen's obsession with that ideal. "The isolation from the earth is seemingly as complete as if you were sailing in a balloon," he wrote, "as if the rocks upon which you stood were floating in air." Strother then reveled in Porte's response to his companions: "Girls, there must be something in our altitude calculated to produce a corresponding loftiness of sentiment. I am in a state of exaltation—overflowing with patriotism." Strother's humor found its way into one of the illustrations that he drew, for which he provided a fitting caption (fig. 2.8):

On the rock they formed a group at once picturesque

and characteristic. Every eye kindled as it swept the boundless horizon, and, by a common impulse, Crayon took off his cap, and the girls spread scarf and kerchief to the breeze, waving an enthusiastic salute to the fair and generous land.—Dead indeed must be his soul, who, standing upon that peak, could not feel full justification for such enthusiasm.[35]

Another landscape that inspired thoughts of the Sublime in the mind of the nineteenth-century Virginia traveler was that of the subterranean cave. Following the discovery around 1804 of Weyer's Cave, the many visitors there responded to the darkness, stillness, and sense of isolation that they encountered with the mix of fear and delight that Burke had associated with the passions of self-preservation. At this strange setting the dangers of the unknown and of becoming lost were real, or at least they seemed so. The discovery in 1878 of even larger caverns at Luray carried such thoughts of the Sublime into the twentieth century.

Sometimes it is much easier to describe the sensation of the Sublime than it is to illustrate a landscape that evokes it; this is true certainly with such catastrophic forces of nature as a typhoon, tidal wave, or avalanche, or with the stillness or the vastness of a landscape. It is also true of the subterranean cave. Harry Fenn, working in 1872 for *Picturesque America*, was more successful than most artists in suggesting the darkness and stillness of the interiors at Weyer's Cave (fig. 2.9).

2.9 Harry Fenn, ***Cleopatra's Needle and Anthony's Pillar***, 1872, wood engraving, 9⅛ x 6⅜ in. (Virginia Historical Society)

Written evidence of the nineteenth-century reaction to the Virginia caverns is abundant. In the text that accompanied Fenn's illustration, Sallie A. Brock described her experience at Weyer's Cave: "A chill creeps over one upon entering, and he feels an intensity of awe as he looks forward, beyond the dim, flickering lights in the sconces, to the profound darkness which spreads its impenetrable gloom in the distance"; there is "sullen stillness," "darkness which can almost be felt," and the feeling of being "entirely cut off from the living world." At the so-called Bottomless Pit "a torch dropped in seems to twinkle away into infinite nothingness, and a stone let fall returns no sound to the waiting listener."[36] Caroline Howard Gilman had entertained similar thoughts when she visited: "the darkness, the stillness, and the echo that every sound calls forth in this subterraneous world, were to us most striking; they give the scene its sublimity."[37] Samuel Mordecai listed a plethora of emotions to be experienced there:

Scarcely any scenes can awaken so many passions at once, and so deeply. Curiosity, apprehension, terror, surprise, admiration, and delight, by turns and together, arrest and possess you. I have had before, from other objects, one simple impression made with greater power; but I never had so many impressions made, and with so much power, before. If the interesting and the awful are the elements of the sublime, here sublimity reigns, as in her own domain, in darkness, silence, and deeps profound.[38]

One visitor to Weyer's Cave in 1850 was so inspired by his tour that he penned a six-page poem, calling the setting "majestic, grand, [and] sublime" and christening it "great Nature's grave."[39]

At least a few of the graphic artists who were assigned the formidable task of replicating the grandeur of the larger Luray Caverns settled on a larger format, which proved to be fairly effective (see below, fig. 3.12). When a visitor there at the close of the century evoked the canon of the Sublime, he elaborated in a familiar way, using signal words and phrases like "awe" and "the insignificance of man," and, like a number of the visitors to Natural Bridge and the Peaks of Otter, he tied the sensation directly to a belief in the Divinity:

The majestic grandeur, the awful sublimity, the wonderfully awe-inspiring influence, the marvelous beauty, of this mystical subterranean world, almost leads the visitor to believe himself to be in a land of phantoms and mysterious, unearthly sculptors. . . . The spell-bound and awe-stricken beholder can only gaze upon them in mute amazement. . . . Are you an infidel, or a skeptic? If so, visit this cave. Its ennobling sublimity, its profound grandeur will convince you of the insignificance of man, and create within you a belief in the Supreme Architect. Are you a believer? then go. . . . It will strengthen your faith in, and veneration for the great builder of the Universe.[40]

If the darkness, stillness, and vast size of the Virginia caverns inspired the nineteenth-century visitor, the bizarre shapes of their limestone formations left him at least a little bewildered. These forms were given popular names, like Cleopatra's Needle and Anthony's Pillar at Weyer's Cave (fig. 2.9, above), that only emphasized the oddness of their appearance. Caroline Gilman found the stalagmites and stalactites at that cavern to be in some instances so comical in form as to compromise the otherwise overwhelming sensations that she experienced there: "the impression [of the Sublime] is strangely at variance with the minute examination of perpetually changing objects, and the frequent discovery of ludicrous caricatures." Perhaps for that reason, Harry Fenn sketched a figure who contemplates the scene at Weyer's Cave without recoil, which would have been the state of mind for a mortal to assume in the presence of a landscape that is truly sublime.

According to Edmund Burke, death is "a more affecting idea than pain" and the "king of terrors," in other words, a sublime idea if the viewer himself is not actually threatened with death at the moment.[41] The Civil War photographer Alexander Gardner would have known this even without reading Burke (fig. 2.10). He was protected from what Burke called "being actually in such circumstances" by, in this case, the "distance" of time; Gardner obviously was at the setting long after the armies had retired. Because of the quality of verisimilitude that is inherent in the medium of photography, he could effectively replicate on paper the evocative sight that must have stopped him in his tracks in the woods near Chancellorsville.[42] The subject here is not human mortality, which a depiction of a skeleton by itself might address; instead Gardner tells the story of an horrendous battle. He plays on his understanding of what Burke called the human

2.10 Attributed to Alexander Gardner, *Wilderness Battlefield Scene*, 1863, albumen silver print from original glass plate, 5 x 3¼ in. (Courtesy of Gilman Paper Company Collection)

passions of self-preservation. This landscape image could only have been inspired by the peculiar inclination in the romantic era to pursue man's most basic emotions wherever the thought of terror would carry them.

The Picturesque in Virginia

The American landscape was not overly picturesque, at least to the eyes of the English traveler. It is "far from possessing a fair proportion of what we should term picturesque scenery," wrote Charles Joseph Latrobe in 1835. "You cannot, in speaking of these vast regions, say that the general character of their scenery is picturesque." Not only is there a deficiency of those "abrupt" changes of terrain that are characteristic of Old World landscapes, but in so expansive a setting one has to search out the Picturesque.[43]

When it is found, James Kirke Paulding bemoaned, there are no ruins to be seen that would inspire poets and painters.[44] The American landscape was simply dissimilar from that of the Old World; it also was a frontier that was undergoing development. In such an environment Americans came to develop "ideas of the picturesque [that were] widely different" from those of the English, according to the British writer Godfrey Vigne in 1832. He carped that Americans prefer "a railroad, a canal, or a piece of newly cleared ground" to "the romantic [view]."[45]

Even if the Virginia landscape was not the Lake District of the British Isles or the Roman Campagna of Italy, a number of artists born and trained in England came to the state determined to locate picturesque scenery there, which they in fact found and recorded in numerous paintings and prints. Travelers frequently made reference to the Picturesque as they passed scenery that they found appealing. For instance, the landscapes of the upper James River and those surrounding the springs were often noted. On the route from Richmond to Natural Bridge, "for many, *many* miles you pass through a Gallery of Pictures, most gorgeous and varied."[46] "Nature is seldom seen more picturesque" than near Rockfish Gap.[47] "The scenery near [Balcony Falls] is highly picturesque."[48] "The approach [to Red Sulphur Springs] is beautifully romantic and picturesque."[49]

If William Gilmore Simms was critical of Thomas Jefferson's description of sublimity at Harpers Ferry, at least the two recognized picturesque scenery at that site. Jefferson wrote in his *Notes* that "the distant finishing which nature has given to the picture is of a very different character. It is a true contrast to the fore-ground. It is as placid and delightful as that is wild and tremendous."[50] Simms said that "the scene is undoubtedly a fine one—pleasing and picturesque." This picturesque quality was in fact what appealed to most of the travelers and artists who followed Jefferson's invitation to visit Harpers Ferry. At mid-century Samuel Mordecai would rank the landscape there as perhaps "the most singularly picturesque in America."[51] In 1835 the British watercolorist William James Bennett depicted the type of lyrical scenery that Simms described (fig. 2.11): "Beauty is here, and dignity, and the eye lingers with gratification upon the sweet pictures which are made of the scene, at the rising and the setting of the sun."[52]

Bennett had exhibited in London galleries for more

2.11 William James Bennett, ***View Looking across the Shenandoah towards Harper's Ferry***, 1835, watercolor, 18 x 28 in. (Courtesy of Museum of Fine Arts, Boston, M. and M. Karolik Collection of American Watercolors and Drawings, 1800–75, © 1999)

than fifteen years before he emigrated to New York City in 1826. He was well trained as a watercolorist and had even served in 1805 as a draftsman with the British forces in Egypt and later in the Mediterranean. He is best known for producing an aquatint series of American cities.[53] His title "View Looking across the Shenandoah towards Harper's Ferry" tells us that this is neither a depiction of the town nor a topographical record of rivers and mountains. Instead it is a picturesque view, coincidentally one that is near the famous confluence of two rivers. As in the work of Claude, the warm light and calm weather enhance the peacefulness of this bucolic scene, which is fully developed with rich narrative elements. Coulisses serve to lead the eye gradually across tranquil water to a luminous distance. If Bennett created what resembles a European picture, part of the explanation is that the setting reminded foreign visitors of the Old World. In 1797 Louis Philippe, the future king of the French, described the Shenandoah River near Harpers Ferry in such terms: "The banks of the river are charming, and the whole region looks like Switzerland."[54]

While the Great Falls of the Potomac seemed sublime to the nineteenth-century traveler, the same river both above and below the falls was considered picturesque. Following his successes at painting and publishing views of both Natural Bridge (fig. 2.2) and Harpers Ferry (see below,

2.12 Joseph Jeakes after William Roberts, ***View on the Potomac, Virginia***, 1810, aquatint, 15 1/4 x 19 3/4 in. (Courtesy of Library of Virginia)

fig. 3.3), the English artist William Roberts produced a depiction of the Potomac above the fall line; it was engraved as a colored aquatint in 1810 (fig. 2.12). The Potomac River had attracted interest when the seat of government was developed along its bank, becoming like the gentle Thames below London a destination for at least a few artists. In Roberts's view the landscape is made to resemble a picturesque "English garden" that is punctuated with clumps of trees and a lake. If Claude's narrative elements from antiquity are necessarily absent, at least gentlemen strollers, a building, and a boat are present; these

2.13 Benjamin Henry Latrobe, ***View on the Elizabeth River, Norfolk, Virginia***, 1796, pencil, pen, and watercolor, 6 $^{15}/_{16}$ x 10 $^{5}/_{16}$ in. (Courtesy of Maryland Historical Society)

earth," improving the landscape by repositioning its elements, and presenting "a distant view glittering among near objects." But there is also a topographical purpose that guides this artist. Latrobe in fact was unhappy with the results here; he wrote in his journal that the "river has not an appearance of sufficient width in the drawing." But he was sufficiently accurate for a probable identity of this view to be offered: we look across the Elizabeth River to Portsmouth.[55]

Joshua Shaw, another English artist active in Virginia in this early period, seems to have been determined to transform the entire frontier of America into the relatively tamed and highly picturesque countryside of the Old World, at least on paper. He set out "to visit nearly every State in the Union," arguing that "in no quarter of the globe are the majesty and loveliness of nature more strikingly conspicuous than in America."[56] In looking through his *Picturesque Views of American Scenery*, a bound portfolio of eighteen aquatints that he published between 1819 and 1821, the viewer finds little reference to those "vast regions" of nondescript and untouched landscape that Charles Latrobe would point to and that in fact lie between the settings that Shaw selected; his views range from scenes in New York State to ones in Georgia and as far west as the Mississippi River. To look at Shaw is to believe that America is already fully domesticated and not the new nation that in fact it was, because his overtly Claudian landscapes typically contain evidence of man's presence by their inclusion of well-traveled roads, grazing cattle, boats, or human figures. Shaw presents a fiction, America as a landscape that enthusiasts of the picturesque would find appealing. His vision is entirely different from that of the New York painters who in the following decades would picture America as an undeveloped continent that they would embellish with ideas about Manifest Destiny. Shaw was an accomplished English artist before he emigrated to Philadelphia in 1817, as was the engraver of the series, John Hill, who preceded him there by a year; both were fully conversant with the picturesque tradition.

Five of the eighteen views selected by Shaw are

are proof, it would seem, that this is not a wilderness. The Claudian trees and the play of shadow across the foreground are expected and effective elements. Like Roberts, Joseph Jeakes, the engraver of this view, brought to the project experience with Old World scenery. Jeakes was familiar with landscapes even more distant and exotic than that of Virginia; he had produced the aquatints for Francis B. Spilsbury's *Picturesque Scenery in the Holy Land* (London, 1803), and he would soon engrave those that appeared in Sir William Thorn's *Memoir of the Conquest of Java* (London, 1815).

One of the first English artists to bring to Virginia the ideal of the Picturesque was Benjamin Henry Latrobe. His sketchbooks at the Maryland Historical Society are filled with scenery of this nature, and in 1798 he even penned an "Essay on Landscape" (apparently as a courtship tool). "View on the Elizabeth River, Norfolk, Virginia" (fig. 2.13) is a typical Latrobe watercolor in that the artist presents at the same time both a picturesque composition and a topographical record. If anything, the scenery is rough, irregular, and characterized by sudden variation. Latrobe was inspired by the landscapes of Claude. "Words cannot describe his pictures. They live. The spectator can travel in them," he wrote. "You almost feel the Warmth of his Sun; or the coolness of his breeze, which appears to wave the vegetating foliage." Latrobe routinely borrowed Claude's formula for composition, stepping back "within the Grove" to establish a foreground in the form of "trees, and shadowy

2.14 John Hill after Joshua Shaw, ***Lynnhaven Bay***, 1819–21, aquatint, 9³/₄ x 14¹/₂ in., published in *Picturesque Views of American Scenery.* (Virginia Historical Society)

2.15 John Hill after Joshua Shaw, ***Oyster Cove***, 1819–21, aquatint, 9³/₄ x 14¹/₂ in., published in *Picturesque Views of American Scenery.* (Virginia Historical Society)

Virginia scenes. The first landscape that he presents is "Washington's Sepulchre, Mount Vernon." The artist said that he had chosen "the best and most popular Views"; the tomb of the nation's "father" was no doubt offered as an example of the latter. Among the "best" landscapes are his views of "Lynnhaven Bay" (fig. 2.14), "Norfolk, from Gosport, Virginia," "Oyster Cove," (fig. 2.15) and

"Bolling's Dam near Petersburgh, Virginia." Shaw had devoted disproportionate attention to the Virginia Tidewater, no doubt because in 1819 this was the most domesticated landscape in America. The area had been settled for two hundred years and on a rural rather than an urban basis. There the artist could with some legitimacy include reference to man's enjoyment of the land in peaceful simplicity, over an extended period of time. "Lynnhaven Bay" is a landscape that composes itself in the best Claudian manner; the sky above is so softly lit as to make the scene idyllic, as opposed to the Edenic views in the North that New York painters would visualize as they derived ways to suggest the newness of the land.

It is ironic that at the time of Shaw's visit the Virginia Tidewater was not an Arcadia, but instead in the midst of an agricultural depression that drove thousands of residents to emigrate from the state. Landscape art does not record reality but instead gives visual form to aspirations; Tidewater Virginia, the birthplace of the nation, should have been idyllic even when it was not. Had it been more like an Arcadia in the early nineteenth century, perhaps the tradition of the Picturesque would have taken better root there; certainly a significant number of artists were present to sow the seeds.

The town of Petersburg, which had lured Joshua Shaw to its outskirts, dates back nearly as far as those other sites that he depicted that lie more in the immediate region of the first settlement. The development of Petersburg began following the establishment of a trading post at the site in 1645. Nearly two hundred years later an unidentified artist saw fit to depict a portion of its waterfront, along with a view of the adjacent village of Blandford, as if the scene

there was as picturesque as a setting in the Old World (fig. 2.16). The artist presents only "A partial View of Blandford & Petersburg" because his principal concern clearly was not topographical accuracy, which in fact he compromised, but instead to arrange a Claudian composition. As we have come to expect, there are giant trees that serve as coulisses, an expanse of water, and a luminous distance. Admittedly, there is a poetic beauty to this image that has been so carefully composed, but no doubt the picture is a better indication of how the residents wanted to view their town than how it actually looked in the early nineteenth century.

The Petersburg scene may date to around 1834, which is when George Cooke painted a view of Richmond. He also manipulated the elements of the landscape to compose a scene that is both masterful and an obvious adaptation of the Claudian model (fig. 2.17, p. 8). The Virginia capital, which was given an identity when Jefferson designed a classical temple to stand on its acropolis, is shown to be aglow like the Roman Campagna; cows graze in this pastoral setting and the gentry parades within it. Admittedly, the view from the spot chosen by the artist, which would soon be the site of Hollywood Cemetery, is on its own highly picturesque in that it is expansive, irregular, varied, and sufficiently rough. But the exact view that Cooke presents cannot be seen in actuality; the artist has in

2.16 Unknown artist, ***A partial View of Blandford & Petersburg from the Appomattox below the Magazine***, c. 1830, engraving, 9 3/4 x 12 1/2 in. (Virginia Historical Society)

2.18 Lefevre Cranstone, *James River, Richmond, Virginia*, 1859, watercolor, 6½ x 12 in. (Virginia Historical Society)

fact repositioned the land to fit the Claudian mold. Cooke was an American artist who was born in Maryland and married into a Richmond family, but from 1826 to 1831 he had studied art in Italy and France, where he learned about the Picturesque at its source. Cooke's canvas is now lost; the aquatint derived from it was produced by William James Bennett, the artist who pictured Harpers Ferry and published the aquatint series of American cities into which this view of Richmond fit.

Not surprisingly, this vista "from the Hill above the Waterworks" was singled out a half-century later in the book *Picturesque America* as "the most commanding and comprehensive view of Richmond" and "one that never tires the eye." While the author of this entry, J. R. Thompson, was disappointed when he inspected the Capitol to find "the meanness of its architectural details and the poverty of its materials," he concluded that "for all the purposes of the picturesque" it served as well "as if it were the Parthenon restored."[57]

In the distant sunlight of Cooke's image are the uncommonly picturesque bends of the James River; these fill the required final plane of Claudian space. A century earlier this scenery had caused William Byrd II to locate the city there and name it after a similar view that he remembered near London, of Richmond on the Thames. It is a setting that was rendered by a number of mid-nineteenth-

2.19 Huestis or George Cook, *Richmond on the James River*, c. 1860–80, gelatin silver print from original glass plate. (Courtesy of Valentine Museum)

century painters, as well as by photographers who now entered the field of landscape art. Lefevre Cranstone, an English painter who traveled throughout Virginia in 1859, recognized the obvious Claudian possibilities of this landscape when he saw the morning sun rise above it to evoke a poetic mood (fig. 2.18). Cranstone's most significant paintings are his records of slave auctions that he witnessed in Richmond and rendered on canvas, but he left as well a sizable body of smaller watercolors of the Virginia landscape before he continued his travels, which carried him so far as Australia. Cranstone's watercolors form a topographical journal of the lands that he visited. They appear to be drawn with a concern for accuracy that would have precluded any significant alteration of the landscape, such as the invention of coulisses to add into the empty foreground of this view. But the artist did step back far enough to select a vantage point from which the architectural clutter of the port's waterfront did not intrude upon the idyllic scenery of Charles City County that looms in the distance. Cranstone painted the background landscape in such a Claudian manner that it seems to echo with wistful memories of its two centuries of English habitation.

A decade or two after the Civil War, the Richmond photographer George Cook, or more probably his son Huestis, selected virtually the same view along the James River that Cranstone had painted (fig. 2.19). The artist was not averse to allowing his camera to record the architectural evidence of how the city had expanded to the east in the

2.20 William Winston Valentine, *Seven Bends of the Shenandoah River*, c. 1890, oil on canvas, 64 x 42½ in. (Virginia Historical Society, Lora Robins Collection of Virginia Art)

intervening years. But to do so required a trade-off; the camera could not simultaneously record detail and give a subtle tonality to atmospheric conditions in the way that Cranstone did. Cook was able to expose his plate for sufficient time to create a remarkable visual record of the buildings along the river, but in the process he lost definition in the river and in parts of the sky. Of course what is most striking in comparing the two views is how the photographer set out to arrange and balance his composition in the prevailing picturesque manner, which was so pervasive a philosophy at this time that it guided the early photographers as much as it did the painters. When put together, the picturesque views by Cook and Cranstone tell us not only how the landscape of Richmond appeared in actuality but also how the nineteenth-century viewer perceived that it looked.

The idea that scenery must be arranged into a Claudian composition if it is to be a worthy subject for a finished landscape painting permeated all levels of artistic activity in nineteenth-century Virginia. Some of the resulting canvases are so far removed from their Old World models as to be unmistakably American. In a view taken late in the century of what is believed to be a portion of the Shenandoah River, where its "seven bends" form a picturesque landscape, the Richmond artist William Winston Valentine chose to shift Claude's horizontal stage to a vertical format in order to match his subject better, while he retained the Frenchman's palette and formula for recession to a luminous background (fig. 2.20). Valentine traveled and studied in Europe; there he learned about the tradition of the Picturesque. He chose to ignore the fact that the emphatic horizontality of Claude's compositions has much to do with the sense of calmness that is integral to a bucolic scene.

An unknown artist working in southwest Virginia in the late nineteenth or perhaps the early twentieth century left a canvas that is even more remarkable evidence of the pervasiveness of an ideal (fig. 2.21). The debt to Claude is unmistakable here in the inclusion and treatment of familiar elements; there is a giant tree, an expanse of water, and a spectacular sky that rivals the vision of Joshua Shaw at Lynnhaven Bay. This painting was found at Vinton in Roanoke County, which is located not far from a town that is actually named Arcadia, after the mythical community of antiquity where life, lived close to nature, was purported to

2.21 Unknown artist, *Landscape*, found in Vinton, Roanoke County, c. 1900, oil on canvas, 20 x 26 in. (Courtesy of Ed Bordett)

be simple and easy. Although the painter clearly was unschooled and untrained in both draftsmanship and the mixing of oils, he understood that the Claudian tradition was an appropriate and effective formula to apply to the western Virginia landscape, parts of which seemed as idyllic as the Roman Campagna. Many artists in Virginia, however, would reject the picturesque tradition and move far beyond the confinement of its rules.

An American Approach to the Landscape

Painters everywhere who were attuned to Edmund Burke's theories about the Sublime and the Beautiful found out soon enough that few of the elements of nature that are truly sublime lend themselves to the paintbrush, and that even less of the Beautiful lies within the domain of the landscapist. Many artists in Virginia recognized as well that the ideal of the Picturesque actually impeded their frequent interest in topographical accuracy and that it made little allowance for the clarity of vision that they encountered in the field. It was perhaps inevitable that a new approach to the landscape would emerge. The old ideals of course survived; it is not surprising that some of the early artists in Virginia wavered between painting picturesque scenes part

of the time while on other occasions they approached the landscape in more innovative ways.

The Virginia landscapist faced a dilemma when the European ideals matched up inadequately with the subject matter that he wanted to record. There were those "vast regions" that Charles Latrobe said spread out between the infrequent changes of terrain. Parts of those expanses could be viewed for great distances from a single vantage point; a Virginia writer in 1870 boasted that the state's natural scenery "surpasses that of Europe in the breadth of its panoramas."[58] There were new towns rising on the landscape that also were neither sublime nor very picturesque. There was Godfrey Vigne's "railroad, canal, or piece of newly cleared ground."

The artist also faced a decision about style. Under the European ideals, he was to work in the somewhat painterly manner of Claude or the even looser technique of Gaspard Poussin. But was that style appropriate for the provincial conditions that still characterized early Virginia? In the colonial period the ruggedness of life in a wilderness setting had contributed to the development there of qualities of forthrightness, simplicity, and honesty that helped to shape a different kind of imagery, one that was acceptable to New World patrons. The forms that emerged in colonial portraits,

2.22 Benjamin Henry Latrobe, *York River, looking N.W. up to West Point*, 1797, pencil, pen, and watercolor, 6 $^{15}/_{16}$ x 30 $^{9}/_{16}$ in. (Courtesy of Maryland Historical Society)

2.23 Russell Smith, *View of the Blue Ridge from the Mansion of Jno. C. Carter, Esqr Albemarle Co. Virginia*, c. 1844, ink, 12 x 33 in. (Courtesy of Library of Virginia)

up and down the eastern seaboard, tended to be linear and less modeled than their English prototypes, even flat in their surface quality. Artists in Virginia and America would perpetuate this linear, reductive style, through the nineteenth century and up to the present.

A final issue that confronted the Virginia landscapist involved light. Nature is more brightly lit on this continent than in England, and under the right atmospheric conditions (not the haze that comes with the intense heat of summer) distant features of landscape can be distinctly visible. Would not this fact of vision have to be addressed? The tenets of both the Sublime and the Picturesque provided little allowance for clarity of vision, because under the former man does not enjoy godlike sight but instead is humbled by

his human limitations, and although a landscape by Claude is certainly luminous, he used light to convey mood rather than topographical accuracy.

Given the expanded field of subjects that were to be painted, the less-than-cosmopolitan conditions in the New World that rejected pretension for simplicity of style, and the intense light there, some artists working in Virginia chose to develop an alternative philosophy to carry to the landscape. The new approach was simply to pursue clarity of vision. No one wrote an essay about this American philosophy; to compose a "philosophical enquiry" about forthrightness would not be forthright. Artists who would follow this creed would endeavor to replicate the visual world with directness. They would paint in a linear style that

would be free of the artificial mannerisms of the painterly tradition; their scenes would be bathed in a bright light. The goal was to convey freshness, cleanness, frankness, and an illusion of accuracy.

The occasional use in Virginia of a different format for an image of the landscape signals in an instant the dilemma that was faced by the artist who carried old landscape ideals to the New World. Benjamin Henry Latrobe may have championed the Picturesque, but on occasion he felt compelled to adapt that traditional ideal in order to respond to the landscape of the Tidewater. To record on paper the remarkable panorama that spread before him on the York River at Airy Plain estate, the artist

pieced together three sheets of paper, thereby creating a New World composition where the width is five times that of the height (fig. 2.22). In his "Essay on Landscape" Latrobe wrote about the kinds of thoughts that were inspired in his mind when he looked across the broad Tidewater rivers. When you stand upon the summit of almost any hill and consider the countryside before you, you see it with pleasure, he said. But if you reposition yourself so that the view includes a "wide expanse of Water," as is so easy to do in Tidewater Virginia, then the enjoyment is considerably heightened because "an historical effect" is produced: "The trade and the cultivation of the country croud into the mind, the imagination runs up the invisible creeks, and visits the half seen habitations." "A thousand circumstances are fancied which are not beheld," he added.[59] Latrobe's drawing of the view up the York River to West Point was conceived as much as a means to record interesting topography as to evoke thoughts about man's settlement of the region.

A half century later Russell Smith, a Pennsylvania artist who traveled extensively in the eastern states, encountered a similar landscape in the Virginia Piedmont that seemed so vast to him that he reacted in virtually the same manner (fig. 2.23). Like Latrobe he felt compelled to put together multiple sheets of paper in order to create a surface broad enough to suggest the expansiveness of the scene that lay before him, in this case a view looking west to the Blue Ridge Mountains from Albemarle County. As with Latrobe's sketch, there is a topographical quality to this

2.24 Victor Huggins, ***Forks of Buffalo***, 1981, acrylic on canvas, 10 ½ x 25 ½ in.
(Courtesy of David Young)

2.25 Russell Smith, *South fork of the south Branch of the Potomac*, c. 1844, pencil, 12 x 16 ½ in. (Courtesy of Library of Virginia)

drawing, in that Smith notes on it such landmarks as Buck's Elbow, Turk's Gap, Pasture Fence Mountain, and Brown's Cave. But he is every bit as interested in the clarity of vision that contributed to the sense of spaciousness in this landscape. His simple medium of pen and ink, which allowed linear exactitude but minimal detail, served his purposes well.

In 1981 Victor Huggins, resident in southwest Virginia as a professor of art, arrived at a similar solution for suggesting the vast scale of the landscape near Blacksburg, where mountain ranges are visible at great distances (fig. 2.24). Rather than simply construct one wide canvas, Huggins placed two beside one another, to emphasize horizontality. The artist said that by their "beauty and calm force," the Appalachian Mountains had "thrust their way, as relentlessly as they came from the earth, into my consciousness and onto my canvas." He could "no longer resist their temptation."[60] In order to stress that everything in his field of vision, from the sky to even the ranges of trees, seemed to contribute to the sense of expansiveness that is the essence of this landscape, Huggins chose to be reductive in both his selection of colors and his rejection of detail, and his style is emphatically linear. He was dealing with nature of a type that was unknown and unanticipated by Old World practitioners of the Picturesque.

Russell Smith spent considerable time studying the landscape of western Virginia when he accompanied a geological expedition led in 1844 by the acclaimed scientist

William Barton Rogers of the University of Virginia. While in the field Smith noticed that the colors and light that he saw in nature were different from what he saw in art, specifically in paintings that are derived from the European landscape tradition. Along the bottom of his pencil drawing of the "South fork of the south Branch of the Potomac" (fig. 2.25), Smith jotted down notes that are evidence that in his field sketches he strove to be entirely accurate. He charted which trees in his drawing were tulip, black walnut, and sycamore. He noted the position of shadows and sunlight. He labeled the sky as "Constable like or English like," to remind himself when he returned to the studio about the type of cloud formations that he had observed and that John Constable had painted in England earlier in the century. Finally, Smith made reference to a group of canvases by the noted New York painter Thomas Cole: "From the presence of so much walnut and Sycamore I see none of the cold heavy greens noticed in Cole's 2nd picture of the 'Voyage of life' but all is warm and harmonizing with the shadows." Cole's series of four paintings illustrates the perils and pleasures of man's life "voyage" from the cradle to the grave; these were the talk of the art world in 1842.

The influence of that art world was sufficiently strong in mid-century America for Smith to be influenced by the pervasive tradition of the Picturesque. In his finished oil painting of the south fork of the south branch of the Potomac (fig. 2.26), which was produced in the studio, away from the influence of the scientist William Rogers, the artist sacrificed the accuracy of detail and the clarity of vision that characterize his field sketch; he altered the types, positions, and heights of trees, and he shifted landscape features in order to construct what he considered to be a proper finished painting, one with the appropriate coulisses and a sense of gradual recession. Smith's finished oil has virtues that are different from those of the pencil sketch.

To modern eyes, Smith was perhaps most effective when he worked in watercolor (fig. 2.27). There he could retain the freshness that characterizes all of his field work and at the same time produce a record in color of those vast

2.26 Russell Smith, *South Fork of the South Branch of the Potomac River*, c. 1848, oil on canvas, 17 x 24 in. (Courtesy of Lora Robins)

landscapes in Virginia where the eye can reach for miles. In some of the watercolors it is clear that Smith looked for opportunities for the landscape to compose itself in a picturesque composition, but his overriding concern, which he could never put aside in the field, was that the scenery of western Virginia was simply different from the landscapes of the Old World.

Just as the vastness of the Virginia landscape sometimes challenged the artist to devise a different format for his subject, the newly emerging towns there inspired a new, more straightforward type of imagery. Lefevre Cranstone had been nourished by the flourishing watercolor tradition in his native England to be attuned to the atmospheric conditions of the landscape, as we saw in his view of the James River, where he was sensitive to light in a picturesque context. The English watercolorists also painted remarkably accurate and linear

2.27 Russell Smith, *Landscape*, unidentified view of the Piedmont, c. 1844, watercolor, 12 x 16 ½ in. (Courtesy of Library of Virginia)

views of their architecture. But they never encountered in the homeland an emerging urban landscape made up of simple buildings illuminated by a bright light that seemed as fresh and clean as the new city itself. Cranstone would be but one in a long succession of artists in Virginia to paint city views in a style that is linear and attentive to crisp

illumination that allows clarity of vision (fig. 2.28).

On the one hand Cranstone's remarkable view of Richmond is a topographical record. But more than that, the artist is excited by the details of this landscape and eagerly seeks them out and feasts on them, lovingly. It is through love, writes Kenneth Clark, that the facts of vision are turned into art, and in the landscape it is through light that this love is expressed; the landscape painter's greatest gift is an emotional response to light.[61] Light, more than anything else, separates topographical imagery from landscape art;

here it sets Cranstone in the latter category. He quickly attuned himself to the intense brightness and clarity of American light, which reveals crisp details of scenery. He recorded the shapes that it illuminates, the shadows that it casts, and even its distinct quality.

Edward Beyer, a German artist, worked at the same time and in the same way as Cranstone, but in the medium of oil (fig. 2.29). In response to both the setting and the uncomplicated taste of his American patrons, who wanted pictures that honestly replicated the environment that they knew, Beyer also moved in a direction entirely different from the ideals of the Sublime and the Picturesque. It might be argued that as a German Beyer was inclined to be precise, but German art as practiced in Düsseldorf in the mid-nineteenth century was characterized instead by an interest in dark tonalities and mood, and Beyer had studied at the Düsseldorf Academy. Contrary to this training, he gave not only the details of the American towns that he painted but he also conveyed the beauty of those new scenes as they were bathed in light. The artist did not shroud details in mist that might convey mood but instead allowed bright light to reveal them, in all of their linearity. Beyer can be said to have used both a telescope and a microscope in order to present to his patrons what they wanted, usually a flattering record of a burgeoning market town wherein both individual buildings and the surrounding countryside are in focus, painted in detail that never seems trite because it is so lovingly rendered. Kenneth Clark explains that when an artist enlarges the range of our physical perceptions, which is what Beyer accomplished with the magic spectacles that he gives us, the artist heightens our sense of well-being.[62] Beyer's patrons may not have understood that the artist was engaged in such artifice, but they knew that they liked what they saw. Art that answered an artificial ideal was of little interest to either Beyer or his patrons.

In the early twentieth century, artists of the Regional-

2.30 Walker Evans, *Frame Houses, Fredericksburg*, March 1936, gelatin silver print from original negative. (Courtesy of Library of Congress)

ist period, which was isolationist and attuned to those traditional American ideals of forthrightness and simplicity, were also inclined to produce an art that has no reliance on European ideals but instead emphasizes and celebrates clarity of vision and directness. The camera encouraged this development because the medium of photography lends itself to the pictorial development of those qualities. The official job of the Farm Security Administration photographers was to document conditions and so prove the effectiveness of Franklin Roosevelt's New Deal programs, designed to stimulate recovery following the Great Depression. But these artists were inclined also to editorialize. Walker Evans found beauty in the simple and sharply defined abstract shapes of small row houses in Fredericksburg (fig. 2.30); he used the camera to emphasize their architectural merit. In this way Evans was able to convey the same sort of pride of place that Beyer celebrated in his scenes that also show rows of houses. The low social level of the Fredericksburg homeowners was what inspired the artist to make a statement about the dignity of their way of life.

Charles Sheeler, one of the most accomplished of the Regionalist painters, also worked as a photographer; in that way he learned to develop imagery that is characterized by a sharpness of vision. The crisply defined edges in canvases like his view of

2.31 Charles Sheeler, *Bassett Hall*, 1936, oil on canvas, 20 1/2 x 24 1/2 in. (Courtesy of the Colonial Williamsburg Foundation)

Bassett Hall in Williamsburg earned this style of painting the term "Precisionism" (figs. 2.31 and below, 3.59). In the view of Bassett Hall the canvas is even "cropped" like a snapshot and the imagery pushed forward to the picture plane, within what would have been the camera's depth of field, all of this in defiance of the rules of the then long-outdated picturesque mode. In 1936 Sheeler had been invited to newly restored "Colonial Williamsburg" to record scenery there in his straightforward, linear method of painting. That style seemed appropriate because it epitomized the American ideal of clarity of vision that had its origins in the colonial era in places like Tidewater Virginia.

Sheeler's paintings no doubt influenced the work of Rockwell Kent, whose 1956 canvas "Child under Tree, Virginia" even bears a compositional similarity to the view of Bassett Hall (fig. 2.32). Like Sheeler, this artist also was internationally acclaimed, he traveled widely, and he worked in a related medium, in this case printmaking. Kent's passion to find and paint landscapes that were pristine caused him to develop a style that would suggest the freshness of nature as viewed in the clearest light. Clean and vivid color was integral to his vision. Kent's style seems distinctly American: it is linear and reductive, with

attention to basic geometric shapes and relationships that are dynamic because of their simplicity. The simplicity moves Kent's work far beyond topography.

Kent found in Nelson County an unspoiled portion of the Virginia landscape. The setting he depicts is part of Oak Ridge, a large estate south of Charlottesville that was developed by the industrialist Thomas Fortune Ryan, whose grandson became a patron of Kent. The artist gave the foreground of his painting to the enormous oak tree and ridge for which the estate was named. Beyond lies the vast landscape of the Blue Ridge Mountains, the horizontality of which is emphasized as it is in the work of Russell Smith and Victor Huggins.

The style of Robert Stuart, who paints today in Rockbridge County, is also linear, reductive, and attentive to light that can crisply define distant features of the landscape (fig. 2.33). A half-century earlier, at least one of the Farm Security Administration photographers worked the same rural landscape in a manner similar to the style developed by Stuart. In a view near Marion, farther south, Marion Post Wolcott emphasized the role of light as it played across a scene, bringing objects and nature to life (fig. 2.34). She knew that the camera can accentuate the contrast of light

2.32 Rockwell Kent, *Child under Tree, Virginia*, 1956, oil on canvas, 28 x 34 in. (Virginia Historical Society, Lora Robins Collection of Virginia Art)

2.33 Robert Stuart, *Afternoon Light at Gordon's Farm*, 1994, oil on resin-coated paper, 26 x 40 in. (Collection of McGuire Woods Battle and Boothe, Richmond, Virginia, courtesy of Reynolds Gallery)

and shadow and that it can place zones of space in or out of focus. Here Wolcott made the corn stacks seem almost capable of motion as the sun begins to bring them out of darkness and introduces a sharpness of vision to the scene; the background fades out of view.

The similarities in Stuart's and Wolcott's views are coincidental. Both artists were attuned to the transitoriness of light and to the simple beauty of the landscape. But Stuart was not influenced by photography; instead he speaks admiringly about the reductive style of early Italian Renaissance painters, like those

2.34 Marion Post Wolcott, *Field of Shocked Corn Enclosed by Rail Fences near Marion*, 1940, gelatin silver print from original negative. (Courtesy of Library of Congress)

of Siena. Like Claude and those even earlier painters of the Italian landscape, but with no interest in the conventions of the Picturesque and with a palette appropriate to Virginia, Stuart pursues aesthetics and looks to capture the poetic moods that are evoked by the landscape. Wolcott had to be more pragmatic; the photographer utilized the same beauty

and mood to emphasize instead the bounty of the harvest of the American farmer, and implicitly to credit the help of federal programs. Both artists responded to the distinct light and landscape of western Virginia to develop imagery that is innovative and far removed from the old ideals of European art.

2.35 Grandma Moses (Anna Mary Robertson Moses), *Virginia*, 1954, oil and tempera on panel, 18 x 24 in. (Private collection)

Untrained artists active in Virginia also have worked in what is essentially a linear style, in that the forms that they paint are flat and little modeled. Their canvases tend to be simplistic, straightforward, and unpretentious. The most famous and the most accomplished of these "Sunday painters" was Anna Mary Robertson Moses, who became popularly known as Grandma Moses when her paintings began to receive widespread acclaim around 1940.[63] This was late in her life when she was eighty years old and living in New York State. With bright colors and a naive understanding of drawing and composition, she put onto more than a thousand canvases her entirely cheerful memories of her life as a farmwife for more than half a century. A number of the paintings are Virginia scenes that recall the landscape around Staunton, where she had lived during her early married life, from 1887 to 1905 (fig. 2.35). She was inclined to introduce many details of the landscape and the human activity on it, but she possessed both a vivid imagination and a remarkable, instinctive understanding of pattern that enabled her to weave those elements into strong images that perpetuate a traditional belief in the virtues of American rural life.

An artist who has approached Grandma Moses in popular success and imagination is P. Buckley Moss, who works in the Valley and also has pictured farm scenes there,

often in the cold and quiet of winter. She, however, has developed a different linear style that is more subtle than simple. Of the visions of the Virginia landscape crafted by Moses and Moss, the former is the one that is based more on fact than fantasy. Both are pleasing and far removed from European academic traditions and the ideals of the Sublime and the Picturesque.

International Styles of Modernism

By the mid-nineteenth century artists in England and on the Continent looked beyond the ideals of the Sublime and the Picturesque, which they judged to be inadequate means of expression in a modern age. In France in particular different ideas about how to paint the landscape were developed in a wave of creativity that lasted a hundred years, until around 1945 when New York City replaced Paris as the center of the art world. These new styles of painting quickly became international; artists in Virginia throughout the twentieth century have worked in and still practice many of them. It is useful here to introduce the modern styles and review the philosophies that underlie their origins, if for no other reason than as a way to approach a large body of landscape paintings that have been produced in this state.

Following the Civil War a number of American art

patrons favored contemporary European works, especially French academic scene paintings and Barbizon landscapes. Those painters who worked in the French village of Barbizon at mid-century had been influenced by the philosophy of an English landscapist, John Constable, who celebrated the simple, rustic life with devotion akin to that of William Wordsworth; like the poet he searched for moral and spiritual qualities in nature. While both Constable and Wordsworth, and in turn the American Hudson River School painters, believed that the many elements of the landscape, from flowers and rocks to brooks and trees, bear so strongly the imprint of God's intentions that they can be read as pages in a book, the Barbizon artists were concerned more with understanding the moods of nature as a way to help recover traditional values and a simpler rural past that were threatened in an age of urbanization and mechanization. The Barbizon paintings are factual, based on actual observation, but the elements have been composed into poetic and often solemn and grand compositions, with topography subservient to mood. This style has been called Naturalism; American artists studying in France in the late nineteenth century were the first to carry it to our shores.

Richard Norris Brooke of Warrenton trained in Paris under the academician Léon Bonnat; thus the solid craftsmanship of his paint surfaces (fig. 2.36). Back home in post–Civil War Virginia, which had suffered greater social change than France, Brooke realized that Barbizon traditions were compatible with a new southern valuation of the land, so he painted in that style. Like the French artists, he found renewal and inspiration in the order and energy of the landscape.

Today the Richmond artist and teacher Durwood Dommisse paints landscapes that have the gentle rusticity of those by Constable and the grandeur if not the solemnity of some of the Barbizon canvases (fig. 2.37). This is not to say that Dommisse has copied from those earlier painters or even studied their works, only that he shares their optimistic ideology. Like the Barbizon artists, he is active in an age when rapid change threatens older values, and like them he works, in his own words, "to capture the spirit of a place, the poetry, the mood."[64] With Dommisse, as with all in this school, to study the landscape is to examine the qualities of

2.36 Richard Norris Brooke, *Virginia Scene*, c. 1910, oil on canvas, 20 x 30 in. (Virginia Historical Society, Lora Robins Collection of Virginia Art)

2.37 Durwood Dommisse, **The James River in June**, 1996, oil on canvas, 31 x 45 in. (Courtesy of Ken and Virginia Dawson)

its light, forms, colors, and textures in order to reach some sort of understanding about nature and man's place in it. Below we will see that Dommisse is but one of a sizable group of contemporary Virginia painters who work with essentially the same approach to nature demonstrated by the early practitioners of Naturalism.

The French Impressionists, who were active primarily in the last quarter of the century, followed in the wake of the Barbizon artists, overturning many of the rules of traditional landscape painting. According to the philosophy that underlies Impressionism, the subject of a landscape painting need not have grandeur, but instead the preferred scene is commonplace and familiar, and thereby engaging to the viewer. The artist's response to it is spontaneous; he records only an "impression" of the landscape. There is no narrative. The finish to the canvas remains unfinished. The Impressionists carried Naturalism to an extreme; their sole goal was to capture on canvas what the French painter Camille Corot at mid-century had called the "envelope of air," by which he meant the unity of atmosphere and tone in a landscape. In submitting the notion that visual perception is sufficient subject matter, the Impressionists introduced the novel idea that the artist need not comment about his subject but simply record what his eye perceived from one place in one moment of time. Their research into the nature

of color and light yielded joyous landscapes that inspired American disciples to follow their movement, both in the late nineteenth century and through much of the twentieth, when this once radical style, eventually and ironically, was seen to be a conservative one.

Adele Williams, a Richmond artist who in the late 1880s and early 1890s studied in New York and Paris, was an early practitioner of Impressionism in Virginia. It was in New York that she first saw paintings in the new style; in France, despite her study at the conservative Académie Julian, her initial visit was to Claude Monet's studio at Giverny. In 1903 she was with Childe Hassam and other American Impressionists at the art colony in Old Lyme, Connecticut; on several later occasions she persuaded Hassam and other colleagues there to exhibit Impressionist works in Richmond.[65] Her view of Reveille garden, probably painted not long after the turn of the century, is an ambitious exercise in the radical new style (fig. 2.38). American artists generally felt comfortable with Impressionism only if its bold brushwork and color could be structured atop an underlying academic armature, in this instance two large trees that anchor a path. This scene, then, is not entirely spontaneous, which the French paintings tended to be. Nor is the subject commonplace; Reveille was a sizable private estate in Richmond with grounds that were atypical

2.38 Adele Williams, *Reveille Garden*, c. 1900, oil on canvas, 26 x 22 in. (Private collection)

of the local landscape. But the style survives in this adaptation of it to Virginia soil; the canvas is radiant with vivid hues dabbed on an unfinished surface to suggest the "envelope of air" that envelops a joyous landscape.

Another Richmond-born artist, Nell Blaine, carried the style of Impressionism into the second half of the twentieth century in canvases that have become highly popular and widely collected. Most of her work, however, was produced outside of Virginia, because early in her career Blaine settled in New York City. Presumably some of her unidentified landscapes are Virginia scenes, but the commonplace subjects of Impressionism can elude definition, so that the question is unanswered. Predictably, because she lived at a later date than Adele Williams, at a time when the history of art was easily known through museum exhibitions and photography, Blaine was influenced as well by the even more radical French styles that emanated from Paris in the early twentieth

century. She worked with even greater spontaneity than the first French painters, using larger, longer, and bolder brush strokes, with color that is just as freely applied. Blaine's style of painting is perhaps better described as somewhere between Impressionism and Expressionism; the latter movement is examined below.

Just as revolutionary as the work of the Impressionists were the paintings of Paul Cézanne, perhaps even more so in that this Post-Impressionist French artist opened avenues to abstraction that enabled later artists to paint in new ways. Like the Impressionists, Cézanne set out to capture on canvas the sensation of nature, but instead of offering only a spontaneous response, he looked to convey the vitality of objects that occupy space. He tried simultaneously to envision both pattern and depth, and to avoid excessive modeling of form that would diminish the effect of color and design.

Janet Niewald has adapted Cézanne's style to the fertile green landscape of western Virginia, where she teaches at Blacksburg. In her depiction of Paris Mountain, she is attentive to patterns that weave across the picture plane of the canvas and yet at the same time reverberate into space (fig. 2.39). She has modeled the trees and even the mountain with color, so as to convey their precise positions in the landscape and to establish that each of these objects occupies its own segment of space, with the result that the

2.39 Janet Niewald, *Paris Mountain*, 1990, oil on canvas, 26 x 36 in. (Courtesy of the artist)

2.40 Arthur Rothstein, *A Fertile Plateau in the Blue Ridge Mountains, Shenandoah National Park*, 1935, gelatin silver print from original negative. (Courtesy of Library of Congress)

his medium to the new way of seeing things. Arthur Rothstein may never have studied the paintings of Cézanne, but in 1935 he composed a view in the Shenandoah National Park (fig. 2.40) in a way that would have been unthinkable before Cézanne revolutionized the visual arts. Rothstein thrust one stack of corn so much in the picture plane that it almost invades the space of the viewer, while it looms nearly as tall as the hills that rise behind it. Where the photographer differed radically from the French painters who preceded him was that he was more interested in a social message than in aesthetics. As the title reminds us, this "fertile" site has yielded a bountiful harvest to the government-supported farmer. But in looking to establish the position of objects in space and to develop a visual tension between them, Rothstein put into play the same dynamics that are at work in a canvas by Cézanne.

The Expressionist approach to painting was developed in Paris around 1905 in the circle of Henri Matisse and his colleagues whose radical brand of art caused one disenchanted critic to label them *fauves* (wild beasts). Expressionist painters also were active in Germany in the same years. The French variety was first carried to America by artists who lived in or had visited Paris in the first half of the century, and variations of it persist in Virginia today. Much more brash than the Impressionists, the Expressionists were uninterested in replicating on canvas visual perception, which their predecessors already had pushed to its extreme. Instead they chose to liberate color from the limitations of visual reality by utilizing bold hues and an emphatic handling of line and form to "express" their feelings and thereby stir the viewer's response.

Pierre Daura painted in Virginia in an Expressionist manner, albeit sometimes in a more conservative strain than he had seen in Europe, perhaps because he felt that it would be better received in his new homeland (figs. 2.41 and 4.116). Daura was a native of Spain who had traveled to

overall illusion of depth is entirely convincing. From Cézanne also comes the device of positioning a tree branch high above the landscape and in the picture plane, with the mountain juxtaposed in the distance but pulled forward by the tree, to create a tension in the canvas. Niewald's landscapes, however, owe as much to the influence of her subject matter as they do to Cézanne. She speaks about "the wild aspect of [the landscape of] America that is gone or fast disappearing"; this attracts her interest and inspires a harsher realism than would be found in a French painting.[66] It was critical of course that she move far beyond the style of the French artist, which she has done, if for no other reason than the fact that his landscapes have been reproduced so frequently that they are now clichés that are difficult to enjoy. Niewald's canvases are still fresh and vital; their ample forms and clean colors seem infused by the same nourishing environment of western Virginia that makes the trees there grow so full and green.

The developments in modern painting that originated in France eventually made their way into other forms of twentieth-century art, including photography. Camera artists inevitably became attuned to the fact that avant-garde painters were questioning the old ways to handle form and space, while creating innovative solutions that were appropriate in the modern era. The photographer in turn adapted

2.41 Pierre Daura, *Winter Landscape*, c. 1950, oil on masonite, 18 x 24 in. (Virginia Historical Society, Lora Robins Collection of Virginia Art)

Paris in 1916, a pivotal time for the arts because Expressionism had newly liberated painters to move far from the realistic rendering of their subjects. There he associated with some of the most renowned modernists, including Wassily Kandinsky, Fernand Léger, and Piet Mondrian. He even formed with them in 1930 a short-lived group (the Circle and Square) that exhibited geometric and abstract canvases. Daura learned well their use of vibrant color and dynamic form to invigorate the two-dimensional surface of the canvas. Daura married Richmonder Louise Blair when she was in Paris studying art; at the outbreak of World War II the couple relocated in Virginia. The artist taught painting and the family settled at Rockbridge Baths.

   The Expressionist style as it was developed by the *fauves* survives today in the work of a

2.42 William White, *Pink Creek, Summer Afternoon*, 1993, oil on masonite, 11 x 12 in. (Courtesy of Tom and Anna Lawson)

2.43 Maryann Harman, *Beaver Meadow*, 1995, oil and acrylic on canvas, 48 x 72 in. (Courtesy of the artist)

Roanoke artist and teacher, William White, who paints landscapes with alluring colors and the kind of explosive yet varied and subtle brushwork that transforms objects into expressive shapes. His "Pink Creek" (fig. 2.42) appears as if it might have been painted at almost any time or place in the twentieth century. It is an actual site near Roanoke that White sketched on location, on a summer afternoon when the direct sunlight and deep shadows of the setting evoked an "air of mystery" (his words) and made the trees seem almost to gesture. White calls himself a "realist painter," because his scenes are entirely derived from nature. As a "realist," he strives to "simply express what I see." To do that, he utilizes techniques and philosophies of the early Expressionists and their precursors. White is one of too few artists in Virginia today who understand the expressive potential of oil paint, the appeal of its "luscious visual and tactile quality," and how to manipulate it to build up the surface of a canvas; in his hands unmixed, vibrant color is a sensuous material that can convey feelings. White "tr[ies] to paint with innocence and sincerity," which is what the Post-Impressionist artist Paul Gauguin set out to do. In his disdain for narrative, and in "want[ing] the images I make to seem as if they were seen with a sidelong glance," White follows the lead of the Impressionists. He weds these European ideas about painting to the landscape that surrounds him. The subjects are scenery that "I often pass on

my daily routines." Painting them is an "an act of discovery," an experience that he is able to pass along to his viewers.[67]

The Armenian painter Arshile Gorky, who spent several years in the mid-1940s at his wife's family farm in Hamilton in Loudoun County, carried the Expressionist impulse almost to abstraction in his canvas titled "Virginia Landscape" (Cincinnati Art Museum).[68] In Gorky's vision of Virginia scenery, only the space of the landscape survives. Gorky influenced the development of Abstract Expressionism, a movement that emerged after 1945 primarily in New York City. The title of the style is self-explanatory; form and color are presented with spontaneity, boldness, and the absence of reference to the visual world, all for the purpose of expression. At least a few landscapists active in Virginia have been influenced by the style.

Maryann Harman, who lives in Blacksburg and has taught there, was initially an abstract painter. When as a professional she rediscovered the mountain landscape that she remembered from being raised in Virginia, the artist envisioned this scenery as nearly abstract, but not so far as to mask either the identity of her subject matter or its structure. In "Beaver Meadow" (fig. 2.43), the mountain ranges near Blacksburg are entirely recognizable in the panoramic view that the artist spreads before us. Painted with energy and spontaneity, they suggest not only the fecundity of the plant life that is sustained on their fertile slopes and the light that brings out their colors, but also the colossal forces that eons ago crumpled these ranges out of the earth's crust, akin to what Jefferson envisioned at Harpers Ferry. But at the same time, these hills are alive with vivid hues and vigorous brushwork that seem to have an existence of their own, independent of their subject. Clement Greenberg, one of the prominent New York critics whose arguments in the 1950s gave validity to the Abstract Expressionist movement and did much to establish it as a legitimate art form, has championed Harman for "flirt[ing] with the abstract"; he sees that the forms, colors, and frenetic lines developed by her do not lie lifelessly on the canvas but instead establish a "tension" between themselves that gives the image its strength.[69] Harman's paintings are more lyrical and perhaps more appealing than the canvases by the first generation of Abstract Expressionists, in that they are warmer, more luscious, more inviting, even beautiful; they are rendered with a feminine touch akin to that of the abstract painter Helen Frankenthaler.

Harman has developed an entirely personal style of landscape painting that has received international acclaim. It in no way diminishes her accomplishment to point out, as we will see below, that in 1961 Theresa Pollak anticipated Harman's vision of the Virginia mountains, at least to an extent. This was on Pollak's return from studying under Hans Hofmann, the New York painter and teacher who had influenced the Abstract Expressionists as much as Arshile Gorky did.

Other artists in Virginia have felt the influence of another abstract and avant-garde American movement of mid-century, that of Color Field painting. In this style the canvas is large and filled with only color, shapes, or lines that usually have no direct visual reference to the actual world. In a work of 1959, Kenneth Noland, one of the leading practitioners of the style, reduced the Virginia landscape to large concentric circles of the colors blue, black, yellow, and white, set against the field of the unpainted canvas (collection of Joseph Helman, New York). The hues in this painting, titled "Virginia Site," may or may not refer to ones

seen in the landscape; the work may simply have been painted on a Virginia site.[70]

Isabel Bigelow, an Alexandria artist now resident in New York, has moved Color Field painting into the actual fields of the landscape. Her "Field 13" (fig. 2.44) is a large canvas like Noland's. The image is not cold and lifeless; instead the lines and shapes suggest the graceful, even majestic sweep of nature; we can read into it the waves of a lush field that is planted with its crop of wheat or corn, as in one of the Farm Security Administration photographs from the Shenandoah Valley (see below, fig. 4.110). Gradations in the color entice us to believe that we are looking at something that is real, an actual landscape, rather than simply an abstract image into which the rhythms of nature are instilled. Bigelow seems to make the point that the shapes and graduated colors say enough about the land; no details are necessary. The same message is conveyed in James Bradford's "Snow Scene" (fig. 2.45), half of which is filled only with a field of color. Bradford, who lived and taught in Richmond, states in the clearest terms the choice, or perhaps the dilemma, of the modern artist, who must decide whether to work as a realist or to paint abstractly. This canvas functions almost in a didactic manner to demonstrate the

2.44 Isabel Bigelow, *Field 13*, 1999, oil on panel, 60 x 60 in.
(Collection of the artist, courtesy of Reynolds Gallery)

2.45 James Bradford, *Snow Scene*, 1997, oil on board, 7 x 20³/₈ in.
(Courtesy of Reynolds Gallery)

similarities in two styles of painting that are less different than they appear to be. One point Bradford makes is that if the abstract portion of his canvas were presented by itself and titled "Snow Scene," to identify the subject, would it not tell as much about the landscape that inspired it as does the realist image at the left? Landscape, as Arshile Gorky stated with his scene from Virginia, is first and foremost space; space is defined in both of Bradford's views. One additional Virginia artist who works with abstract fields of color in a way that would have been unthinkable before the work of Noland and his colleagues is Ryan Russell, who is active today in Lexington. Although Russell's landscapes are more realistic than not, he is willing to exaggerate those expanses of color that suggest the essence of the scenery that surrounds him in the Valley.

Ray Kass, another of the landscapists who teach and paint in Blacksburg, has approached the nearly abstract landscape from another direction. He has painted a number of traditional watercolor views of distant mountains, but in looking at his entire body of work, which started out with abstraction, one senses that the artist anticipated that he would inevitably grow tired of imitating the panorama of the landscape when nature abounds with patterns that are limitless in number and that await examination. Adventuresome and original artists can lose interest in simply painting facts. In his recent polyptychs, which are assemblages of small panels, Kass in effect has sliced apart those realistic renderings and reassembled the pieces, which are rich with pattern, his purpose being to present a painting that is as

dynamic as his subject, and one that is appropriately large in scale (fig. 2.46). As every advocate of modernist art knows, even the ancients, according to an often-cited passage in Socrates, recognized that colors can give "a pleasure of their own" and that in the same way "straight lines and curves and the shapes made from them, by the lathe, ruler or square" are beautiful.[71] Kass puts color and geometry to use in these landscapes. The patterns that he has found from scrutinizing the landscape appear in his panels to float like beautiful veils in a Color Field painting. With a kind of resonance and repetition more associated with the structure of classical music, those patterns are in turn arranged to form yet a larger pattern, a geometric grid that is made up of the edges of the panels.[72] These landscapes have the cleanness and freshness of nature as illuminated by bright sunlight. For that reason they turn our thoughts back to nature, their inspiration and subject.

The hints of imagery in Kass's painting suggest elements of a particular landscape that is identified in the work's title, "Sinking Creek Polyptych." The naturalist who has hiked the Appalachian Trail through Sinking Creek Valley, or the reader of Steve Sherman and Julia Older's account of such a journey in *Appalachian Odyssey* (1977), knows of the abundance of life in that region, which is the site of the Great Eastern Divide, of the botany and zoology, the trees and grasses, the large rattlesnakes and abundant frogs.[73] He is reminded by Kass's painting that Sinking Creek is a special place; the painting serves to inspire him to count the ways. In this manner the imagery functions almost like Benjamin Henry Latrobe's view of the York River. That earlier sketch also showed only part of what the artist knew was there; it was produced to stimulate thoughts about the larger landscape.

With the teaching of art history in colleges at the beginning of the second half of the twentieth century, both artists and their audience have become cognizant of the best works by both old and recent masters. Admittedly, French artists of, say, the nineteenth century could visit the Louvre to look at the work of Claude or the paintings of the Dutch landscapists, but the mining of art history is much easier and much more prevalent today, when artists like Joellyn Duesberry are as well versed in art history as a museum curator of art. Duesberry's morning view near Middleburg (fig. 2.47) coincidentally bears a superficial similarity to Pierre Daura's view at Rockbridge Baths (fig. 4.116), no doubt because both of these artists derived their landscape styles at least partly out of the French tradition.

It is not easy to pin down sources for Duesberry's art, because she has successfully incorporated influences into a personal style and because a good part of her inspiration obviously comes from nature itself. Duesberry pictures trees indistinctly, with as little regard for the accuracy of their forms as was demonstrated by the first Expressionists,

but with so much more delicate a hand that a comparison with those early modernists fails. A more significant relationship is perhaps to be found in the work of Camille Corot, the artist who so lovingly replicated the "envelope of light" in a landscape and simplified its forms, at least as much as was thinkable in the mid-nineteenth century. Corot also painted with delicacy, and like this French artist Duesberry is able to convey a sensation of the landscape, which is no little accomplishment. She does this partly by a superior eye and instinct for color that is as clean and pure as the atmosphere that envelops her scenes, and partly by a sensitivity to the seasonal transformations of nature and to the regional differences of the broader American landscape.[74] Duesberry revisits sites at different times of the year, and she paints in different states of the union, from Maine to Alaska, from Colorado, her residence, to Virginia, her birthplace. Photography has so familiarized us today with the styles of the past that the question arises as to whether an artist today can approach nature without difficulty and without becoming sentimental; Duesberry's canvases seem to suggest that he or she can.

The audience for landscape paintings is well enough grounded to recognize at least the overt references to canvases from the past, just as viewers of recent motion

2.46 Ray Kass, *Sinking Creek Polyptych*, 1994, watercolor on rag paper, under beeswax, on wood panels, 49 x 56 in. (Collection of Steve Skinner, courtesy of Reynolds Gallery)

2.47 Joellyn Duesberry, *September Morning Near Middleburg, Virginia*, 1996, oil on linen, 30 x 40 in. (Courtesy of the artist)

pictures can identify in the occasional staged scene an obvious and intentional borrowing from an old master painting, such as an interior by Jan Vermeer or a landscape by Winslow Homer. James Warwick Jones, a resident of Tidewater Virginia who has a remarkable eye for recognizing geometry in the natural world and adapting it to his compositions, chose to pay tribute in 1976 to Vermeer's "View of Delft," a canvas that was painted in the 1650s and is itself strongly abstract. Because of the close visual debt to an old master, Jones's landscape is as much about art history as it is about Hampton, its subject (fig. 2.48). Jones provides us a new context in which to view art from the past, as well as a new way to look at Virginia scenery. He has succeeded in riveting our attention to his canvas and, in turn, to the Tidewater landscape. We are inspired to look anew at the great skies and broad expanses of this region,

and to understand and appreciate that the simple abstract structure of marine scenery has a dramatic and timeless force. It will command attention if the viewer will only look at it. This message is by now a familiar one; we have seen that it underlies the imagery of those earlier artists, like Benjamin Henry Latrobe and Joshua Shaw, who carried the ideal of the Picturesque to the Tidewater.

2.48 James Warwick Jones, *View of Hampton*, 1999 (first painted by the artist in 1976), acrylic on canvas, 16 x 20 in. (Courtesy of the artist)

3.39 Flavius Fisher, ***Natural Bridge***, 1882, oil on canvas, 49 x 34¹/₂ in. (Virginia Historical Society, Lora Robins Collection of Virginia Art)

III

Identity from the Land

"History, romance, nature, these make Virginia attractive."
—Wallace Nutting, *Virginia Beautiful (1930)*

The importance of Virginia's exceptionally rich historical landscape was recognized at an early date. Even in 1789, when George Washington first took the oath as president, every schoolboy knew that the first permanent English settlement had been at Jamestown, that Mount Vernon also was in Virginia, and that the Revolutionary War had ended at Yorktown. Tidewater Virginia was "the classic American land," in the words of an author in 1861.[1]

In 1789 Virginia also was becoming known for its remarkable natural landscape. Even thirty years earlier, the Reverend Andrew Burnaby had written,

> I was almost induced to make a tour for a fortnight to the southward, in Augusta county, for the sake of seeing some natural curiosities; which, the officers assured me, were extremely well worth visiting.

Nine attractions were cited to Burnaby, including a beautiful cascade, two curious hot springs, a mineral spring, a most extraordinary cave, a natural bridge, and a river that disappears under a mountain.[2] Although rumblings of trouble with the Cherokees prevented Burnaby from seeing most of these places, even before 1760 a tour of Virginia's natural wonders was in incipient form.

It took the first American guidebook, however—Thomas Jefferson's *Notes on the State of Virginia*, available after 1787—to give Virginia's natural wonders the status of national treasures and make them known internationally. By 1791 Virginians such as Lawrence Butler of Westmoreland County, on the Northern Neck, were working their way through Jefferson's list. Butler records "a description of some curiosities which I saw last summer in my Travels," or, what I did on summer vacation: "The first is Natural Bridge. . . . The second is a falling spring. The third is a cave called Madison's Cave."[3]

By 1837, when a booklet called (in translation) *Something about the Natural Wonders in North America* was published in St. Petersburg, Russia, two of the four engravings were of Virginia sites—the Natural Bridge in Virginia, the Natural Tunnel in Virginia, the Mammoth Cave of Kentucky, and Niagara Falls. There were two diagrams—of Kentucky's Mammoth Cave and of Virginia's Weyer's Cave. There were twice as many entries for Virginia than for any other state.[4]

By the mid-nineteenth century, Virginia was identified in the public imagination throughout the world as much by the natural landscape of western Virginia as by the historical landscape of the east. When a network of roads connected the natural wonders, a southern version of the European Grand Tour emerged, with travelers going from place to place because "Western Virginia offered natural attractions in a condensed locale."[5]

Some of those who made the full circuit of Virginia's world famous natural wonders began in Washington, D.C., took in the nearby Great Falls of the Potomac, then Harpers Ferry, the caves of the Shenandoah Valley, the mineral springs in the Blue Ridge and Allegheny Mountains, the New River gorge in what would become West Virginia, then the Peaks of Otter and the Natural Bridge. The latter became the most renowned "natural curiosity"—to use the language of the day—equal to the state's foremost "artificial curiosity," Mount Vernon. Those who began instead in Norfolk would first take in the nearby Great Dismal Swamp—Virginia's exotic other—in most every way the antithesis of the western wonders.

A writer in the 1790s, Isaac Weld, noted that "a variety of pleasing landscapes are presented to the eye in almost every part of the route from Bottetourt to the Patowmac."[6] In the 1890s Emory A. Allen wrote of the western region, "In the years to come, when the charms of American scenery shall be acknowledged, tourists will not rush to foreign lands until they have visited this beautiful section."[7]

He was wrong. Writing in 1870, the editor of *The*

Virginia Tourist reported that

> It is a subject of complaint, and a sore reflection with Virginians, that the natural scenery of their State, which they claim excels in interest any equal area of the Union, and surpasses that of Europe in the breadth of its panoramas and in many other effects, has been so long neglected, obtaining hitherto so small a patronage of the traveler and the artist. . . . In years before the war these scenes were visited from abroad to some extent. This awakening interest must have been cut short by the war, or, for some other reason, curiosity has resiled from the mountains of Virginia.[8]

There was a brief resurgence after 1872, when the popular book *Picturesque America* declared that "Picturesque America may be said to find almost an epitome in the State of Virginia. Her scenery—infinitely varied, exceedingly beautiful, and sometimes truly grand—repeats in her own boundaries features which would have to be sought in places widely separated."[9] But, generally speaking, interest in Virginia's natural landscape peaked before 1860. To be sure, the Valley and mountains of Virginia attract more visitors today than ever before because of population growth, but the relative position of the region within the larger picture of national and international tourism is a diminished one. No longer do people think instantly of the Natural Bridge when they think of Virginia.

By contrast, the historical sites—Jamestown, Williamsburg, and Yorktown—were well known but hard to visit in the 1800s because of lack of access, accommodations, and amenities. In the late 1800s and early 1900s, however, the Colonial Revival movement refocused attention on Virginia, where many colonial homes and churches had survived. Indeed, the fact that so many eighteenth-century structures were extant in Williamsburg made the re-creation of the town as it looked in the 1700s seem achievable. The problems of access and accommodations were overcome and today Yorktown, Mount Vernon, Jamestown, and Colonial Williamsburg each host a million people annually; and Monticello draws in excess of half a million tourists. By contrast, Natural Bridge attracts only 250,000. Although visitation to natural sites is very large, it seems that things have come full circle. Today Virginia is identified in the public consciousness, first and foremost, for its historical landscapes, not only the long-revered

Revolutionary War sites, but also the hallowed grounds of the Civil War. No one Civil War battlefield, however, has achieved the status of an icon that gives identity to the commonwealth, as Weyer's Cave and Natural Bridge once did, and as Mount Vernon and Williamsburg still do.

NATURAL LANDMARKS
The Great Falls of the Potomac

George Washington believed that the Potomac River was the natural corridor for linking the mature east to the developing west. He advocated a canal system around the falls of the Potomac, a picturesque obstruction, but an obstacle nonetheless. The river then would transport western produce to the east and take eastern settlers to the west, strengthening Washington's case for situating the new federal city on the banks of the Potomac.[10] The vote to move the seat of government was one of Washington's proudest accomplishments during his first term as president. During those same years he became one of the earliest, if not the first, collector of American landscape paintings. In 1757 he had ordered from a London merchant "A Neat Landskip" for the chimneypiece of his Mount Vernon parlor, but as president he chose instead imagery that spoke of American destiny. In 1793 he bought two idealized Hudson River scenes by William Winstanley, an English artist, whom he rated "a celebrated Landskip painter." He encouraged the artist to paint the falls of the Potomac.[11] There is no evidence that Winstanley did, but on 30 January 1797 Washington bought a landscape of the Great Falls of the Potomac by another Englishman, George Beck, who had briefly worked in Norfolk.[12] The president hung it in the Green Drawing Room of his executive mansion in Philadelphia, and later at Mount Vernon, where it remains today. Almost immediately, Beck produced a second oil painting, which, in order to provide scale for the natural wonder, included tiny figures fishing. A hand-colored aquatint was published of this second view.[13]

The scene was a popular one with artists in the early republic. On 6 April 1795 William Strickland of Yorkshire, later sixth baron of Boynton, produced a sketch of the falls in watercolor, which was the favored medium of those making quick excursions from the national capital (fig. 3.1). Like Beck, he painted the falls from the front to maximize

3.1 William Strickland, *Gt. Falls of the Patomak*, 1795, watercolor, 8 x 13 in. (Courtesy of the New-York Historical Society, ©)

the extent of the torrent.[14] On 15 September 1809 Benjamin Henry Latrobe made two watercolors taken from the Virginia side of the river, which offered the finest views. One showed the falls from "one mile distant" while the other was a close-up view that included the ruins of an iron forge. His vantage point was known as Matildaville, which was founded by "Light-Horse Harry" Lee and named for his wife. Like Washington, Lee hoped to capitalize on the establishment of the capital along the Potomac and the projected canal. The town did not thrive, however, and never had more than six houses.[15]

The boundary of Virginia and Maryland was the southern edge of the Potomac, so legally the Great Falls were in Maryland. However, those making a circuit of Virginia's natural wonders from Washington, D.C., usually began there. The falls lay just fifteen miles upriver from the federal city. In 1810 Arthur Middleton wrote that "The Falls of the Patowmac, a few miles from this city, were too attractive to be neglected."[16] Another visitor noted that "they are well worth a visit."[17] "From the place where we landed to the Falls," wrote Isaac Weld, "which is a distance of about three miles, there is a wild, romantic path running along the margin of the river, and winding at the same time round the base of a high hill covered with lofty

trees and rocks."[18] On 26 August 1819 a foreigner "With a large party of ladies and gentlemen" visited the Great Falls. "On my way thither I saw no good farms," he wrote, but "About the rocky falls of this river all is wild, romantic, savage, and sublime, to a degree beyond my power to describe." He was not so swept away, however, as to miss the economic possibilities of the region, noting with almost equal fervor, "Here are pits, or quarries of marble, an infinite supply!"[19]

"The view of the small cataract is not unusual," wrote Carlo Vidua, "but that of the large one merits observation."[20] Arthur Middleton described it: "water rushes down with tremendous impetuosity, over a ledge of rocks, in several different cataracts, winding afterwards, with great velocity, along the bottom of the precipices, whose rocky crags are so intermixed with trees as to produce a beautiful effect."[21] The Great Falls of the Potomac, however, would never be the ultimate American waterfalls. "I did not turn out of my way to see them," wrote Godfrey Vigne in 1832. "I have seen a great many, and purposed visiting Niagara."[22] By the time of William MacLeod's painting of 1873 (fig. 3.2), the reputation of the Great Falls as a natural wonder had declined considerably. It

3.2 William MacLeod, *Great Falls of the Potomac*, 1873, oil on canvas, 34 x 45 in. (Courtesy of Corcoran Gallery of Art)

was not included in either *Picturesque America* or *The Great South*, both published in that decade. The opening of the Far West and the grandiose canvases of Albert Bierstadt and Thomas Moran made it seem merely quaint. It is too little visited today.

Harpers Ferry

Another place that experienced the vagaries of popularity was Harpers Ferry. It was not the town itself that was at first an attraction, but the nearby confluence of the Shenandoah and Potomac Rivers. For several decades after the founding of the republic, most visitors made reference to Thomas Jefferson's memorable description of Harpers Ferry in *Notes on the State of Virginia*, privately printed in Paris in 1785 but not generally available until the London edition appeared in 1787.

As discussed in the preceding chapter concerning the Sublime, Jefferson called Harpers Ferry "perhaps one of the most stupendous scenes in nature" and "worth a voyage across the Atlantic." One of the first to disagree was Isaac Weld, who visited about 1795 with a copy of Jefferson's *Notes* in hand. Jefferson had written that the rivers Potomac and Shenandoah, dammed up by the mountain, suddenly "tore the mountain asunder from its summit to its base" and then flowed together unvexed to the sea.[23] Weld complained that Jefferson wrote as if he had been there when it happened but that at present it gave no such impression. "To find numberless scenes more stupendous it would be needless to go farther than Wales," he concluded.[24]

Weld overlooked the psychological factors that come into play in viewing grand scenery. The romantic imagination was not limited to the scene "in its present state," wrote Henry Gilpin in 1827. Rather, "such a scene does not astonish you simply in itself, but you cannot see it without reflecting on the means by which it was caused—you are at a loss to conjecture whether it is the work of some sudden convulsion or the effect of gradual and long continued causes."[25]

Still, some tourists felt that Jefferson had misled them. Jerome Bonaparte was well aware of "Mr. Jefferson's singular description," which Bonaparte quotes extensively in his journal of a visit to Harpers Ferry. The Frenchman juxtaposes it, however, to one by an unnamed author, who ridiculed the idea of "two quiet rivers joining and in a moment rending asunder the solid mountain!" Bonaparte then concludes, "Quite a different description, is it not?"[26] Godfrey Vigne, writing in 1832, also dismissed Jefferson's cataclysmic scenario: "After all I had heard, I was disappointed with Harper's Ferry." He supposed the rivers had gradually worn a gap through the mountains "without the least appearance of exasperation."[27] The Italian count Carlo Vidua wrote, "Harper's Ferry owes its notoriety to ex-president Jefferson, who, in his *Notes on the State of Virginia*, a much admired work, gave a very exaggerated description of the picturesque scene." He would concede only that it was "a very wild and rustic view," hardly a cause for crossing the ocean.[28]

Jefferson's language was even satirized in a poem:

> Ah! Tell me not of heights sublime,
> The rocks at Harper's Ferry,
> Of mountains rent in the lapse of time—
>   They're very sublime, oh very!
> I'm thinking more of the glowing cheek
>   Of a lovely girl and merry,
> Who clim'd with me to yon highest peak—
>   The girl of Harper's Ferry.[29]

But not everyone felt humbugged by Jefferson. Henry Gilpin wrote that, "I was very sorry I had not with me Mr. Jefferson's notes in which is a short but vivid account of Harper's Ferry, which the girls must read—everybody has been telling me it is *too* vivid, & that I should be disappointed . . . but I have found that many people never find the wonders of nature sufficiently wonderful."[30] On viewing the rivers' junction, John Edwards Caldwell wrote, "The mind is lost in wonder and admiration, and my pen in vain attempts a description of the scene itself, or the feelings I experienced in contemplating this great work of nature."[31] William Faux, an Englishman, virtually paraphrased Jefferson: "The romantic and stupendous scenes of nature are here unrivalled. No travellers should return from America without seeing Harper's Ferry, which is very well sketched by the late president Jefferson in his notes on Virginia."[32] Another Englishman agreed that "the scenery of Harpers Ferry is very grand" and "inexpressibly beautiful," but for sublimity felt that "I have seen bolder and more sublime scenery and scenery of more exquisite loveliness in our own country."[33]

3.3 William Roberts, *Junction of the Potomac and Shenandoah, Virginia*, c. 1808–10, watercolor, 12 x 15¹/₂ in. (Courtesy of the Museum of Early Southern Decorative Arts)

Jefferson's celebration of Harpers Ferry attracted foreign and American artists to the site. One of the first was William Roberts, a native of England or Ireland who had a brother in Norfolk and who, in one letter to Thomas Jefferson, described himself as a Virginian. During his presidency Jefferson received oil paintings by Roberts of both Natural Bridge and Harpers Ferry. A few years later, feeling that those paintings "were not I think altogether worthy of the subjects," Roberts tried again. His vantage point was the top of the hill from which Jefferson had surveyed the scene below. In the pen, pencil, and wash sketch executed on the site, Roberts gives some suggestion of sublimity by emphasizing the height of the mountains, but the federal arsenal founded in 1794, adjacent houses, and ferry boats carrying both humans and animals domesticate the scene, rendering it more picturesque. The regular lines and crisp details of the buildings suggest that Roberts used a camera obscura or, less likely because patented just a

year earlier, a camera lucida. The initial sketch was the basis for a finished watercolor that was sent to the etcher Joseph Jeakes (fig. 3.3). To reduce the sense of vertigo, Roberts's "studio" watercolor is a more close-up view in which both the mountains and rushing water are diminished. As compensation, boulders were added to the river as sublime hints of the dangers of navigation. Cannons were added to clarify which building is the arsenal. These changes were maintained and, to a degree, extended in the aquatint by Jeakes, except that the cannons became logs. Published in London in 1808 or 1809, the etching bore the title "Junction of the Potomac and Shenandoah, Virginia."[34]

The American artist Rembrandt Peale painted the watercolor shown here (fig. 3.4) about 1812 as a study for a four-by-six-foot oil painting that he displayed for a viewing fee. He announced in the Philadelphia *Aurora* of 9 January 1812 that "REMBRANDT'S NEW PICTURE GALLERY" had "his large view of HARPER'S FERRY at the junction of the Shenandoah with the Potomac." At so early a date this canvas was probably better known than any other painting of an American landmark. Because it essentially illustrated Thomas Jefferson's description in *Notes on the State of Virginia*, Peale chose to mention it in his application to Thomas Jefferson in 1825 soliciting a post teaching fine arts at Mr. Jefferson's new university in Charlottesville.[35] Peale's painting was not the largest of Harpers Ferry. On 1 December 1808 a notice in the *Federal Gazette & Baltimore Daily Advertiser* placed by Cole & Bonsal, auctioneers, reported that they "are now exhibiting a collection of Paintings, intended to be disposed of by Subscription; among others, is a representation of Harper's Ferry, with the adjacent Scenery, this painting, which is elegantly framed is 11½ by 7½ feet."

In 1806 William Winstanley exhibited in London his view of the confluence of the Shenandoah and Potomac. George Washington had encouraged him to paint "the Great and little Falls [of the Potomac]; the passage through the Blue [Ridge] Mountains, the Natural Bridge, &c. as grand objects."[36] Francis Guy, a landscapist in Baltimore who produced views of gentlemen's seats, also was lured by Jefferson's account and did several views of Harpers Ferry, including a large canvas now in a private collection. Unlike William Roberts's mountaintop view, Winstanley and Guy painted the scene from the water's edge, and the latter's inclusion of cattle followed precepts of the Picturesque. Charles Bird King sketched the site c. 1815–20, as did Thomas Doughty in the next decade. Thanks to Thomas

Jefferson, Harpers Ferry became an internationally recognized landmark of Virginia; thanks to George Washington, it was easily accessible by water from the new national capital.

Nathaniel Willis had another kind of experience at Harpers Ferry—a guilt trip. Standing at Jefferson's summit he thought,

> It is difficult, at least for me, to stand on any eminence commanding a landscape, wild, yet formed for a blest human residence, without seeing in it the forfeited inheritance of the red man. The unpicturesque new village of the white man, his mill, and his factory, does not convey to my imagination an image of happiness and I regret the primitive rover of the wild, who neither blackened nature with smoke, nor violated her harmony with brick and shingle.[37]

Here is an early manifestation of the myth that the American Indians never "blackened nature with smoke" when in fact, in Virginia at least, slash-and-burn agriculture had been their agricultural modus operandi for centuries before European contact. As to Willis's praise of the Indians for resisting "brick and shingle," as an Englishman Willis might be excused for not knowing that it was such disdain for the white man's ways that led to their expulsion or even extermination in America. No such tender solicitude as Willis's was shown them while they were still around. There was no place for romantic sentimentality about the Indians until they were killed or safely removed beyond the Mississippi. Thereafter, guilt about the "vanished race" could be indulged in the more lavishly because unencumbered by need for redress or fear of their return.

Willis had his epiphany at the top of a high hill overlooking the rivers, the gap, and the town. Upon that summit, "probably the first object in point of celebrity, though not in real natural interest, that claims the attention of the stranger, is Jefferson's Rock," wrote Ele Bowen in 1855. In a post–Civil War painting by C. B. Ogden, the famous rock already is held in place by artificial supports (fig. 3.5).[38] "This juts out at the side of a steep hill," wrote James K. Paulding in 1816, "a little way up the Shenandoah, and from it there is a fine view of the chasm in the mountain, and the noble

3.4 Rembrandt Peale, **Harper's Ferry**, 1812, watercolor, 8¼ x 13¼ in. (Courtesy of Maryland Historical Society)

landscape seen through the vista."[39] The rock reportedly bore Jefferson's signature until, Jeffersonians claimed, a dastardly Federalist erased it. Hundreds of others have signed it since. Perhaps this anecdote had its origin in a specious story of which Jefferson was the author. In 1802 Dr. Samuel Latham Mitchell asked Jefferson the location of the exact spot from which he had first surveyed Harpers Ferry. Jefferson replied that it no longer existed—having been blown up by government soldiers during the Federalist regime—from political considerations he supposed.[40]

Ele Bowen described Jefferson's Rock:

3.5 C. B. Ogden, *Jefferson's Rock* (at Harpers Ferry), 1887, oil on board, 18 ½ x 12 in. (Virginia Historical Society, Lora Robins Collection of Virginia Art)

It is probably about twelve feet square, on the top, by five feet in thickness. Its shape, however, is very irregular. It will be observed that it lies directly over the fissure which detached a larger rock below, and that, very nearly in the centre, it supports another rock. . . . This rock is supported in equilibrium in a very singular manner, and it is this which constitutes its most interesting feature. Broad and massive at the top, it rests on a rock less than one-fourth its size and weight, and this, in turn, instead of lying flat, is nicely poised on its rear. The whole thing looks very much like a huge tortoise bearing a heavy incumbrance on its back!

The sublimity of the scene lay partly in its precariousness. "The whole assemblage," wrote Bowen, "appears ready, at any moment, to march down the precipice and woe to the humble tenements 'down below' if it ever does."[41]

Some tourists wrote as though they would have

3.6 Ferdinand Richardt, *Harpers Ferry*, 1858, oil on canvas, 28 ½ x 48 ½ in. (Private collection, lent in memory of Mr. and Mrs. William E. Crawford, Jr.)

welcomed the flattening of the town. Thomas Cather insisted that

> The view from the top of the rock on either side of Harper's Ferry is indeed glorious, but there is scarcely a pleasure in this world without an alloy of pain. No blessing without a curse upon it, and this scenery is subject to the general rule. There is a most abominable little village just in the pass between the mountains. . . . Here is the Government Manufactory of Firearms, and the smell of coal smoke, and the clanking of hammers obtrude themselves on the senses and prevent your enjoyment from being unmixed.[42]

The artist Ferdinand Richardt had a different attitude. He turned his back on the junction of the rivers and made the town the focus of his paintings, whether in close-up (fig. 3.6) or distant (fig. 3.7) views. The town of Harpers Ferry was among the first places in Virginia to be reached by a railroad, as is shown in an oil painting by the English artist George Harvey about 1836 (fig. 3.8). Harpers Ferry became a transportation nexus, and even in Harvey's early view one sees traffic by foot, horseback, canal boat, and railway.

In October 1859 Harpers Ferry began a new phase of its history when abolitionist John Brown made a raid on the federal armory to secure weapons for slaves whom he assumed would revolt once they were armed. In a sense, the Civil War was ignited at Harpers Ferry, as much as at Fort Sumter. Although the raid was a complete failure, it polarized attitudes throughout the nation. Southerners were livid to learn that the man who would have had them killed in their beds was being lionized in the North as a Christian martyr and hero. In the ensuing war the town changed hands several times.

A guidebook published after the Civil War declared that "Nature, the Federal Government, and the Baltimore & Ohio Railway Company have done a great deal to make Harpers Ferry beautiful and prosperous." After admiring the new railway bridge more than any natural features, the writer continued that, "War, flood, and fire have done a great deal to injure and destroy it. The result is a remarkable combination of sublimity and dirt, magnificence and ruin. If there were nothing else to interest a tourist, the historical associations would attract him."[43] As Harpers Ferry receded

3.7 Attributed to Ferdinand Richardt, *Harpers Ferry*, c. 1859, oil on canvas, 32 1/4 x 35 in. (Courtesy of the Glen Burnie Museum, Winchester, Virginia)

3.8 George Harvey, *Harpers Ferry*, c.1835–41, oil on board,
18 x 24 in. (Courtesy of Raymond E. Holland Collection)

3.9 Andrew Melrose,
Near Harpers Ferry,
c. 1870–80s, oil on
canvas, 21 x 35 ½ in.
(Courtesy of Lora
Robins)

in the public consciousness as a natural wonder it simultaneously came to the fore as a historical attraction. Andrew Melrose's oil painting from the 1870s or 1880s alludes to Harpers Ferry's duality by placing in the foreground a cannon so grotesquely oversized that it seems to belong at the Kremlin (fig. 3.9). It reminds the viewer that the scene has not always been a peaceful and bucolic one. By 1887 *Raymond's Vacation Excursions*, a popular guidebook, described Harpers Ferry almost wholly in terms of its historical importance rather than its landscape.[44]

Caves

"The Alleghenies, or endless mountains, are divided into small, nearly parallel chains, notable for their natural phenomena, including the numerous grottoes," wrote Jacques Gérard Milbert in 1828.[45] One of the first caves to become a significant tourist attraction was Madison's Cave, named for the father of Bishop James Madison of Virginia, one-time president of the College of William and Mary. It is located seventeen miles north of Staunton, in Augusta County, near the south fork of the Shenandoah River. "It has long been known," wrote Henry Gilpin in 1827, "and I believe it is described by Mr. Jefferson in his Notes on Virginia—a book by the bye, I have a thousand times regretted that I forgot to bring with me." Madison's cave, however, was "so less remarkable than Weyer's, that it is now seldom visited."[46] Once attendance declined, it was mostly given over to the manufacture of saltpeter, the stench of which kept most everyone away.

About 1804 a German farmer named Bernard Weyer (or Weir) discovered another cave in the same hill as Madison's Cave. It became one of Virginia's foremost natural attractions and today is known as Grand Caverns. The German artist Edward Beyer included a torchlit view in his series of lithographs called *The Album of Virginia* (fig. 3.10). "The Artist has selected the Tapestry and Drum Room," wrote Samuel Mordecai in the textual accompaniment to Beyer's lithographs, "which is perhaps the greatest of its Wonders."[47] The famous mid-nineteenth-century travel writer and illustrator David Hunter Strother, whose nom de plume

was Porte Crayon, was an enthusiastic proponent of "Nature's Great Masterpiece." In "Virginia Illustrated," a five-part series of articles published in *Harper's New Monthly Magazine* between December 1854 and August 1856, Porte Crayon described and drew the natural wonders of Virginia. At Weyer's Cave he wrote that "The richest arabesques of a Persian palace, or the regal hall of the famed Alhambra are but poor and mean in comparison," but for actual description words failed him and he took refuge in his art:

> Indeed, but for the sketches, the disheartening task of description would probably not have been undertaken, for how can mere words portray scenes which have no parallel among the things of upper earth? . . . Language fails frequently in conveying correct impressions of the most commonplace objects, and in the hands of its most skillful masters is sometimes weak, uncertain, false. Combine it with graphic art and how the page brightens! Well have our fathers called it the art of Illumination. Most books without illustrations are but half written.[48]

"We went into the cave about three o'clock and remained until nearly six. I cannot describe it," wrote Mary Jane Boggs in 1851.[49] Henry Gilpin, a visitor in 1827, noted that "Various names are given to the different rooms."[50] "The association of the beautiful and sublime with the vulgar and hackneyed" was how Samuel Mordecai dismissed the silly names given the thirty-five "apartments."[51] This was, after all, the heyday of P. T. Barnum. A writer for *Scribner's* referred to some of the names in this flowery

3.10 Edward Beyer, ***The Drum's. The Tapestry Room. Weyers Cave***, 1858, lithograph, 10 x 15¾ in. (Virginia Historical Society)

description:

> a vast subterranean labyrinth of glittering grottoes and iridescent galleries, where stalactites of extraordinary brilliancy sparkle in the torch light and hang from the fretted roof like corbels and foliated pendants of a gothic cathedral. Here are pulpits and organs, audience chambers, and throne rooms; here the ceaseless petrification takes all manner of beautiful and fantastic shapes, throwing its drapery around the form of a vestal or fastening its jewels to the person of a queen, as the visitor passes along its crystal colonnades and stops delighted before its frozen cataracts.[52]

How did visitors rank Weyer's Cave as a natural wonder? Mary Jane Boggs "was not quite so much struck with it as Natural Bridge and the Peaks of Otter," but thought "it is really a wonderful place."[53] By contrast, Gen. Calvin Jones remarked, "The Bridge affords only two or three views—the Cave a thousand."[54] Charles Cramer remembered in 1837 that "an English painter who visited the cave remarked that it would take him years to create drawings that would even come close to doing it justice."[55] One ambitious artist who felt equal to the task was Russell Smith, who in 1844 painted "Scene in Weyer's Cave looking toward the mouth" (fig. 3.11). An 1861 article in *De Bow's Review* called Weyer's Cave "scarcely inferior in mysterious grandeur to the celebrated Mammoth Cave of Kentucky."[56] A Confederate soldier wrote, "It is certainly the most beautiful hole in the ground I was ever in, and the environments on the outside are strikingly picturesque."[57] *The Virginia Tourist* in 1870 listed it as "one of the greatest sights in Virginia."[58] Dr. John Jennings Moorman in his 1846 book *Virginia Springs* went further: "It would be difficult to convey an adequate idea of the vastness and sublimity of some, or the exquisite beauty and grandeur of others of its innumerable apartments . . . Weyer's cave is one of the great natural wonders of this New World, and for its eminence in its own class, deserves to be ranked with the Natural Bridge

and Niagara, while it is far less known than either."[59]

In the 1870s the American public was reminded of Weyer's Cave when a chapter was devoted to it in *Picturesque America* accompanied by several illustrations by artist Harry Fenn.[60] Within six years, however, the discovery of Luray Caverns in Page County eclipsed Weyer's Cave almost as thoroughly as Weyer's had displaced Madison's Cave after 1804. A restrained but significant testimonial of Luray's importance came from the Smithsonian Institution: "Comparing this great natural curiosity with others of the same class, it is safe to say that there is probably no other cave in the world more completely and profusely decorated with stalactite and stalagmite ornamentation than that of Luray."[61]

3.11 Russell Smith, *Scene in Weyer's Cave looking toward the mouth*, 1844, watercolor, 8 ½ x 12 ½ in. (Courtesy of Calder Loth)

3.12 Joseph Becker, *Virginia-The Grandest of American Caverns-A Visit to the Newly Discovered Cave at Luray, Page County-The Sultana Column in the Giants' Hall*, 1878, woodcut, 13 ¾ x 20 ½ in. (Virginia Historical Society)

Visitors were amazed. "That rigid stone should lend itself to so many delicate, graceful, airy shapes and attitudes rivaling the flexible flower of the organic world, fills the mind with astonishment and bewilders the eye," wrote Ernest Ingersoll.[62] An Englishwoman considered it "unrivaled in the whole known world, and far surpassing in interest of every kind, the great 'Mammoth Cave' of Kentucky, gigantic in size, but almost bare." A pair of travelers who had seen both caves agreed. "No pen can describe it; no pencil can depict it," they wrote.[63]

Some attempted it nonetheless. A supplement to *Frank Leslie's Illustrated Newspaper* for 18 January 1879—within months of the discovery of Luray—included one double-page and two full-page engravings—each entitled "The Grandest of American Caverns" (fig. 3.12). Few painters would ever depict Luray Caverns. It belonged to the age of photography. It also had electric lights by 1882, at least in the summer. An 1884 guidebook to attractions along the Baltimore & Ohio Railway said, "mystical is the influence of the atmosphere permeated by electricity; for the bright light is everywhere, and with its characteristic shadows produces effects of the most impressive description."[64] Nature, at least underground, could now be theatrically lit.

The Springs

From the mid-eighteenth to the early twentieth century, western Virginia was dotted with spas. People traveled to them not only from the Tidewater and low country regions of Virginia and other states, but also from northern cities, as a refuge from the sultry summer heat and malarial fevers or simply as a summer excursion. One went for sightseeing, sport, business, courtship, matchmaking, to see and to be seen.

There were thermal springs, such as Warm Springs and Hot Springs, where the water's temperature as well as its mineral content made it appealing. At the mineral springs, the chemical content of the water was supposed to cure, or at least alleviate, a range of ailments and conditions. Some of the spas were denominated Warm, Hot, Sweet, Sweet Chalybeate, Healing, or Boiling Springs, and others Red, White, Blue, Grey, Yellow, or Salt Sulphur. They were not interchangeable. Some springs were thought best for childhood illnesses, others for problems of the aged.

Beginning with Dr. John Rouelle's *Complete Treatise on the Mineral Waters of Virginia* in 1792 and continuing with Dr. John Jennings Moorman's *Virginia Springs* in 1846, a propagandist literature set out to analyze the healthful properties of each spa and extol the benefits of mountain living. In the first edition of *Notes on the State of Virginia*, however, Thomas Jefferson expressed a more measured view, noting the "several medicinal springs, some of which are indubitably efficacious, while others seem to owe their reputation as much to fancy and a change of air and regimen as to their real virtues."[65] Even more skeptical was Capt. Frederick Marryat, who wrote, "We drank of every variety of water except pure water—sometimes iron, sometimes sulphur; and, indeed, every kind of chalybeate." He came to doubt their efficaciousness but "did not like, however to interfere with the happiness of others, so I did not communicate my ideas to my fellow-passengers."[66]

James Kirke Paulding, traveling to the Warm, Hot, White Sulphur, and Sweet Springs during the summer of 1816, wrote that

> very few people visit these springs, remote and difficult of access as they are, except to avoid the autumnal season, which is unhealthy in the lowlands; or, in the hope of arresting the progress of some dangerous malady. Few come there for pleasure—and even fewer to exhibit their fine clothes. Indeed, the greater proportion of the company consists of invalids; and, of course, little amusement or gayety is to be found at these places.[67]

The middle decades of the nineteenth century, however, witnessed a dramatic rise in the number of visitors to the springs because of turnpike construction, improved stagecoach travel, and eventually the railroad. Moreover, once a network of decent roads connected the various springs, "something like a Southern version of the tour" emerged, with high society going from spring to spring.[68] Drawn from across the Old Dominion, the United States, and even Europe, articulate travelers reported their impressions, favorable or otherwise, in such popular standards as George W. Featherstonhaugh's *Excursion through the Slave States* (1844) and Mrs. Anne Royall's *Southern Tour* (1830). One of the South's most celebrated female travelers, Mrs. Royall, an Englishwoman, supported herself in widowhood by publishing a series of guidebooks based on her tours through the United States. She was unabashed in voicing her opinions. Of the springs region of western Virginia she wrote, "How admirably has Providence provided resources for every part of the globe. This bleak, inhospitable, and dreary country, remote from commerce and navigation, destitute of arts, taste, or refinement, derives great advantages from these springs. Thousands of dollars are left here annually by those wealthy visitors."[69]

Virginia's resorts also became the setting for romantic fiction and the inspiration for poems. Antebellum writers, eager to defend the traditions of southern society, played out their romantic fancies against a springs backdrop that characterized an aristocratic lifestyle sympathetically. These books, in turn, contributed to the mythology of the Old South that, after defeat in the Civil War, fused with that of the Lost Cause.

Approximately fifty miles southwest of Washington, D.C., Fauquier White Sulphur, or Warrenton, Springs lay far off the beaten path to Virginia's mountain resorts. This drawback was in some measure offset by its proximity to the nation's capital, a fact that brought it such distinguished visitors as John Marshall, James Madison, James Monroe, Martin Van Buren, and Henry Clay. In 1849 the Virginia legislature took refuge there from a cholera outbreak in Richmond.

If Fauquier White Sulphur Springs did not achieve preeminence among its sister spas, it was not because it lacked aesthetic appeal. In that regard many thought Fauquier White Sulphur surpassed all others. The accommodations were excellent. The four-story brick hotel and sixteen buildings that stood around it in a semicircle enclosed a park ornamented with fountains and formal gardens, if an engraving on the resort's stationery is to be believed (fig. 3.13). These were not present, however, when Edward Beyer depicted it for his *Album of Virginia* in 1857. Either the continental garden had disappeared or it had never been built. Nonetheless, Beyer shows "a well shaded ground" that was "beautifully laid out, or ornamented by walks, flowers, and shrubbery." The notes to Beyer's *Album* point out as well the deer park, where a pack of sixty or seventy fallow deer afforded the pleasure of the hunt over a one-mile track stretched along the Rappahannock River.[70] On nearby flat land mock medieval tournaments were staged.

The surrounding landscape was neither wild nor romantic. Nonetheless, visitors were moved by the setting and the view. An anonymous visitor wrote,

> There are few scenes upon which I have gazed with so much delight and rapture, as that presented occasionally, at sunset, from the top of the Pavilion. Art indeed, has done but little for the enhancement of the prospect, but there Nature unfolds her beauties to the spectator, in many of her most fascinating and lovely forms. . . . How rapturous would have been the sensation of Claude, or Poussin . . . at seeing some of these autumnal sunsets![71]

The Civil War hastened the decline of Fauquier White Sulphur Springs. In 1862 Union troops firing on Confederates encamped there reduced the hotel to ruins. It reopened in the late 1870s but could not recapture its former grandeur. The property became a military academy in 1895, but when the main building burned it went out of business. It reopened as a recreational center, then became the home of the Fauquier Springs Country Club.

To the northwest lay one of Virginia's earliest spas, Berkeley Springs, now in West Virginia's eastern panhandle. It was first named Frederick Springs and the nearby town Bath after England's premier watering place, and in 1756 Lord Fairfax gave the land containing the springs to Virginia for the benefit of the public. The Berkeley Springs was established in 1776 and became one of the earliest fashionable watering places in the South.

Another early spa was Shannondale Springs in the northern end of the Blue Ridge Mountains. George Washington went there in 1748, at age sixteen, while surveying for Lord Fairfax.[72] The print shown here, however, depicts buildings not built until the early 1800s (fig. 3.14). From this vantage point William Burke wrote, "Ascending to the summit you have in view the whole scene, including two-thirds of the horizon . . . . Landscape should be seen by glimpses . . . . In this respect, Shannondale is favored, being studded with fine elms, oaks, sycamores, and other indigenous trees."[73]

In his *Narrative of a Tour in North America*, published in 1831—as was the Shannondale image—the British traveler who called himself Henry Tudor visited the Virginia springs and described the setting and architecture of another of the early springs. This was Sweet Springs, on Pott's Creek, a tributary of the James. It lay in Monroe County, just into the region that would become West Virginia in

3.13 *Stationery* letterhead from Fauquier White Sulphur Springs resort, before 1849. (Virginia Historical Society)

1863. Jerome Napoleon Bonaparte wrote in 1846, "The Sweet Springs is one of the most ancient and celebrated watering-places in the United States."[74] The spectacular natural setting and the arrangement of buildings at Sweet Springs was like that at Shannondale and, indeed, was typical of the mountain springs. Tudor was traveling in winter, however, which was atypical.

> Half frozen to death, after having passed over a continued succession of four or five mountains, I reached, for the night, one of the fashionable Virginian watering-places, called the 'Sweet Springs,' situated at the foot of one of them, and by which, indeed, and by others, it is entirely surrounded, having a handsome and extensive sweep of verdant ground spread out in front, of the dimensions of a park. Nothing can exceed the romantic seclusion of this beautiful spot; of which the finely sheltered situation, and many natural advantages, render it a crowded and favorite resort during the summer months. The accommodations, nevertheless, are very indifferent, inasmuch as the sleeping apartments are altogether separated from the hotel, in which are the public rooms, and where are carried on the ordinary functions of eating and drinking. The dormitories are erected at some little distance from the latter, in the form of a continued line of cottages of a single story, and in each of those, one, and sometimes two beds are placed. It is obvious that such an arrangement must be exposed to much inconvenience, particularly for invalids, and for all in rainy weather.[75]

Just a few years later, George Cooke depicted on canvas a neighboring resort in the same county that was similar in its architecture and setting. This was Red Sulphur Springs (fig. 3.15). "The approach is beautifully romantic and picturesque," wrote Dr. Henry Huntt. "Winding his way around a high mountain, the traveler is charmed by the

sudden view of his resting place, some hundreds of feet immediately beneath him, into which he descends to a verdant glen, surrounded on all sides by lofty mountains."[76] Cooke presents the resort at sunset, when Huntt's tired traveler would have reached what he perceived as an idyllic setting, all the more welcome as the sun set. By the use of dramatic lighting and by exaggerating the slope or pitch of the mountains, the painter evokes visually what Huntt described in words. The artist includes himself at an easel in the foreground of the painting, his attention directed to the dormitory rows that are still lit by sunlight.

Beyer visited Red Sulphur Springs two decades after George Cooke; the resort had changed surprisingly little, although the social hall, the building on the right that is elevated above the others, had apparently lost its classical balustrade by 1857 and had become a less elegant structure. The notes to the *Album of Virginia* refer to the "picturesque" nature of this region and to the "steep Mountain" above the spring, but the mood of the landscape and its unusual terrain were not the principal concerns of this artist. Instead, Beyer shows Red Sulphur under the midday sun, and he focuses on the distinguishing feature of the resort, the spring to the left that is sheltered by an elegant and huge classical temple. The notes to the *Album* explain its importance: "The pavilion over the Spring is a dome 42 feet in diameter, supported by twelve columns." With a height of "about 52 feet," it was "the largest of any in the Mountains of Virginia."[77] It was designed by the notable Philadelphia architect William Strickland. In his series of lithographs Beyer depicts fourteen of these world-famous springs; his

3.14 C. Burton, for Fenner Sears & Co., London, *Shannondale Springs, Virginia*, 1831, engraving, 4 x 5 ½ in. (Virginia Historical Society)

3.15 George Cooke, *View of Red Sulphur Springs, Virginia*, 1836–37, oil on canvas, 32 ¾ x 48 in. (Private collection)

purpose with this imagery was to differentiate the resorts from one another by pointing to the unique elements of each.

The approach to the Warm Springs in adjoining Bath County also was impressive. A Miss Sedgwick wrote:

> We ascended for four miles, winding up a road resembling the ascent in the Catskill, but affording glimpses of far more beautiful mountain scenery. When we reached the summit the grandest scene my eyes ever lit on, save Niagara, was under my eye. An amphitheatre of deep, deep glens below, mountain rising over mountain, one stretching beyond another, some in conical peaks, others in soft, wavy lines, and others broken into fantastic shapes, the sunbeams here and there piercing the dark flying clouds and giving to the whole scene the elegant effect of a painter's pencil.[78]

One of the travelers who sketched Warm Springs was Sir William Fox, who would become the first prime minister of New Zealand (figs. 3.16 and 3.17). With its straight roads and many support buildings, Warm Springs more resembled a town than the other resorts. Edward Beyer, the principal painter of Virginia's towns at mid-century, in effect had only to repeat that formula when he added a view of Warm Springs to his *Album of Virginia* just a few years after William Fox's visit. In Beyer's lithograph a sizeable hotel stands at the center of the composition, like the college

building in his view of Salem (fig. 4.4 below).

A few miles from Warm Springs lay Hot Springs. In 1832 Thomas Goode, physician and entrepreneur, acquired the property and developed a resort. By 1848 there were so many visitors to Hot Springs that Goode was compelled to build a large hotel, which he named the Homestead. According to the notes to Beyer's *Album*, the accommodations for 250 guests were "first class" and the scenery was "wild, romantic, and beautiful." By the 1850s the Homestead was easily reached from eastern cities. But more than the location and the architecture, it was the waters that set this resort apart. There were nine separate baths of varied temperatures. The waters were said to be "excelled by nothing ever known to the human race. Their alternative and curative powers are unsurpassed by those of any mineral water on the face of the Globe."[79]

Bathing, of course, was what lured travelers to the mineral springs in the first place; water was the principal topic of their written accounts. The landscape was impressive but, after all, was much the same everywhere in the western counties. Many descriptions seem interchangeable. Berkeley Springs was a "pleasant rural situation at the foot of a steep mountain."[80] Shannondale Springs was "most beautiful and magnificent."[81] Augusta Springs was "extremely picturesque."[82] At Sweet Springs, "Nature indeed has not been sparing in embellishing with her choicest beauties this enchanting spot."[83] Of Sweet Chalybeate Springs in Alleghany County William Burke wrote, "The situation of these Springs is a beautiful one, overlooking one of the most fertile and best cultivated farms in Virginia."[84] At Blue Sulphur "The mountain scenery is indeed rich and romantic . . . . The painter may find employment in sketching the bold outline of nature's work."[85] An Englishman traveling from west to east, passing from the Kanawha country to the White Sulphur Springs, also was moved by the landscape to make a reference to art: "For one hundred and sixty miles you pass through a gallery of pictures most exquisite, most varied, most beautiful—one that will not suffer in comparison with a row along the finest portions of the Rhine."[86]

The springs at White Sulphur were well known to the Indian inhabitants of what now is Greenbrier County, West Virginia. After the Revolution reports of the miraculous recovery of an invalid woman who had taken the waters spurred the first arrival of white visitors. Soon cabins dotted the landscape as Col. Michael Bowyer, owner of some ten thousand acres surrounding the springs, sought to accommodate travelers "to take the cure."

About 1818 Bowyer's son-in-law James Calwell became proprietor of the White Sulphur. Calwell, with his industrious son William, constructed new cabins and a tavern and so launched the springs on its rise to prominence. One of the first artists to portray it was John H. B. Latrobe about 1832. Among the first authors to extol it was John Jennings Moorman, the resident physician at White Sulphur Springs. His *Virginia Springs*, in multiple editions after 1846, gave other springs their due but claimed primacy for the Greenbrier White Sulphur.

If the healing properties of its waters attracted its first visitors, the "high and refined social qualities" of its clientele were responsible for the White Sulphur's achieving a reputation as *the* Virginia spa of the nineteenth century. The socially, politically, and financially eminent from all parts of the North and South, as well as from foreign shores, set the White Sulphur

Springs as their principal destination as they sallied forth on their annual trek to the cooler, more healthful environs of the Virginia mountains.

Among the foreigners was Jerome Napoleon Bonaparte, nephew of the French emperor. "The White Sulphur is decidedly the most agreeable of the Virginia springs," he wrote. "The White Sulphur is in an elevated valley on the western side of the Allegheny ridge, and is surrounded by hills. The middle of the valley, where the buildings stand, is cleared of trees, with the exception of some noble oaks, left for the purpose of ornament and shade. . . . The 'tout ensemble' produces a most pleasing appearance."[87]

3.16 Sir William Fox, *Near the Warm Springs. Virginia*, 1853, watercolor, 9¹⁄₂ x 13⁴⁄₅ in. (Courtesy of National Library of New Zealand)

3.17 Sir William Fox, *The Warm Springs. Virginia*, 1853, watercolor, 9¹⁄₂ x 13⁴⁄₅ in. (Courtesy of National Library of New Zealand)

3.18 Edward Beyer, *Greenbrier White Sulphur Springs*, 1853, oil on canvas, 26 x 50 in. (Courtesy of The Greenbrier, White Sulphur Springs)

Edward Beyer depicted the resort twice in the 1850s (figs. 3.18 and 3.19), when Marianne Finch echoed the consensus that it was "the most central and celebrated of these establishments."[88] The notes to Beyer's *Album of Virginia* make clear why White Sulphur Springs was an obvious choice for the artist's attention: "The beauty of its location, the medicinal virtues of its waters, and its enlarged accommodations, have conferred upon it the title of 'The Queen of Springs' in the Mountains of Virginia; and hundreds flock to it every season from all sections of the Union." In the year preceding the publication of Beyer's *Album*, "great improvements" had been made to the resort: "Many of the cabins have been removed, and magnificent buildings and handsome cottages have been erected in their stead." The architect for these changes, a Mr. Ellis, "kindly furnished" his "design" (in the form of drawings) to Beyer, who it appears simply revised his image of 1853 without actually seeing the new buildings. The central structure, the "hotel," was touted as "the largest in the mountains": its classical structure, details, and fine proportioning made it as handsome as carefully designed urban architecture. The first floor was given to

3.19 Edward Beyer, *White Sulphur Springs, Greenbrier County*, 1858, lithograph, 11 1/8 x 19 1/8 in. (Courtesy of Chiles Lawson)

"the office, reception rooms, a dining room sufficient in dimensions to seat 1,000 persons, a ball room sixty feet square, and other smaller rooms. The second and third floors are for visitors." There were as well "fine and well shaded walks, and admirable views." The writer then excused further comment: "But it is not necessary to describe this famous place minutely, as it is well known in every portion of our country."[89] Greenbrier White Sulphur, then, was like Mount Vernon; as the grandest of the Virginia springs and thus a symbol of the whole group, it was sufficiently famous to give identity and renown to the state.

Edward Beyer observed that in 1857 the railroad ran to Covington but would "soon be finished to the [White

Sulphur] Springs."[90] Eventually the railroad deposited visitors virtually at the front door of the Homestead in Hot Springs. The White Sulphur Springs in Greenbrier County, West Virginia, and in Virginia the Warm Springs and the Homestead at Hot Springs in Bath County are the sole survivors from the golden age of Virginia's spas. The Red Sweet Springs in Monroe County is operated by the state of West Virginia as a home for the aged. Most of the springs are in ruins or have disappeared altogether.[91]

The ravages of fires and the Civil War, the postwar impoverishment of the South, wider travel opportunities, and a certain disinclination of northerners to travel to the South after the war all contributed to the demise of the Virginia springs. Perhaps more important were medical advances, a discountenancing of the purported healing powers of the waters, and the emergence of the germ theory as the reigning medical paradigm. Under the germ theory, communal bathing seemed more likely to cause diseases than to cure them.

Hawk's Nest and Crow's Nest

Heading west on the turnpike from White Sulphur Springs to Charleston one passed the Hawk's Nest and Crow's Nest overlooking the New River gorge—among the most westerly of the attractions on the circuit of Virginia's natural wonders. They are in Fayette County, now West Virginia, 324 miles from Richmond. An 1836 gazetteer reads:

> Before reaching the valley of the Kanawha, the traveller is feasted by the sublime and picturesque scenery from the cliffs of *New River*, which is one of the principal tributaries of the Kanawha. One of these cliffs has been long known by the name of the *Hawk's Nest*—but more recently called *Marshall's Pillar*, in honor of the venerable Chief Justice who as one of the State Commissioners in 1812 stood in person upon its fearful brink and sounded its exact depth to the river margin. Every one has heard of the far famed falls of Niagara—and yet I doubt if the beholder of that wonderful cataract ever experienced more of the true sublime, than the grand and elevating prospect from *Marshall's Pillar*, is apt to inspire.[92]

This was not an isolated or exaggerated opinion. It was shared by Harriet Martineau, an Englishwoman whose *Society in America* was widely read. "I had never heard of it," she writes, "and I never heard of it again," but she was moved by it almost as much as by Niagara Falls.[93]

In 1843 the young artist Worthington Whittredge traveled to Charleston in search of portrait commissions. Enchanted by the scenery, he soon returned to Cincinnati determined to specialize in landscapes.[94] Among his earliest views are several of the New River gorge. Whittredge may well have decided to visit this particular site after reading a description akin to the one cited above; the artist is known to have been an avid peruser of guidebooks. The two scenes shown here (figs. 3.20 and 3.21), painted in 1846 and 1848, record not only the landscape near Hawk's Nest but also the artist's developing skills, which at this point in his career progressed with each canvas. Prior to his departure for Europe in 1849, Whittredge exhibited several of his western Virginia views at the National Academy of Design in New York City, where he would later serve as president, and at the American Art-Union.[95] In New York he learned much about the work of Thomas Cole and the landscape movement that Cole had founded. "Crow's Nest" in particular is composed in the manner of the early Hudson River paintings; the viewer is placed low in a wild and bountiful landscape through which he senses that man can easily progress. Not far beyond is a mountain that towers toward heaven. In both landscapes Whittredge includes Cole's ubiquitous storm-blasted tree, a

3.20 Worthington Whittredge, ***View of Hawk's Nest***, 1846, oil on canvas, 17 x 24 in. (Courtesy of the Executive Mansion, Commonwealth of Virginia)

3.21 Worthington Whittredge, *Crow's Nest*, 1848, oil on canvas, 39 ³/₄ x 56 in. (Courtesy of the Detroit Institute of Arts, Gift of Mr. and Mrs. William D. Biggers, ©)

motif emblematic of the destructive force of nature and evidence that this Edenic landscape is still the domain only of explorers and hunters.

An 1836 gazetteer identified both "sublime and picturesque scenery" at the New River gorge. Writers gravitated to the former, artists to the latter. The element of fear, often found in written accounts of Hawk's Nest, is entirely missing from Whittredge's canvases. The writer of 1836, for example, invited the reader to "Imagine yourself standing upon the projecting point of a perpendicular rock, 1200 feet from the valley below. . . . From the flat rock forming the summit, to the agitated waters below, the view is fearfully grand: few of the many who visit it, can look over this dizzy height but in a reclining position."[96] A year after this gazetteer was published, Harriet Martineau wrote, "We issued suddenly from the covert of a wood, upon a small platform of rock; a Devil's Pulpit it would be called if its present name were not so much better;—a platform of rock, springing from the mountain side, without any visible support, and looking sheer down upon an angle of the roaring river, between eleven and twelve hundred feet below. Nothing whatever intervenes."[97]

These writers had carried to the Hawk's Nest region the European ideal of the Sublime, an idea that was of little interest to Whittredge because Thomas Cole had developed

an entirely different and nationalistic agenda that the young artist found more appealing. Cole's purpose was not to address man's sense of humility before nature, by showing a terrifying view from atop a "Devil's Pulpit," but rather to depict the land—with particular attention to the majesty of mountain scenery—as God's gift to a people who must seize the opportunity to develop in this unspoiled setting a vast and great nation. In this myth of a new American Eden that Cole and his followers put to canvas, man is ever mindful of the omnipotence of the Creator, but he is entirely comfortable in this environment.

The old approaches to the landscape had survived in Virginia. Partly for that reason the *Album of Virginia*, which was the work of a European artist, was well received there. Edward Beyer included in it a lithographic view from Hawk's Nest. The accompanying text read, "The view, astounding in such variety of grand and lofty scenery—woodland and vale untouched and untrod by the foot of man—is well calculated to inspire ennobling emotions."[98] No mention is made of an American Eden, nor is there evidence of even an awareness of the nationalistic viewpoint of the New York landscape school. The construction of a bridge across the New River gorge by the Chesapeake and Ohio Railway effectively destroyed the impression of seeing an "untrod" wilderness, but the railroad furthered settlement of this portion of the American Eden.

3.22 Unknown artist, *Falls of the Pedlar Virginia*, 1831, aquatint, 9 x 5 in., published in *The Souvenir*. (Courtesy of Dr. and Mrs. Lewis Wright)

3.23 Unidentified artist, *A West View of the Falling Spring, Bath County, Virginia*, c. 1830–50, engraving, 9 x 7¼ in. (Courtesy of Dr. and Mrs. Lewis Wright)

3.24 Russell Smith, *Falls of the Kanawha*, 1844, ink, 12 x 16½ in. (Courtesy of Library of Virginia)

Prints and paintings of many of the falls in Virginia were produced in the nineteenth century. One of the earliest depictions is that of Pedlar's Falls in Amherst County (fig. 3.22), but the artist for this 1831 print is unknown. Between 1830 and 1850 there appeared the color lithograph "A West View of the Falling Spring, Bath County, Virginia" (fig. 3.23). It depicts a falls of the Jackson River, which rises in the Warm Springs Mountains about twenty miles southwest of the town of that name. Less than a mile from its source "the water falls over a perpendicular rock about 205 feet high—50 feet higher than the Niagara Falls," according to Edward Beyer, who included a stylized view of Falling Spring in his *Album of Virginia*. According to Beyer, "Jefferson visited this spot, and mentions it in his manuscripts as a sublime natural curiosity. At that time the river rolled over the rock in a solid mass. Since then, many canals for driving mills and other works have taken from the Fall much of the water."[99] Both in the view shown here, and in Beyer's view, the water clearly falls in several separate streams. In fact, Jefferson had written, "The only remarkable Cataract in this country [by which he meant Virginia], is that of the Falling Spring in Augusta [later Bath County] . . . . This Cataract will bear no comparison with that of Niagara, as to the quantity of water composing it."[100]

Beyer's *Album of Virginia* also included Kanawha Falls in what soon would become West Virginia. Russell Smith sketched it in 1844 (fig. 3.24). "The scenery is truly romantic," wrote Lucius Venus Bierce about 1822, "On each side are lofty mountains, rugged in the extreme . . . behind is a noble river winding its course among the hills, which appear to unite, and in front is the lofty mountain whose height seems unmeasurable, through which the river breaks its way and rushes down the precipice as if in joy at its deliverance."[101] Although the falls were as wide as the Kanawha River, the "precipice" of which Bierce spoke was just twenty-five feet, so there could be no comparison to Niagara. Peyton Falls in Alleghany County had the opposite problem (fig. 3.25). The text accompanying an engraving in *The Illustrated London News* extolled it as "the highest cascade or waterfall in

3.25 M. Jackson, **Peyton Falls, Alleghany County, Virginia**, 1864, woodcut, 8 ½ x 6 in. (Virginia Historical Society)

America, being 200 ft. in height, while that of Niagara is only 150 ft.," but the writer conceded that at "only about ten yards wide at the top," any comparison to Niagara was futile.[102] It is almost as if the idea was that if enough of these waterfalls were celebrated in print or on canvas they would collectively match Niagara in both quantity and sublimity.

Currier and Ives published a color lithograph with the generic title "Valley Falls—Virginia" (fig. 3.26) that possibly is a composite view of several cataracts—a distillation of the many extant views. Or maybe the Currier and Ives audience cared only that they were somewhere in the Valley of Virginia. Likewise, R. Hinshelwood's engraving after a sketch by Harry Fenn, prominently placed in *Picturesque America*, is identified merely as "Cascade in Virginia" (fig. 3.27).

Besides waterfalls, the western reaches of Virginia were filled with oddly shaped rocks and other features deemed worthy to be given names. In the 1850s David Hunter Strother visited one such place—the Natural Chimneys near Mount Solon. Two engravings of them—based on Strother's sketches—appeared in "Virginia Illustrated" in *Harper's New Monthly Magazine* (fig. 3.28). "Although these rocks are highly picturesque, curious, and not wanting in grandeur," wrote Strother, "yet there

3.26 Currier and Ives, **Valley Falls—Virginia**, mid-19th century, lithograph, 8 x 12 ½ in. (Virginia Historical Society)

3.27 R. Hinshelwood after Harry Fenn, **Cascade in Virginia**, 1872, engraving, 11 x 9 in., title page to *Picturesque America*. (Virginia Historical Society)

3.28 David Hunter Strother, **The [Natural] Chimneys**, 1857, wood engraving, 3 ½ x 4 ½ in., published in *Harper's New Monthly Magazine*. (Virginia Historical Society)

3.29 David Hunter Strother, **The Cliffs at Seneca**, c. 1853, pencil, ink, wash, on paper, 10 5/8 x 14 1/2 in. (Courtesy of West Virginia and Regional History Collection, West Virginia University Libraries)

was nothing about the Chimneys to excite enthusiasm—in short, they were wanting in the quality of sublimity" that distinguished the merely curious from the first rank of natural wonders.[103] A sight that Strother did consider sublime was the cliffs at Seneca in Pendleton County. His sketches, although done c. 1853, were not published until 1872, when the site had become West Virginia (fig. 3.29).[104] The Seneca Rocks appear in *Picturesque America*, where the text is by Strother but the illustrations by William Ludwell Sheppard. Strother describes it as a magnificent "sheet of rock, half a mile long by five hundred feet broad, set up on edge" with its surfaces "stained with varied colors, white, yellow, red, brown, gray, and purple." It was "a scene in which all the elements of curiosity, beauty, and sublimity, seem to have been accumulated and combined." Attributing to it the ultimate accolade of sublimity called, he thought, for a fuller explanation: "When the sun gilds its painted and festooned sides, we glory in its beauty; when a passing cloud veils it in shadows, we are awe-struck by its weird sublimity."[105]

Natural Bridge

Perhaps the first written mention of Natural Bridge is by the Reverend Andrew Burnaby, who visited Virginia in 1759. He regretted that trouble with the Cherokees deterred him from visiting various "caves, springs, torrents," but especially "a natural arch or bridge, joining two high

mountains, with a considerable river running underneath."[106]

The first person to give a full account of Natural Bridge was Philip Vickers Fithian of New Jersey, who was tutor to the Carter family of Nomini Hall in Virginia. On 16 January 1776 he saw what he called "that great American, natural Wonder, called 'High Bridge' or 'Cedar Bridge.'" His language would become characteristic when describing the scene:

It is indeed a Work divine. Description by Language, or by Imitation in Colour, can never afford to the Mind a Conception so great as the Truth. . . . Such stupendous Grandieur presented to the Mind by Painting or Description, may for a While amuse.—But the Sight of such supernatural Workmanship, removes from the Mind every little Idea. . . . I shall be thought romantic, but I must declare my Conceptions. . . . We viewed it also from the Top. This also is astonishing! Neither of us had so great Resolution as to stand on the Border & Look over—For the whole Colony I would not do it—I dare not venture nearer than six Feet.[107]

Fithian does not mention the story of George Washington climbing to carve his initials on Natural Bridge, but he does cite Washington as one of only three men who succeeded in hitting the underside of the arch with stones thrown from the ravine below. By the time of Fithian's visit in 1776, Natural Bridge had become associated with another Virginian, whose fame was less than five months away. Thomas Jefferson was its owner. He had bought it and 157 adjoining acres from George III in 1774, the same year, ironically, in which Jefferson penned his radical treatise *A Summary View of the Rights of British America*, which provided the rationale ultimately adopted for the Revolution.

Jefferson regarded his purchase "in some degree a public trust, and would on no consideration permit the bridge to be injured, defaced or masked from the public view." To William Carmichael he wrote, "I sometimes think of building a little hermitage at the Natural bridge . . . and of passing there a [part] of the year at least."[108] Not until 1803, however, did he build any structure, and then it was not for himself. One of Jefferson's slaves, who had taken the name Patrick Henry, lived there with his wife and gave tours.

Probably there was a room for guests. Jefferson may also have had commercial motives. When the bridge proved a poor investment he wrote of it in 1809 as "dead capital" and proposed offering it for sale, but in the same letter he reiterated his belief that it was "undoubtedly one of the sublimest curiosities in nature."[109] The main reason it did not generate income was the absence of any public accommodations at a time when it would have been considered ill-bred for Jefferson to charge for his private hospitality. No hotel was built until 1815.

Many tourists after 1787 were familiar with Jefferson's panegyric in *Notes on the State of Virginia*. John Marshall, who seldom agreed with Jefferson, declared Natural Bridge to be "God's greatest miracle in stone." When, in 1778, Botetourt County was subdivided and a non-English name needed, the new county in which the bridge lay took its name from the natural wonder—Rockbridge.

In 1782, with Lord Cornwallis's army safely in captivity, the Marquis de Chastellux, a major general under the French commander Rochambeau, was enticed by Jefferson to visit Natural Bridge, the name used increasingly through time and universally by 1830. Chastellux was the victim of a trick long used on travelers. At a certain point on a nondescript road his guide asked rhetorically, "You desire to see the *Natural Bridge*, don't you, sir? You are now upon it, alight and go twenty paces to the right or left, and you will see this prodigy." The marquis dismounted and soon espied through the trees that the road was on the narrow top of the famous arch. He "enjoyed this magnificent but tremendous spectacle, which many persons could not bear to look at," including Jefferson, whose vertigo gave him a violent headache.[110] Chastellux arranged for another Frenchman, Baron de Turpin, a skilled mathematician and draftsman, to visit the bridge to take measurements. It was determined to be 215 1/2 feet high. Three engravings that resulted from Turpin's excursion were published in the Dublin edition of Chastellux's *Travels in North America* and apparently are the first published views (fig. 3.30). One of the Chastellux images

was almost immediately appropriated by an American publication, the *Columbia Magazine*, in 1787 (fig. 3.31). Another early engraving appeared in the three editions of a travelogue by Dublin-born topographical artist Isaac Weld, published between 1798 and 1800 (fig. 3.32). Weld's engraving, too, was soon reproduced in other publications, including as the frontispiece to Daniel R. Preston's *The Wonders of Creation; Natural and Artificial*, published in Boston in 1807. Weld's close-up vantage point also would become the one favored by most subsequent artists.

For at least fifty years after Chastellux, most people knew Natural Bridge through black-and-white engravings and aquatints (technically etchings). Many of those who came to Natural Bridge having seen these prints pointed out how inadequate they were. In 1855 Mary Jane Boggs wrote, "As to attempting a description of the Bridge, it would as preposterous an idea as that of making a picture of it."[111] John Disturnell echoed her sentiments: "No adequate idea of this magnificent work of nature can be obtained from the efforts of either pencil or pen; and though both have been employed in its delineation, yet neither has done full justice to the subject."[112] Two clergymen wrote, "Look at that masonry. Is it not like the perfection of art; and yet what art could never reach? Look at that colouring. Does it not appear like the painter's highest skill, and yet unspeakably transcend it?"[113]

Although many doubted pen or pencil could do justice to Natural Bridge, many tried all the same. Some of

3.30 Baron de Turpin, *Perspective Taken from Point A* (Natural Bridge), 1786, engraving, 5 1/2 x 8 3/8 in. (Virginia Historical Society)

those familiar with Jefferson's *Notes*, such as Thomas Chapman in 1795–96, and John Edwards Caldwell in 1809, could think of nothing original to say.[114] James Kirke Paulding observed that "The late President Jefferson deserves the ill-will of every traveller in this part of the world, by having in his Notes on Virginia, a work now become classical, given a description of this bridge . . . that none can expect to rival him."[115]

A book that Jefferson kept at the bridge for visitors to record their "sentiments" was unfortunately destroyed in 1845. Among the luminaries who visited were presidents James Monroe, Andrew Jackson, and Martin Van Buren, Missouri senator Thomas Hart Benton, Texas's president, governor, and senator Sam Houston—a native of Rockbridge County—and Virginia native Henry Clay, Speaker of the House, senator from Kentucky, and Whig Party presidential candidate. The centerpiece of Clay's political program—the American System—was internal improvements, so it is not surprising that he should think of Natural Bridge as "the bridge not made with human hands, that spans a river, carries a highway, and makes two mountains one."[116]

Less exalted travelers differed in what feature of Natural Bridge was most compelling. To a majority it was the design of the arch. "One of those scenes never to be forgotten," wrote Henry Bright in 1852. "The guides tell you of people [in profile] in the rock, of Washington's name written on it, and fifty other equally important personalities. One doesn't care for them, or think of them, while staring upwards in stupid amazement at so grand a work of the Great Architect."[117] Ernest Ingersoll wrote, "The first impression is the lasting one—its majesty! It stands alone. There is nothing to distract the eye."[118] The artist David Hunter Strother, while writing of the bridge's "unique and simple grandeur," differed with Ingersoll about the first impression being the lasting one: "While the sentiment of awe inseparable from the first impression may be weakened or disappear altogether, wonder and admiration grow with time."[119]

To Henry Gilpin, it was the vista from the top of the bridge that excelled: "The view from it looking down Cedar Creek is one of the most magnificent imaginable. It extends over hills, & valleys, green, beautiful, & fertile, some rising into mountains, some sloping into little dells, and the former gradually increasing till the scene is closed by the romantic summits of the Blue Ridge."[120] By contrast, a Congregational minister who visited in 1816 thought that "on the summit of the hill, or from the top of the bridge, the view is not more awful than that which is seen from the brink of a hundred other precipices."[121]

Undoubtedly, the sense of danger in being atop the bridge was part of its sublimity. One visitor wrote, "I rode over it but would not recommend a shy horse."[122] Another tourist believed that "to look down into the vast abyss" from atop the bridge "would shake the stoutest heart."[123] Without explicitly citing the concept of the Sublime, or the role that surprise and terror played in it, David Hunter Strother nevertheless made it part of a story about himself as Porte Crayon and his cousins visiting Natural Bridge. Knowing he is on the road atop the bridge, he pushes aside some branches and suddenly reveals to one of his female relations the abyss below. She shrieks, recoils, and "No, No, not for the world!" will she take a second look.[124]

Another aspect of the Sublime at Natural Bridge related to the manner of its creation. Jefferson had supposed, as with Harpers Ferry, some cataclysm. Indeed, one visitor almost quotes Jefferson's remarks on Harpers Ferry to explain Natural Bridge: "Some violent convulsion of nature is supposed to have suddenly cleft a mighty mountain asunder, from top to bottom."[125] Samuel Mordecai

declared with conviction that "Its formation by some terrible convulsion of Nature, is undoubted."[126] Some of the religious-minded, however, were creationists who thought the Natural Bridge was no accident of nature. The bridge "has remained nearly as it is now since the creation or the flood, notwithstanding what Thomas Jefferson hath said to the contrary," wrote the Reverend Robert Miller in 1811.[127] Both Jefferson and Miller were wrong. A more nearly correct explanation was given by Francis William Gilmer in a paper read on 16 February 1816 to the American Philosophical Society, of which Jefferson was a member. Gilmer argued that water erosion had produced Natural Bridge.[128] Nearly twenty years before Gilmer, however, Louis Philippe, later king of the French and no intellectual, had surmised after his 1797 visit to Natural Bridge that it "seems to have been hollowed out by the water's steady action, perhaps like the rifts of the Rhône."[129] In fact, the current hypothesis is close to that of Louis Philippe. A cavern produced by erosion mostly collapsed, leaving the Natural Bridge as a remnant of a much larger vaulted roof.

Had the current hypothesis been known in the early nineteenth century, the sudden collapse of the cavern would have been a sublime thought. As it was, however, the Gilmer hypothesis of slow erosion by water became the reigning orthodoxy. But vast and almost infinite time was a sublime concept too. Considering it led Lady Howard of Glossop to write, "it would be impossible to imagine anything more magnificently grand than this portentous and wondrous monument—of the gradual and insidious disintegrating power and might, in the long course of ages, of a stream of water!"[130] Even so, the eclipse of the theory that the bridge was created by an unknown and unimaginable catastrophic event diminished that intangible sense of awe that had sustained Natural Bridge in the first rank of natural wonders.

The efforts of authors to convey Natural Bridge were soon matched by those of artists, perhaps heartened by the conviction that one of their pictures would be worth a thousand of the authors' words. The English artist William Constable painted the bridge in watercolors in 1807. On three occasions Thomas Jefferson invited his friend Maria Cosway to come from England to paint the bridge, a subject he thought "worthy of immortality." He also failed in his efforts to entice John Trumbull.[131] Within a few years of

3.33 Currier and Ives, *Natural Bridge*, c. 1860, lithograph, 12⅞ x 17 in. (Virginia Historical Society)

Jefferson's death in 1826, however, improved roads made Natural Bridge more accessible, and the railroad soon would make it more so. Perhaps the first oil painting of significance was that by Jacob Ward about 1835. That year it was exhibited in the American Academy of Fine Arts, listed as "Lent by L. P. Clover, For Sale." Lewis P. Clover, Sr., a New York framer and sometime landscape artist himself, had Ward's painting published as a hand-colored aquatint by William James Bennett in 1839.[132] The image attained its greatest circulation, however, when Currier and Ives pirated the Bennett print and produced an image by the new medium of lithography (fig. 3.33).

Many artists followed in Jacob Ward's wake. In 1839 George Cooke exhibited a "View of the Natural Bridge, in Virginia, at sunrise" at the Apollo Association in New York City. In 1853 it belonged to Daniel Pratt of Prattsville, Alabama, but its present whereabouts are unknown. In 1852 one of the leading American landscape artists of the day, Frederic Edwin Church, tried his hand at painting Natural Bridge. His traveling companion Cyrus Field doubted Church could duplicate the colors of the bridge that arose from minerals in the soil atop the bridge leaching down into the limestone arch, but when Church succeeded admirably, Field felt obligated to buy the picture, now at the University of Virginia.[133] In 1855 John Moran, three of whose brothers also were artists, painted a close view of Natural Bridge in

oils, now at the Governor's Mansion in Richmond.

David Johnson, a second generation Hudson River School artist who worked on a smaller scale than Church but whose skills rivaled those of his New York colleague, was perhaps drawn to Natural Bridge by an affinity for rock studies. Boulders that suggest the mood of a setting are often prominent in his paintings of falls and rivers; sometimes they even stand alone as the subject.[134] In any case, Johnson produced three paintings of Natural Bridge in 1860; he exhibited one of them in 1862 at the National Academy of Design in New York. It may or may not have been the canvas that is a distant view showing the bridge in a wider panorama, now at Reynolda House in Winston-Salem, North Carolina. There, in an almost picturesque composition, Johnson presents the surrounding landscape that Thomas Jefferson had termed "delightful"; the artist conveys the sense of "peace and calm" that was noted by many visitors to the site. He was true to his usual manner, which was not to overwhelm the viewer with the grandeur of nature but instead to offer the city dweller an escape into a bucolic world. In the remaining two canvases that give the traditional view of the bridge from Cedar Creek, the artist broke free from his usual manner, no doubt in response to his subject, to invoke the Sublime (fig. 3.34). The bridge is shown to be a magnificent rock formation that seems infused with energy, or at least it still bears the imprint of

3.34 David Johnson, *Natural Bridge*, 1860, oil on canvas, 30 x 24 in. (Courtesy of C. Kevin Landry)

some cataclysmic force. It slants and twists, not as much as in the Roberts view that it in some ways resembles (fig. 2.2), but in a more credible manner, so that the viewer can only tremble before the reality of it. The small figures inserted for scale are removed to the middle ground, where they seem minuscule beneath a giant arch. The foreground is given to rocks. No previous artist had so effectively used this array of nature's rubble to suggest the upheaval that had put it there. The canvas is slightly larger than the panoramic view and it presents Natural Bridge as comparable to Niagara Falls, which had been painted by Church only three years earlier in a painting that had been almost universally admired. Of Johnson's views, this may be the canvas that was exhibited at the academy; it was the one that was engraved by Samuel Valentine Hunt and published in *The Ladies Repository*.[135]

Even at mid-century, the vast majority knew of Natural Bridge from prints such as those by Samuel Hunt and Currier and Ives. The engravings of David Hunter Strother alone, in *Harper's Monthly*, were seen by far more

people than ever viewed oil or watercolor originals. Virtually all of these prints were captioned "Natural Bridge, Virginia." Some people also knew of Natural Bridge from a famous map. A guidebook of 1855 asserts that "One of the best representations of the Natural Bridge yet attempted, is contained in a Map of North America, published some years ago in Philadelphia."[136] Probably the map referred to is Henry S. Tanner's "Map of the United States," published in 1823 in *A New American Atlas*. It features a magnificent and large cartouche picturing Natural Bridge towering over a puny Niagara Falls (fig. 3.35). Although folk artist Edward Hicks did visit Natural Bridge, this map was the pictorial source he used for Natural Bridge in six of his "Peaceable Kingdom" paintings in the 1820s.[137]

Just as Henry Tanner had done on his map half a century earlier, so former Confederate general John Esten Cooke, writing in *Picturesque America* in 1872, grouped Natural Bridge and Niagara Falls in a unique category. "The Falls of Niagara and the Natural Bridge," he declared, "are justly esteemed the most remarkable curiosities in North America."[138] The pairing of these natural wonders had a long history. Hester Liston, wife of Great Britain's first minister to the United States, wrote that Natural Bridge was "most certainly, after the Falls of Niagara, the most extraordinary production in America."[139] A French wallpaper called

3.35 Henry S. Tanner, *Map of the United States*, 1822, 46 ½ x 59 ¾ in., detail showing cartouche. (Virginia Historical Society)

75

"Picturesque America," produced in 1834, featured both Natural Bridge and Niagara Falls. To the Reverend Moses Hoge of Richmond, "Natural Bridge is among the cliffs what Niagara is among the waters—a visible expression of sublimity—a glimpse of God's great strength and power."[140] To Henry Gilpin, "It is not perhaps as sublime as Niagara . . . but a person may form an idea of Niagara infinitely nearer the truth than of the Natural Bridge, and I confess if I were called upon to say which was the most worthy of a voyage to America I should hesitate considerably before I preferred Niagara."[141] "It approaches Niagara in grandeur and excels it in height and in awful mystery," declared a guidebook of 1887.[142] To Ele Bowen "Natural Bridge . . . deserves to take precedence of Niagara itself.—first, because of the great rarity of such scenes in comparison with water-falls; secondly, because of its much greater height; and thirdly, because of the greater phenomenon of its structure throughout."[143]

Of course, there were dissenters. "There we found the bridge—and disappointment," wrote the author of *Dick's Trip through Virginia on Horseback* in 1899. "It is wonderful, yet it does not come up to the expectations that one derives from reading and seeing pictures of it."[144] Others damned it with faint praise. "It was not frightful or stupendous," wrote Mary Allan-Olney, "but was very wonderful as a freak of nature, and made a very pretty picture."[145] Louise Closser Hale, who visited in 1916, objected to the fee: "The French Government open to the public the greatest natural bridge in the world, that of Constantine in North Africa. The Spaniards offer the Alhambra without fees; the Forum in Rome is for the people. But in America, we had to pay . . . to view Niagara Falls, and the enjoyment of an arch of rock still cost us a dollar."

Having vented her spleen, Hale further observed,

> I had a very definite picture in my mind of Natural Bridge, due to my father's Cousin Laura's stereopticon views with which I was always entertained in my youth. . . . However, Natural Bridge with its glory of young colour was admitted without question as 'better than my father's Cousin Laura's,' and I suppose if anything is better at [age] thirty-seven than it was at seven—it was worth a dollar.[146]

Mrs. Hale was a New Yorker, and for a time after the Civil War visitation to Natural Bridge by non-Virginians plummeted. "There was a time when the Natural Bridge was esteemed among the greatest wonders of the continent," lamented the editor of *The Virginia Tourist* in 1870. "Of late it has languished in obscurity and neglect," he continued, "visited only by stray travelers from the Virginia springs, or, as we may judge, by frugal picnic parties from the near town of Lexington and the neighborhood."[147] *Raymond's Vacation Excursions* observed in 1887 that the site was "one of which northern visitors know but little, except from the pictures in their old geographies."[148] The recognition of Natural Bridge in *Picturesque America* and *The Great South* in the 1870s produced a brief upsurge of tourism as well as a new burst of artistic creativity.

This national rediscovery of Virginia's picturesque scenery led George Douglas Brewerton, a native of Rhode Island who had served with the military in California and New Mexico before the Civil War, to Natural Bridge in 1872. How could he depict this overly familiar subject? It had been portrayed from both sides, from a distance, and close up. The artist's solution was the novel idea of a snowscape (fig. 3.36). Also in the 1870s, Paul Schulze from

3.36 George Brewerton, **Natural Bridge**, 1872, pastel on paper, 22½ x 28 in. (Virginia Historical Society, Lora Robins Collection of Virginia Art)

Brooklyn chose to depict a little-known nearby cave (fig. 3.37) paired with a watercolor (fig. 3.38) that embodies the observation of one visitor that "The arch forms a beautiful picture frame around the landscape."[149]

In the 1880s Vermonter James Hope and Canadian Thomas Wilkinson painted the bridge. Flavius Fisher, however, had only to travel from Lynchburg to paint it (fig. 3.39, p. 48). A native of Wytheville, Fisher had studied in Paris in 1860 and in Berlin during the Civil War. William W. Valentine of Richmond, who saw Fisher in Berlin, wrote that, "as he receives no orders and is unable to get to the South, to which he is devotedly attached—he is quite sad."[150] After the war, Fisher quickly returned to Virginia and set up a studio in Lynchburg. A correspondent from Lynchburg wrote to the Richmond *Whig* in 1867 to report that

> You will be gladder still to know that his [Fisher's] skillful pencil is employed in illustrating the magnificent scenery of Virginia. He is, as you know, the best portrait painter in the whole country, North or South. . . . but he is ambitious to excell in historical and landscape painting, and his ambition is not misplaced.

The writer went on to observe that "the picture of the Roanoke Valley, near Big Spring, now on the easel, promises a new triumph."[151] Of Fisher's identified works, however, "Natural Bridge" seems to be his masterpiece. After its completion he moved to Washington, D.C., where he died in 1905.

Because of railroads, Natural Bridge was more accessible than ever to tourists when Fisher painted it in 1882. More than a dozen visitors, including women and children, are pictured at the base of the arch. To them the bridge was a spectacular but not mysterious site, for it had become accepted that the bridge was created by slow erosion rather than some unfathomable cataclysmic event. To maximize the sense of the bridge's height, Fisher gives the viewer an extremely low perspective and renders the figures on a tiny scale. The limestone was millions of years old, but the blasted trees that climb the cliffs of the arch are rendered with a vigor that suggests newness and the regenerative forces of nature. Fisher's most effective tool is light, which he uses both to capture the subtle hues of the stone and to lure the viewer beyond the bridge itself into a distant

3.37 Paul Schulze, *At the Cave, Natural Bridge Va.*, c. 1875, watercolor, 18 x 13 1/2 in. (Virginia Historical Society, Lora Robins Collection of Virginia Art)

verdant view. A decade later an oil of Natural Bridge by local artist Fanny Lecky Paxton won first prize at the World's Columbian Exposition in Chicago in 1893.

By then, however, the Indian summer of heightened awareness of Natural Bridge was at an end. The establishment of Yellowstone National Park and the production of huge panoramic paintings of the Grand Canyon had given a new dimension to the term wonder of nature, and by this new standard Natural Bridge did not seem to measure up. The Richmond publisher of *Raymond's Vacation Excursions* argued that "This vast wonder impresses the beholder more and more, the longer he gazes upon its grand proportions, in the same manner that Niagara, the Yosemite Falls, the Cañon of the Yellowstone, and the Grand Cañon of the Colorado grow in grandeur."[152] But the attempt was futile. That which in 1795 had been called "the greatest natural Curiosity in America and perhaps in the whole World," and in 1853 "the wonder of the state—the natural bridge of Virginia," after 1900 descended permanently into a secondary role among the works of nature.[153] Even some works of

3.38 Paul Schulze, **Natural Bridge, Va.**, c. 1875, watercolor, 18 x 13 ½ in. (Virginia Historical Society, Lora Robins Collection of Virginia Art)

man, such as the Panama Canal, seemed as marvelous as Natural Bridge to many eyes. None of those other wonders, however, could claim the distinction of being used as a metaphor in one of the greatest of American novels, *Moby Dick*. Describing the great white whale, Herman Melville wrote,

> But soon the fore part of him slowly rose from the water; for an instant his whole marbleized body formed a high arch, like Virginia's Natural Bridge, and warningly waving his bannered flukes in the air, the grand god revealed himself, sounded, and went out of sight.[154]

The Peaks of Otter

Unlike Natural Bridge, it is not immediately apparent why the Peaks of Otter were regarded as major natural wonders. In *Notes on the State of Virginia*, Thomas Jefferson supposed them to be the highest mountains in the United States or even North America.[155] This misconception was a long time a-dying. In fact, the Peaks were not even

the highest mountains in Virginia. Even Jefferson conceded they were "but a fifth part of the height of the mountains of South America."[156] Isaac Weld, who saw them in 1796, doubted they equaled Mount Snowden in Wales.[157] Travel accounts suggest that their appeal lay in their shape, the sublime view from the Peaks, the precarious situation at the summit, and "Owing to the circumstance that the country on one side is nearly level, and that the surrounding mountains are comparatively low, their appearance is exceedingly imposing."[158]

Of the view of the Peaks approaching from Botetourt, James K. Paulding wrote, "you have a full view of the famed Peaks of Otter, towering high above the surrounding mountains, one rising to a point, the other flattened at the top."[159] Another traveler wrote, "You see them rising above the very peaks of the Blue Ridge . . . as blue as the sky above, and remarkable in their shape," which yet another tourist likened to "the form of Sugar loaves."[160] Another tourist recorded that, "soon the Blue Ridge comes plainly into view, where two sharp and prominent heights, easily dominating the range, loom up ahead and catch every eye."[161] The Marquis de Chastellux, a French major general in the Yorktown campaign of 1781, characteristically chose an analogy from the science of fortification—the Peaks "advanced from the Blue Ridge as a kind of counter-gard."[162] The fact that the Peaks lay nearly equidistant between the Blue Ridge and the Alleghenies and "over-topped them" was appealing to artists, although not many of them came in the nineteenth century.[163]

The Englishman William Strickland made a pencil sketch in the spring of 1795 entitled "View of the Pike of Otters from the window of Bedford court house" (fig. 3.40). Charles De Wolf Brownell of Connecticut visited in 1848 on a tour that included sketching Natural Bridge.[164] He was commissioned to paint "The Peaks of Otter from Mount Prospect, Residence of the Honorable Robert Allen" (fig. 3.41) and one of identical small size showing Allen's home in the composition (fig. 3.42).

Edward Beyer must have had commissions, too, because he painted four oils of the Peaks entitled "Bedford" as well as the one shown here, which is inscribed "The Peaks of Otter and the Town of Liberty," a onetime name of the town of Bedford (fig. 3.43). As always with this artist, it is the extraordinary details of the town that engage the

3.40 William Strickland, *View of the Pike of Otters from the window of Bedford court house, the highest Pike, N: W: by N: distant at the foot about 8 miles, the summit may be ascended in about 3 miles*, c. 1794–95, pencil, 8 x 12 in. (Courtesy of the New-York Historical Society, ©)

3.41 Charles De Wolf Brownell, *The Peaks of Otter from Mount Prospect, Residence of the Honorable Robert Allen*, 1848, oil on canvas, 3 x 5½ in. (Virginia Historical Society, William Anderson Hagey Fund purchase)

3.42 Charles De Wolf Brownell, *View of Prospect Hill, at the Base of the Peaks of Otter*, 1848, oil on canvas, 3 x 5½ in. (Virginia Historical Society, James H. Willcox, Jr., Fund purchase)

viewer. In every inch of the depiction of Liberty—in the trains, the houses and public buildings, the tilled fields, the people at work or play—the viewer finds reason to linger in front of the canvas. Of the inhabitants of Liberty, one

traveler probably familiar with *William Tell* wrote, "They, indeed, are the very princes of freemen; breathing, as they do, the pure breezes of their own blue mountains, and daily learning lessons of liberty and independence from the wild bird that soars in unobstructed flight and proud defiance about the towering summit of the Peaks of Otter."[165] Liberty was the point of departure for excursions to the Peaks, and in *Picturesque America*, the author of the chapter about southwest Virginia wrote a passage that seems to describe Beyer's panorama:

I noticed but little life or activity in the long street on Liberty hill; some negroes were at work in one of two tobacco warehouses; farmers were bustling in on the red country roads leading toward the purplish hill-background; and miles away two sharp, yet symmetrical peaks, connected by a gap, perched high up on the Blue Ridge chain, sprang into view. They were the mighty twins! Two splendid guardians of the sweet valley spread out at their bases, they rose in indescribable grandeur.[166]

Although all of Beyer's oil paintings are *of* the Peaks, two of the three plates in his *Album* show the vista *from* the Peaks:

They afford the Artist and Tourist one of those grand land-marks, which, once seen, are ever after remembered. The eye from the summits may lose itself in admiration of the magnificent Panorama which outspreads beneath on all sides, and floats onward far within the distance, until the shadowy outlines, earth and sky, are mingled. From this elevation the eye can command the horizon, for the distance of at least one hundred miles. . . . Near the summits vegetation ceases, and huge Cyclopian boulders lie piled on one another, as though it might have been the fabled works of the Giants, in their vain ascent to Heaven. . . . This [southern] Peak is the one generally ascended, and the panoramic view is said to be the finest in the world.[167]

One traveler remarked that "The view overlooks what is called the Piedmont of Virginia, and can hardly be surpassed."[168] Another agreed, writing,

We now, however, stood on the wild platform of one of nature's most magnificent observatories—isolated, and, apparently, above all things else terrestrial and

3.43 Edward Beyer, *The Peaks of Otter and the Town of Liberty*, 1855, oil on canvas, 26 ³/₄ x 58 ³/₈ in.
(Virginia Historical Society, Lora Robins Collection of Virginia Art; partial gift of Mildred Edmunds Long)

looking down upon, and over, a beautiful, variegated, and, at the same time, grand, wild, wonderful, and almost, boundless panorama! Indeed, it was literally boundless; for there was a considerable haze resting upon some parts of the 'world below,' so that in the distant horizon, the earth and sky seemed insensibly to mingle with each other.[169]

From the Peaks Samuel Janney foresaw a great national destiny for the United States and offered a "fervent prayer" to the nation, "That like thy scenery may thy virtues shine,/And bear the impress of a stamp divine."[170] In 1844 the Whigs of Bedford County had a more prosaic, if still patriotic, objective when they unfurled a party banner at the summit. The orator touted the virtues of their candidate for president: "Fellow citizens—in standing here this morning on the topmost rock of this far famed Peak of Otter, I propose with this pure rain water, which has just fallen from the heavens, to drink the health of Henry Clay, that fearless Tribune of the people and born leader of Men."[171] Virginia-born Clay lost to James K. Polk nonetheless.

The Great Dismal Swamp

The name of the Dismal Swamp is "almost as familiar as Niagara or the Rocky Mountains," wrote an Irish poet who visited the site at the end of the nineteenth century.[172] By that date swamps throughout the American

South had attracted considerable attention in folklore, where they had become associated with sin, decay, and death. The Great Dismal, which straddles the North Carolina border below Norfolk, had generated its share of that mythology as the setting for stories about disappearance, demons, dangerous creatures, and the unknown.[173] It was a vast setting a century ago, six times its present size.

One legend in particular made the Dismal Swamp internationally famous and set it apart from all other swamps in America. In this story, said to be derived from an Indian tale, a young man refuses to accept the death of his beloved; she has gone not to her grave, he insists, but to the Dismal Swamp. In that uncharted and seemingly boundless tract he joins her, in an otherworldly way. So romantic a tale of unfulfilled love, which recasts the classical myth of Orpheus and Eurydice, was suitable material for a ballad. In 1803, after hearing the story in Norfolk, the Irish bard Thomas Moore published a poem about this "death-cold maid" and the land where "the serpent feeds, And never man trod before":

> They made her a grave too cold and damp
> For a soul so warm and true;
> And she's gone to the Lake of the Dismal Swamp,
> Where, all night long, by a firefly lamp,
> She paddles her white canoe.[174]

Moore's poem became immensely popular and remained so for some time. David Hunter Strother, writing at mid-

3.44 John Gadsby Chapman, *Lake of the Dismal Swamp*, 1825, oil on canvas (fireboard), 34 x 39 in. (Virginia Historical Society, Lora Robins Collection of Virginia Art)

3.45 John Gadsby Chapman, *Lake of the Dismal Swamp*, 1830s, engraving, 4 ½ x 6 ¼ in. (Virginia Historical Society, Lora Robins Collection of Virginia Art)

colonists found little value in a landscape that was useless, unsafe, disordered, and in no way visually pleasing to them. William Byrd II, serving as a commissioner for the Virginia colony with the task of determining the borderline with North Carolina, was the first to call the region "dismal" and its few, wretched inhabitants "Dismalites." In his *History of the Dividing Line* (1728), the master of Westover described the swamp as filthy and noxious, a living hell through which passage was extremely difficult. To him the swamp was a "land of the dead," a place where "the foul damps ascend without ceasing, corrupt the air, and render it unfit for respiration." Not even the turkey buzzards would fly over it, he said. The swamp did have a peculiar attraction, however. Byrd's men clamored to be a part of the first group of white men to enter it, and Byrd himself marveled about the rich soil there, which "makes every plant an evergreen." As a member of the Royal Society ever in search of specimens, he took an interest in the swamp's "natural curiosities."[176] Later in the century George Washington and other planters looked to drain the Dismal Swamp to convert its fertile soil into productive farmland. Their goal was not realized until the twentieth century, when in the process the Great Dismal was reduced to its present size.

century under the pen name of Porte Crayon, claimed that "The Lake of the Dismal Swamp" had been sung to him in his cradle when he was an infant. Robert Frost knew the ballad; following an unrequited love affair, the despairing young poet traveled from Massachusetts so that he might spend an evening in the sympathetic environment of the Dismal Swamp.[175]

Before Thomas Moore penned his poem, the Great Dismal had been viewed only as a wasteland. The first

One of the first artists to depict the Great Dismal was the Virginian John Gadsby Chapman, who in 1825, at the age of only seventeen, painted as a fireboard a scene of Lake Drummond, the swamp's principal feature (fig. 3.44). Chapman no doubt selected this subject partly because of the fame of the swamp that followed the publication of Moore's poem, and partly because Joshua Shaw had recently searched the Tidewater region for picturesque scenery, only to overlook its most renowned landmark (see figs. 2.14 and 2.15 above). Chapman follows the rules of the Picturesque as best he could with a scene of stagnation and decay, which perhaps Shaw simply did not care to depict. In looking beyond the foreground of Chapman's image to the still and expansive lake of the swamp, one senses the special nature of this landscape that had been noted in 1797 by Benjamin Henry Latrobe; he wrote that the first appearance of the lake "absorbs or expells every other idea, and creates a quiet, solemn pleasure, that I never felt from any similar circumstances."[177]

A decade later, in 1835, Chapman repainted the lake. This second canvas is now lost, but it is well known from an engraving after it by James Smillie that appeared in a number of gift books of the period (fig. 3.45). Currier and Ives even published a lithograph based on the image.[178] Chapman's two canvases were essentially the same, except for the prominent addition in the second of a perched

vulture, the figure of which both amplifies the mood of repose and silence in the landscape and injects a feeling of brooding and pain. It is possible that Chapman knew the work of the naturalist William Bartram, who in his travels had noticed how the figure of a bird of prey can somehow encapsulate the ambience of a landscape: "The solitary bird . . . stands alone on the topmost limb of tall dead cypress trees, his neck contracted or drawn in upon his shoulders, and beak resting like a long scythe upon his breast. In this pensive posture and solitary situation, it looks extremely grave, sorrowful and melancholy, as if in the deepest thought."[179] Edgar Allan Poe knew Chapman's print, which he singled out for praise as the sort of image that would adorn his ideal room. The Great Dismal had always intrigued Poe, who in his writings routinely described the same sort of phantasmic landscape that is constricted by stagnation and disintegration.[180]

One reason why Chapman's image was republished so often, as was Moore's tale of catharsis and hope, was that Americans in this era increasingly accepted death as a release from the stress of life. Both painter and poet confront that subject, and both picture an expansive lake that is an otherworldly region of spiritual calm akin to the new rural cemeteries that then were being built. In the 1820s, Henry Inman painted a romantic nighttime view of the swamp as peopled by the two ghostly figures of Moore's poem; Inman's painting is now lost, but an engraving after it, produced by Peter Maverick, appeared in *The Talisman* in 1828.[181] Working faithfully from Maverick's print, an untrained Connecticut painter, George Washington Mark, developed an oil painting of the scene (fig. 3.46). Contemporaries criticized Inman for inventing the setting of a swamp that he had never visited, but Mark's primitive style of painting makes topographi-

3.46 George Washington Mark, ***Dismal Swamp, Va.***, 1840, oil on canvas, 38 x 48 in. (Courtesy of Virginia Museum of Fine Arts, Gift of Edgar William and Bernice Chrysler Garbisch)

cal accuracy irrelevant. The painter effectively illustrates the final verse in Moore's poem:

> But oft, from the Indian hunter's camp,
> This lover and maid so true
> Are seen, at the hour of midnight damp,
> To cross the lake by a firefly lamp,
> And paddle their white canoe!

Those who regarded Dismal Swamp merely as "a vast bog" might at least celebrate a remarkable engineering feat—completion of a twenty-two-mile canal through the swamp.[182] "By means of this canal," wrote William S. Forest, "a communication is opened between the sounds and principal rivers of North Carolina and the waters of the Elizabeth [River], Chesapeake Bay, and the ocean."[183] Soon after the opening of the canal on 31 December 1828, the painter Robert Salmon—best known for harbor scenes—depicted the canal in a small oil painting (fig. 3.47). The festivities seem to still be underway as the steamboat *Lady of the Lake*, flag flying and filled with sightseers, sails northbound through the narrow waters past the "large and commodious" Lake Drummond Hotel. Salmon's view was not strictly accurate but undoubtedly represents a didactic nationalistic art and reflects a mind-set of America's progressive triumph over nature, all at

a time when the issue of federal funding of "internal improvements" was becoming *the* major issue dividing Democrats and Whigs.

At mid-century, Americans reached a point of transition as to how they would evaluate the swamp. Despite their interest in its mythology, many remained reluctant to embrace this peculiar landscape with the seriousness with which they would revere, for example, a Hudson River scene. They might welcome a canal bypassing the Great Dismal Swamp, but the swamp itself still seemed to be an ambiguous region where light and dark, life and death, and

3.47 Robert Salmon, *Dismal Swamp Canal*, 1831, oil on canvas, 10 x 14³/₁₆ in. (Courtesy of Virginia Museum of Fine Arts, gift of Eugene B. Sydnor, Jr.)

3.48 Regis Gignoux, *Sunset on Dismal Swamp*, c. 1845, oil on canvas, 12 x 18 in. (Courtesy of the Ogden Museum of Southern Art/University of New Orleans)

3.49 David Hunter Strother, *The Barge*, 1856, wood engraving, 4 x 4¼ in., published in *Harper's New Monthly Magazine*. (Virginia Historical Society)

good and evil are not so clearly differentiated, and where plant life is excessively prolific, almost like a cancer, symbolizing a breakdown of the very logic and order that underpin civilization. To study the swamp might be to surrender conscious control to intuitive response. And according to popular belief, swamps were the source of miasma, an infectious air then believed to be the cause of deadly typhoid, malaria, and yellow fever. Thus in 1853, in his poem "The Edge of the Swamp," William Gilmore Simms could consider this landscape so dangerous that he warns his reader to avoid its contamination.[184]

Other Americans, however, were ready at mid-century to look anew at the swamp and to study its landscape seriously. Poets and painters, who would still turn to God's "Holy Book" of nature to understand their world, now felt compelled to reconsider landscape types and strategies, given how their society was plagued with such evils as greed and slavery and was changing under the impact of such forces as urbanization, industrialism, and democratization, and given how the new science seemed increasingly irreconcilable with religion. Painters and travel writers were describing, with no ill effects, faraway and exotic lands that were as bizarre as the American swamp. A variety of new landscape types, including prospects of marshes and of other scenes marked by stillness, would be introduced at this time.[185] Thus in the 1840s and 1850s at least a few painters traveled to the Dismal Swamp to

observe and record its landscape. Flavius Fisher painted the swamp in the late 1850s, when he was working out of Richmond.[186] Regis Gignoux, a French artist who established a studio in Brooklyn after 1841 and made repeated visits to Virginia, painted several views of the swamp that he exhibited in New York City. As evidence of the Dismal Swamp's continuing renown, one of the views was commissioned by Lord Ellesmere. Gignoux's view shown here, "Sunset on Dismal Swamp" (fig. 3.48), may date to 1858.[187] The artist employs the traditional structure of the Picturesque canvas, whereby the eye is led over placid water to a warm distant sunset. But instead of a settled Claudian landscape that reverberates with echoes of antiquity, this French artist presents a wilderness filled with the tortured forms of ragged trees and plant life. He invites the viewer to study this previously neglected chapter of God's "Holy Book" of nature.

One writer of national prominence who was willing to analyze this landscape fully was David Hunter Strother, who was taught art by Chapman. In 1856 he sensed that his countrymen were prepared to accept the use of intuition in approaching the landscape, since traditional nature study seemed no longer able to present solutions. At least at the Dismal Swamp, such a primitive approach might be acceptable; this was a setting that for decades had stood as an enigma to him and to many of his readers. Casting Porte Crayon as a member of the traditional school of thought that was guided by discipline and temperance, he leads the reluctant Crayon and his readers to a new understanding of the swamp as a landscape of self-knowledge.

"To the Lake of the Dismal Swamp: Porte Crayon's Inward Journey" recounts for the readers of *Harper's New Monthly Magazine* Strother's visit there (fig. 3.49). As the title suggests, the writer's quest is not only the inner lake of the swamp but also his own inner self. Strother opens with a statement that points to his rejection of traditional approaches to nature: "Man, like the inferior animals, has his instincts, less imperious and less reliable, but oftener controlling his godlike reason than most are willing to admit." Like Poe in the opening passage to "The Fall of the House of Usher," Strother describes a setting that is so dark, still, and gloomy that Porte Crayon can only feel utterly alone there. Like Poe, he points to its uncanny qualities. Crayon attempts to associate this landscape with death, as traditionalists always had done, but he cannot deny its vitality and the superabundance of plant life in the swamp. The monotony is so "wearisome, dreary, solemn, [and] terrible" that Crayon can only surrender to the landscape, to undergo a catharsis that is complete when he reaches the welcoming expanse of Lake Drummond. Stripped of his ego by the intense sublimity of this unique landscape, Crayon emerges from the outing with a better understanding of himself and his world. Strother showed that the swamp is not threatening; instead one might even find sanctuary and self-renewal there.[188]

Because the Great Dismal proved to be a convenient symbol of the slaveholding South, which was itself a landscape out of control, at least in the eyes of northern abolitionists, this swamp became a subject of interest on the eve of the Civil War and throughout that conflict. Henry Wadsworth Longfellow, in his poem "The Slave in the Dismal Swamp" (1855), tells of a runaway who even out of bondage is deprived of his freedom because he is forced to live "Where hardly a human foot could pass, Or a human heart would dare, . . . Like a wild beast in his lair." In Harriet Beecher Stowe's second novel, *Dred: A Tale of the Dismal Swamp* (1856), yet another escaped slave remains entrapped in a landscape that is a metaphor for the institution of slavery. During the war T. W. Higginson described the slaveholding South as "a Dismal Swamp of inhumanity, a barbarism upon the soil."[189] Perhaps appropriately, given this focus of the abolitionists, Union troops patrolled the Dismal Swamp during the Civil War.

Unlike Strother, not every visitor to the Great Dismal was pleased with what he saw there. In 1850 a correspondent for *Chamber's Edinburgh Journal* objected dryly that "this is not the spot which the fairy elves would choose for their revels."[190] This Scottish traveler had been lured to the site by the fame of Moore's ballad. The renown of the swamp was also the cause for its inclusion after the war in *The Great South*, but in that large volume it is dismissed in a brief account as only "a succession of wild and, apparently, irreclaimable marshes" that are of no merit: "For miles the eye encounters nothing save the bewildering stretch of swamp and dead trees."[191] It is omitted entirely from *Picturesque America*. Yet the fame of the Great Dismal persisted to the end of the century and beyond, as long as Moore's ballad was remembered.

HISTORIC LANDMARKS
Mount Vernon

On 10 October 1759 the Reverend Andrew Burnaby visited Mount Vernon and wrote, "This place is the property of colonel Washington and truly deserving of its owner."[192] He knew all about George Washington. We are apt to forget Horace Walpole's remark from London that "the volley fired by a young Virginian in the backwoods of America set the world on fire."[193] A twenty-two year old who starts a worldwide war, fought in North America, Europe, India, and on the high seas, was not apt to be forgotten just five years later with the war still underway. Mount Vernon, however, did not became a major destination for tourists and artists until the American Revolution made Washington the most famous man in the world.

Thereafter, people wanted to see Washington and where and how he lived. The term "father of his country" is too remote to impress us. To his contemporaries, however, Washington had made the words of independence a reality and truly fathered the country. He became the focus of loyalty that hitherto had gone to the king, yet he embodied the virtues that set the infant republic apart from European monarchies. Washington became symbolic of the nation itself. To love the nation was to love Washington, and vice versa, and because Washington loved Mount Vernon, Americans should also. It became our national shrine and held a place in the national consciousness much as Arlington National Cemetery does today.

To Washington's mortification, however, the flood of visitors began in his own lifetime. At one point he remarked that he and Mrs. Washington had not dined alone at Mount Vernon for twenty years. On the occasions when both were away, they instructed their attendant to take visitors through the house. Those who could not visit Mount Vernon could view it, nonetheless, through myriad paintings and prints. One of the first artists to depict the house was Edward Savage, who about 1791–92 produced views of both the land and river fronts. He advertised both paintings in his Philadelphia Museum 1795–1800, at his Columbian Gallery in New York City 1801–11, and in his New-York Museum in Boston 1812–17 as "North-East View of Mount Vernon, Painted on the Spot" (fig. 3.50) and "A West View of Mount Vernon." The fact that he showed these pictures for more

3.50 Edward Savage, *North-East View of Mount Vernon, Painted on the Spot*, 1791–92, oil on canvas, 22 x 36 in. (Courtesy of Mount Vernon Ladies' Association)

than twenty-two years demonstrates the enduring interest in the subject and the likelihood that he executed several such pairs, although only two are known.[194]

The architecture of the house, as opposed to the setting, is not our principal concern here, although it bears mentioning that Washington has been underappreciated as an architect. The Sage of Monticello may have designed the more erudite home, but if imitation is the sincerest form of flattery, Washington's creation has been copied by the American people far more often than Jefferson's. In the 1940s a Frenchman perhaps went too far in comparing it to Louis XIV's Trianon at Versailles.[195] Not every visitor, however, was an admirer. During the Revolutionary War itself, "the external appearance of the mansion did not strike the Baron [Steuben] very favorably," and the general commented that "if Washington were not a better general than he was an architect, the affairs of America would be in a very bad condition."[196]

Mount Vernon deserves to be first in any discussion of historical landscapes in Virginia because it was by far the most visited site throughout the 1800s, and until well into the 1900s it had no rival. Even today, this house attracts

roughly equal visitation to the whole complex at Colonial Williamsburg. The reasons are the preeminence of Washington as a historical figure, the site's proximity to the nation's capital, and the intrinsic charm of the architecture and beauty of the setting.

Washington believed that his house had the most pleasant situation of any in the colonies or new nation. Reverend Burnaby wrote of his 1759 visit that "The house is most beautifully situated upon a very high hill on the banks of the Potowmac; and commands a noble prospect of water, of cliffs, of woods and plantations."[197] Isaac Weld, who visited in the 1790s, remarked that "the scenery altogether is most delightful."[198] After Washington's death in December 1799, however, a visit to Mount Vernon by Americans was less a journey to a picturesque site than a pilgrimage to the American holy land, a place hallowed in the republic's still young historical memory. "The very name of that place has long been dear to me . . . so sweet a name," wrote Theodore Dwight, Jr., in 1834.[199] About 1911 Edith Kimball wrote similarly: "To tread these paths once familiar to the hero of all childhood dreams . . . is a privilege indeed!"[200]

It was not long after Martha Washington's death that the house and grounds fell into disrepair. This was in keeping with the depleted condition of the Tidewater region generally in the early 1800s, when Theodore Dwight, Jr., wrote of the approach to Mount Vernon that "The solitude was as profound as that of any deserted region of Italy; the habitations of men at many parts of the road, seemed as distant; and nature appeared almost as left to herself."[201] Once the historic icon came into view, however, attitudes changed.

Now to a thoughtful mind," wrote one Mr. Kennedy in 1852, "there is not so much to *see* at Mount Vernon as to *think about*. We had seen the 'portrait' of this edifice an hundred times or more: we had seen it in rude prints upon the walls of village bar rooms in the distant valley of the Mississippi; we had noticed it as often as a 'frontispiece' upon the 'clocks' of New England manufacture . . . we had had it in our observation in many forms and variety of pencilling, but here it was now, the thing itself, standing palpably before our eyes: need we say, we recognized it at once?"[202] (fig. 3.51)

Among those who thought about Mount Vernon in the 1850s were the sectionalists, both North and South, who claimed George Washington and his estate as part of their southern or their national heritage. Was the great man's principal legacy independence from outside interference or a union of states? In 1861 the Confederacy put Washington on its great seal, but in 1855 artist William Trost Richards claimed Mount Vernon as a national icon (fig. 3.52).

The holiest of holies at the shrine was the tomb. However, "when we sought out the 'tomb' of the departed patriot," wrote one visitor in 1852, "we were indeed most sadly disappointed." After making invidious comparisons between it and Westminster Abbey, the writer concludes that "there is nothing, positively nothing to elevate one's conception of a sepulcher; indeed, there is much to derogate and to detract from such preconceptions as one might have formed."[203] Others agreed. "The tomb is a sad affair for such a man," wrote the earl of Carlisle in 1851.[204] "The building, if it can be called one, is a miserable looking brick hovel," wrote another Englishman in 1839.[205] "Nothing can be simpler than the tomb in which the first president of the United States reposes," was the observation in *The Great South*, published in 1875. "There is no attempt at decora-

tion," it continued. "One sees nothing but two marble coffins lying on the brick floor."[206] All of these comments, moreover, were made after an even less imposing structure had been replaced in 1831. Of that sad affair, Andrew Jackson wrote in 1815,

> In a small vault at the foot of the hill, overgrown with Cedar, repose the bones of the father of his country. Why is this so! Must the charge of ingratitude ever rest upon Republiks? It is now several sessions since Congress solicited the remains of him whose whole life was devoted to his country's service, in order that a suitable testimonial of a nation's respect might be shewn them. The venerable widow who cherished them as the most precious relict, sacrificed her individual feelings to a nation's wishes, and granted the request. Since then, as though the apparently

3.51 Charles Kirke for George Mitchell (New England), **Clock**, c. 1840. (Virginia Historical Society, estate of William Anderson Hagey)

3.52 William Trost Richards, *Mount Vernon*, 1855, oil on canvas, 29 ¹/₂ x 48 in. (Courtesy of The Newark Museum)

3.53 Russell Smith, *The Original Tomb of Washington*, 1836, oil on board, 15 x 11³/₄ in. (Virginia Historical Society, gift of Nicholas F. Taubman, Alan M. Vorhees, L. Dudley Walker, and Anne R. Worrell)

warm interest they displayed had been a studied mockery, those remains have been permitted to moulder in the "dark, narrow cell" where they were at first deposited.[207]

The romantic imagination of some visitors and artists, however, was moved by this modest republican resting place. Theodore Dwight, Jr., wrote, "There is something much more congenial to my mind in the simple and indeed humble repository of the ashes of Washington than in the most splendid monument of Italy, or even of Egypt."[208] Augusta Blanche Berard wrote in 1856, "I felt nothing but the sacredness of the spot. I stood at the *Tomb of Washington*. It was holy ground."[209] Joshua Shaw, whose image of the tomb was engraved by John Hill and appeared in *Picturesque Views of American Scenery* of 1819–21, saw the small size and unkempt state of the tomb as especially apt and moving. So did Russell Smith of Philadelphia in his oil done after the second tomb had been completed, but nonetheless conspicuously entitled "The Original Tomb of Washington" (fig. 3.53).[210]

As she left Mount Vernon about 1911, Edith Kimball wrote, "It was with thoughts not sad, but distinctly reverential that we descended the lovely winding, wooded path to the river, passing once more the resting place of the nation's greatest and best." The experience moved her to pen a poem:

> Flow gently, Potomac! thou wash-
>   est away
> The sands where he trod, and the
>   turf where he lay,
> When youth brushed his cheek with
>   her wing;
> Breathe softly, ye wild winds, that
>   circle around
> That dearest, and purest, and holiest
>   ground,
> Ever pressed by the footprints of
>   spring!
> Each breeze be a sigh, and each dew-
>   drop a tear,
> Each wave be a whispering monitor
>   near,
> To remind the sad shore of his story;
> And darker, and softer, and sadder
>   the gloom
> Of that evergreen mourner that
>   bends o'er the tomb
> Where Washington sleeps in his glory.[211]

There was the occasional visitor whose recollections were less elevated, or perhaps we should say, more confused. One was the Reverend Newman Hall of Liverpool, who perhaps had seen one too many places along the historic Potomac to keep them straight. He remembered that "I was taken to Mount Vernon, the estate of General Lee."[212] Others knew it all too well. So many paintings and prints had been done of Mount Vernon by 1874 that the editors of *Picturesque America* omitted it from their book because "It is unnecessary to describe the home of Washington, so familiar to every citizen by description if not by sight."[213] In 1940 the novelist Willa Cather was so sure her readers knew Mount Vernon's appearance that she used the house to describe another building in *Sapphira and the Slave Girl*: "The Mill House was of a style well known to all Virginians, since it was built on very much the same pattern as Mount Vernon."[214]

Monticello

Although there are no statistics, Monticello evidently was far less visited in the 1800s than Mount Vernon. It was not near a major city or destination, as Mount Vernon was to Washington, D.C., and whereas Mount Vernon became the nation's first historic house museum in 1859, Monticello was a private home until 1923, although the Levys, who had owned it since 1834, made it accessible to the public. In contrast to Mount Vernon, few artists painted it. The house fared somewhat better in prints. A late example is "Jefferson's Home.—Monticello, Va.," c. 1886, by an

3.54 Unknown artist, ***Jefferson's Home.—Monticello, Va.***, 1886, wood engraving, 12½ x 18 in. (Virginia Historical Society)

unidentified artist (fig. 3.54). In this montage the central view of "Monticello—Seen from Moore's Creek" is surrounded by views of "The Tomb," "Jefferson's Mill," "Carter's Mount," and front and rear views of the house.[215]

For the 1900s, we know from a study of foreign language travel books about Virginia, covering the period 1900 to 1950, that thirty-seven of seventy-seven included passages about Mount Vernon against just five whose authors had visited Charlottesville and, presumably, Monticello. It is worth noting, however, that the only author in the study actually to compare the two houses, Austrian diplomat Ernst Prossinagg, found Jefferson's the more appealing.[216] There has been a sharp increase in interest in Thomas Jefferson and his house in recent times. Possibly his miscegenational dalliances, agnosticism, and dabbling in such fields as wine and architecture have made him far more empathetic than the stoic Washington in an age of talk show television.

Jefferson had many visitors to Monticello during his lifetime. Indeed, Poplar Forest was acquired as a retreat from the bustle of Monticello. In 1782 the Marquis de Chastellux visited and later wrote, "The house, of which Mr. Jefferson is the architect, and often one of the workmen, is rather elegant and in the Italian taste, though not without fault."[217] In 1786 an Italian count observed that "The situation of this villa is very pleasant. From it one can enjoy the view of the Blue Mountains, of the hills, and of the plain; and it overlooks numerous plantations beyond the town. The house, designed by the owner, is after the Italian style, with high, spacious rooms—possibly in accordance with too grandiose a concept, with the result that it isn't finished yet."[218] A decade later Englishman Isaac Weld wrote in nearly identical terms: "It is most singularly situated. . . . At present it is in an unfinished state. . . . The house commands a magnificent prospect, on one side of the blue ridge mountains for nearly forty miles, and in the opposite one, of the low country, in appearance like an extended heath covered with trees, the tops alone of which are visible. The mists and vapours arising from the low grounds give a continual variety to the scene."[219] Strikingly similar language was used a quarter of a century later by another visitor, a testimony to the conventions of pictorial description: "These views are the most extensive I have ever seen in my life . . . but of all the prospects I have ever

beheld the most magnificent is toward the north and north east—it looks over the tops of several mountains—it has the Blue Mountain again on the left—it embraces hills at the distance of a hundred and twenty miles—while at your feet, you look down on Charlottesville, & the valley around it."[220] This mingling of near and distant scenes of different aspects was an important ingredient in the definition of a successful prospect or picture.

Former president John Adams, who differed with Jefferson on so much, promised Richard Rush that if he visited Adams at Montezillo, in Quincy, Massachusetts, "even this Hillock among Mountains will exhibit natural Beauty Superiour to the vast Wilderness you saw from Monticello."[221]

As with Mount Vernon, opinions of the house differed. The occasional visitor found it "too ingenious," but most agreed with Arthur Middleton, who observed in 1810 that Monticello "is thought one of the most elegant private habitations in the United States."[222] As late as 1875 a less picturesque but indispensable "row of negro cabins" still was visible nearby.[223] John Robert Godley summed up the generally rhapsodic views of the landscape when he wrote that "a more extraordinary and original situation it is impossible to conceive."[224] Jefferson, usually identified as a classicist rather than a romantic, anticipated the romantic movement in America by building his abode amid mountain scenery.

After his death, portentously on the fiftieth anniversary of the Declaration of Independence, Monticello became a destination for political pilgrims. In 1939 a visitor wrote disapprovingly: "The house is a shrine for Democrats and in particular Virginians who, I repeat, do not honor Washington as much as we do in New York."[225]

As at Mount Vernon, the grave was especially sacred ground to the faithful. In 1828 Margaret Bayard Smith wrote, "Dear Monticello! my chief inducement to take this long journey was once more to visit its revered shades and weep over the grave of one of the best and greatest of men and of a friend."[226] The "tomb" was even more modest than at Mount Vernon. "A rude stone wall encloses a small square left in a state of nature, full of forest trees," wrote Smith, "[a] lovely and lonely grave in the solitude of the mountains."[227] In 1834 George Cooke visited Monticello and exhibited a painting—"Tomb of Thomas Jefferson"—at the Apollo Association in October 1838. Unfortunately, it is untraced, as is Cooke's "View of Monticello" exhibited at the American Academy of Fine Arts in 1835.[228]

Just two years after Jefferson's death, Margaret Bayard Smith observed that a "desolate mansion now stands—All was silent—Ruin has already commenced her ravages. . . . In a few weeks she [Martha Jefferson Randolph] must leave this dear and sacred spot, for in a few weeks it <u>must</u> be sold."[229] By the 1850s Benson Lossing, traveling the nation doing sketches for his *Pictorial Field-Book of the Revolution*, noted that "This venerated mansion, is yet standing, though somewhat dilapidated and deprived of its former beauty by neglect."[230] Ruins, however, were conducive to contemplation about the transitoriness of life and fame, and William Wirt could not help reflecting that:

> From this summit, the Philosopher was wont to enjoy the spectacle, among the sublimest of Nature's operations, the looming of the distant mountains; and to watch the motion of the planets, and the greater revolution of the celestial sphere. From this summit, too, the patriot could look down, with uninterrupted vision, upon the wide expanse of the world around, for which he considered himself born; and upward to the open and vaulted heavens which he seemed to approach as if to keep him in mind of his high responsibility. Indeed it is a prospect in which you see and feel, at once, that nothing mean or little could live.[231]

Jamestown

Francis Louis Michel of Switzerland went to Jamestown in 1701 and later wrote, "It is one of the largest and most beautiful places in the country, although it does not have more than thirty-five houses."[232] What telling evidence of the overwhelmingly rural character of early Virginia. The capital had been moved to Williamsburg in 1699, however, and Jamestown began an inexorable decline. In 1732 a traveler wrote, "James City was formerly the Capital of the Colony; now not more than two houses left."[233] In 1781 a French soldier in the Yorktown campaign observed, "I saw there but one house standing." He mused that "Tradition still preserves its locality; but the time will come when it will be as difficult to find the place where it stood, as that of the Capital of Old Priam in ancient Troy."[234]

A ceremony was held on the bicentenary of Jamestown in 1807, but by 1838 statesman William Wirt could write, "I find no vestiges of the ancient town, except for the ruins of a church steeple, and a disordered group of old tombstones that give food for thoughts of mortality."[235] Ruins were seldom seen in the United States at that time, but they did foster meditation.

> It is difficult to look at these awful proofs of the mortality of man without exclaiming in the pathetic words of Shakespeare:
> > "The cloud capped towers, the gorgeous palaces,
> > The solemn temple, the great globe itself;
> > Yea, all which it inherits shall dissolve;
> > And, like this insubstantial pageant, faded,
> > Leave not a wreck behind."[236]

Jamestown had left a wreck behind—the church tower. The church had been built 1639–47, then burned by Nathaniel Bacon's rebels in 1676 and rebuilt. It fell into decay along with the town in the early 1700s and became the focus of most paintings of the site. In 1834, Alexandria-born John Gadsby Chapman painted "Ruins of Jamestown, Virginia, America," the title of which perhaps suggests he intended to sell it in Europe, where in fact it was purchased by the Virginia Historical Society in 1990 (fig. 3.55). Chapman was related by marriage to the wife of George Cooke. Cooke's "Ruins of Jamestown," done in 1838, is unlocated. James Warrell, who worked in Richmond, probably did his Jamestown painting at about this time.[237] A generation later, William Murray Robinson chose the same vantage point as Chapman for his watercolor view.[238] There really was not anything else to paint.

In Chapman's painting the artist apparently did little to exaggerate the disarray he depicted, for Bishop William Meade reported in 1856 that "very heavy and strong" and "well cemented" stone and brick tombs there were virtually blasted into pieces by the slow but steady growth of trees.[239] The ruins Chapman depicted produced ambivalent responses among Virginians. They knew from European authors that ruins were considered picturesque, but America was too young a country to have ruins, and they touched a sore spot. Virginians in the first half of the nineteenth century were undergoing a severe and prolonged agricultural depression that hit Tidewater the worst. Between the Revolution and Civil War a million Virginians would leave

3.55 John Gadsby Chapman, *Ruins of Jamestown, Virginia, America*, 1834, oil on board, 11 x 14 in. (Virginia Historical Society)

the commonwealth. Many of the older regions were depopulated as even grand old houses were left to ruin. A Connecticut visitor to Tidewater about the time Chapman was painting wrote, "What a lamentable picture is presented by a country like this, worn out by exhausting crops, and abandoned years ago to sterility and solitude."[240] A whole literature of declension emerged in Virginia. Although the causes of the decay of Jamestown were different, decaying buildings and abandoned cemeteries were reminders that a once glorious civilization was in decline and undergoing an economic and cultural collapse. If Virginians were chastising westward-bound neighbors for forgetting their past and selling the homes and bones of their forefathers, would they not have mixed feelings about the ruins of Jamestown?[241]

Some Virginia writers of this period, of whom Edgar Allan Poe is the best known, found an attraction in the impermanence and decay scattered across Virginia's landscape. Chapman, however, attempted with his painting of Jamestown to reverse the prevailing negative connotations of ruins. To be sure, he manipulates composition and lighting to extract fully from the scene its inherent drama and romantic appeal. This broken landscape was then as evocative as any setting of ruins in England or Italy that might suggest the transitoriness of human life and the passage of time. But there is nothing gloomy in this scene bathed in a warm early evening light. The eye of the viewer is carried instead to a blissful scene of boating on the James. Instead of focusing on dignified dilapidation, Chapman looks forward to a bright future rooted in a glorious past.

Chapman uses ruins as an inspiration to celebrate the extraordinary colonial heritage in which Virginians should take pride. This also was the theme of his paintings of

Yorktown, discussed below. With sectionalist bias, he valued the Jamestown settlement as evidence that Virginia preceded New England, a fact that he would say earned its present inhabitants the right to control America's destiny. Chapman's positive response to the societal crisis in Tidewater Virginia was paralleled by the attitude of a new generation of agricultural writers. To their way of thinking, the Jamestown settlement had made the entire James River valley a sacred place because it was there that Anglo-American farming began. They were appalled by the careless husbandry of the early settlers, but rather than idly condemn those practices, they would revise them. The new agriculturalists would become better stewards of the earth. Similar changes in attitudes toward the land were taking place in New England at the same time, just as sectionalists there were revaluing their history and its landscapes in the same way that Chapman did.[242]

The French soldier who feared Jamestown would go the way of Troy need not have worried, because the great nation founded there remembered its origins. If the colonial period was the childhood of our country, then we were born at Jamestown, and Yorktown was a rite of passage to full adulthood. "It is curious to reflect, " wrote William Wirt, "what a nation, in the course of two hundred years, has sprung up and flourished from that feeble, sickly germ which was planted here!"[243] James Kirke Paulding provided an answer to Wirt's musing and the Frenchman's worry: "The place . . . is one of the most interesting to a reflecting mind (as mine is of course) of any in the country. . . . Nothing now remains but the land they cultivated, and their graves; but the spot is well known, and every century . . . will only render it more interesting and illustrious."[244]

A traveler from the Midwest, crossing Virginia west to east, came upon a tiny brook and, being told by locals that it was the ultimate source of the James, wrote, "I could not but feel a kind of veneration, while I stood on the banks of that stream on which the first settlement was made in Virginia in 1607 . . . Jamestown, the once famed nursery of America, is now no more, or known only in history or song."[245]

American history, however, was coming to be written primarily by New Englanders whose sectionalist agenda seemed to slight Jamestown's role. A New England woman who visited the site in 1835 wrote, "Jamestown, *somewhat*

noted in the old history of this country, is now but a landing for passengers to Williamsburg." Gleefully, she reported that "a hut or two and the ruins of a brick church, the first one built in Virginia, alone designate the locale. The ruin is really quite picturesque. . . . Trees have grown up to quite a good height on the site of the aisles."[246]

Later, another northern visitor, but not from New England, commiserated with the Virginians: "The New England writers who furnish our histories and school-books seemingly desire to dwell upon and keep to the front the Pilgrim Fathers and Plymouth Rock, and leave untold the entire story of the Cavaliers of Virginia." "One enterprising Yankee," he had been told, "sent off to New England two hundred of these relic bricks" from Jamestown church. "One wonders," he concluded, "if they desire to transplant this original landmark and rebuild it upon Plymouth Rock."[247]

There was another threat to Jamestown—erosion. A traveler in 1859 thought that "unless protected by piling or some engineering resource, the ground on which the first successful American settlement had its centre will have disappeared however."[248] He calculated that the cost would be a tenth of that just spent to acquire Mount Vernon for the public. Nothing was done, however, until Jamestown Island was acquired by the Association for the Preservation of Virginia Antiquities (APVA), almost as its first act in 1889. Fears that most of the original James Fort had been washed away recently were shown to be unfounded, and the Jamestown Rediscovery Project is systematically excavating the remains.

Other than stabilizing the site and church tower and erecting some statues, the APVA left the island undisturbed. No museum or other facilities were built. That approach was endorsed by Louise Closser Hale, who visited Jamestown about 1916. "One cannot countenance the thought of a present existence in any other form," she wrote. "A moving picture house opposite John Smith's statue would have been too dreadful to entertain."[249]

Williamsburg

In 1775 the Reverend Andrew Burnaby wrote of Williamsburg, "it is far from being a place of any conse-quence . . . the church, the prison, and the other buildings, are all of them extremely indifferent."[250] He was right about the town's size but not about its importance. It was in Williamsburg that Thomas Jefferson penned a pamphlet that provided the ultimate rationale used for revolution. It was there that the debates took place that led Virginia to declare its independence on 15 May 1776. Its political and economic significance vanished, however, when the capital was moved to Richmond in 1780. Just a year later a French soldier with General Rochambeau's army wrote that "everything there appeared desolate."[251] In 1810 a visitor described it as in a "deserted, forlorn condition."[252] The lunatic asylum was the principal remaining institution, and it was unkindly said that "500 lazy live off 500 crazy."[253]

It is a mistake, however, indeed a myth, to suppose that Williamsburg's *historical* significance was entirely overlooked until the Reverend W. A. R. Goodwin's mission was matched with the means of John D. Rockefeller, Jr., to restore and reconstruct the town in the 1930s. In 1860, on the eve of another war of independence, Englishman Lefevre Cranstone knew enough of Williamsburg's role in the earlier contest to seek it out. Among the sketches he did there was one of the Powder Magazine in an apparently good state of preservation (fig. 3.56). By 1875 it served as the stable for the town's principal inn.[254] In 1890 one visitor noted "The one long street of the straggling town" and remarked that "The principal promenaders are the town's cows." Yet, not only did he write that "Williamsburg is worth a visit," he also acknowledged that it had been the inspiration for his book.[255] Can we resist a comparison to Edward Gibbon who, hearing the monks singing vespers

amid the ruins of the Roman Forum, took up his pen to write *Decline and Fall of the Roman Empire*?

In 1897, in the novel *Diomed*, a dog reports his master giving an electioneering speech in Williamsburg as follows:

> New Yorkers are proud of the growth of their city at trade, wealth, and population. The pride and boast of Williamsburg is that it has no wealth or trade; and that its population is less than it was a hundred years ago. This ambition, or lack of it, is at least unique. . . . Williamsburg to-day is but an insignificant village. Williamsburg of the past is an immortal and glorious spot, around which the affections of every lover of our early history linger with unspeakable veneration.[256]

Artists as well as authors found inspiration in unrestored Williamsburg. Louise Closser Hale, whose husband, Walter, was an artist, wrote,

> It makes no difference what you draw in Williamsburg for every house is historic and every one is a composition. If an artist is doing the old Powder Horn from which Lord Dunmore purloined the powder that blew the cannon ball into St. Paul's of Norfolk, he is fearing he had better hasten to the old Wythe House where Washington once lived. If he begins on the Wythe House he is itching to get at Bruton church next door, and while he works upon Bruton he prays the creator of good architecture to keep the Poor Debtor's Prison from falling into dust before he gets around to it.[257]

Among the artists who apparently agreed with her were Edith Clark Chadwick of Massachusetts, who visited Virginia in the 1890s, and Thomas Harrison Wilkinson, a Canadian who painted in unrestored Williamsburg about 1903. Both did watercolors of the Wythe House (fig. 3.57), the Powder Magazine (which the Hales called the Powder Horn), and Bruton Church.[258] Georgia O'Keeffe's parents moved to Williamsburg in 1903, and as a teenager she sketched the interior of Bruton Church, but no landscapes are known.[259]

"The church is pretty," wrote one visitor in 1732.[260] By 1800, however, it was observed that "the episcopal church, the only one in the place, stands in the middle of the main street; it is much out of repair."[261] The decline of this church building reflected the broader condition of the denomination, which had been disestablished at the end of the eighteenth century and disendowed at the beginning of the nineteenth. The Angli-can Church, re-christened the Protestant Episcopal Church, slowly revived, and by the 1820s its survival was no longer in doubt. This gradual recovery also occurred at Bruton Church. About 1837 or 1838, however, the interior was radically altered by cutting down the high pews, discarding the old high pulpit, and making a Sunday school of the west end—all concessions to the egalitarian spirit that followed the Revolu-tion.[262]

That spirit is not what brought Alfred Wordsworth Thompson to Williamsburg in 1893. By then the Colo-nial Revival movement was well under-way, and Thompson's painting "Old Bruton Church, Williamsburg, Virginia, in the Time of Lord Dunmore" is an artifact of that movement (fig. 3.58). It perhaps began under the impulse of the centennial of American independence in 1876 and

3.57 Thomas H. Wilkinson, **George Wythe House**, 1903, watercolor, 12¾ x 17 in. (Virginia Historical Society)

3.58 Alfred Wordsworth Thompson, **Old Bruton Church, Williamsburg, Virginia, in the Time of Lord Dunmore**, 1893, oil on canvas, 18 x 27⅛ in. (Courtesy of the Metropolitan Museum of Art, Gift of Mrs. A. Wordsworth Thompson, 1899, © 1983)

3.59 Charles Sheeler, ***Governor's Palace*** (Colonial Williamsburg), 1936, oil on canvas, 21 ½ x 23 ½ in. (Courtesy of The Colonial Williamsburg Foundation)

gradually gathered steam, as from the great Corliss engine at the Centennial Exposition, and found expression in painting, architecture, and interior decoration. Granny's old furniture also suddenly became *antiques*.

In this context Thompson's picture was a social landscape more than a natural one. It does not depict worship, but the social rituals that preceded and followed the service itself. The gentry arrive on horseback or in carriages, taking care to make an imposing appearance. They exchange gossip and news and transact business, the Sabbath notwithstanding. The gentry would be seated last, not out of modesty, but rather a sense of theater, like the monarch entering Parliament after the lesser orders were assembled. The interior architecture of Anglican churches powerfully reinforced these accepted norms of social hierarchy, which is why Bruton's interior was radically remodeled later.[263]

The lifestyle of the Virginia gentry in the 1700s exercised a strong appeal to the Gilded Age plutocracy most likely to buy such pictures. First, they were Anglophiles. It was, after all, in 1895 that Consuelo Vanderbilt married the duke of Marlborough, and within a few years Nancy Langhorne of Virginia would be viscountess Astor. The scene is set during the years 1771–75, when John Murray, earl of Dunmore, was royal governor, rather than in Patrick Henry's governorship a few years later, to keep it *pre-revolutionary*. Under Dunmore there was greater stability and social deference of the kind portrayed by Thompson, and those were qualities wistfully sought after by turn-of-the-century capitalists whose workers were flocking to unions and socialism. The Colonial Revival included a strong element of nostalgia not only for a pre-industrial and primarily Anglo-Saxon America, but even for an inegalitarian and undemocratic age. Perhaps that is why it is not called the Jeffersonian Revival.

Colonial Williamsburg itself is an artifact of the Colonial Revival movement, albeit from a more progressive strain that took pride in the achievements of the Revolution itself rather than in the *ancien régime*. Before the restoration, Williamsburg had been a jumble of eighteenth-

and nineteenth-century buildings, many of the former period with accretions of the latter. It lacked architectural purity, but it was an organic thing, a living community. The transformation that occurred after 1930 tidied up and harmonized the village, eliminating the anomalies, but this lessened its charm in the eyes of some artists. It did, however, make Williamsburg far better known than it had been since the halcyon days of the 1770s, both to the general public and to the artistic community.

The principal missing buildings—the Capitol and the Governor's Palace—were reconstructed in the 1930s thanks to the providential discovery in the Bodleian Library at Oxford University of a copper plate showing their original appearance. Among the first artists to visit was Theodore Ballou White of Philadelphia, who did a series of lithographs of Williamsburg buildings as early as 1934.[264] Two years later the precisionist Charles Sheeler painted the Governor's Palace (fig. 3.59). His previous work as a professional photographer led him as a painter to pursue the same sharpness of vision, to look for underlying abstract structure in compositions, and to work in a reductive style

in which, paradoxically, zones of sharp detail coexist with areas without any. He precisely defined his forms by painting sharp edges and creating a clean, smooth surface, seemingly devoid of any personal touches.

J. J. Lankes's approach was diametrically opposed to Sheeler's. Lankes was among the leading practitioners of the revived art of wood block prints. His book *Virginia Woodcuts*, which featured several views of Williamsburg (fig. 3.60), got reviewed in H. L. Mencken's *American Mercury*. The review read in part, "The vigor of Mr. Lankes' woodcuts is matched by the delicate fancy that he so often gets into them. They are never literal records but always poetical evocations of a memory or a mood."[265] Williamsburg would provide subject matter for every artistic taste.

Yorktown

"Did you know that the main product of Yorktown is history?" That was the conclusion of third and fourth graders in one Missouri school after studying Virginia in class.[266] Actually, before the Revolution, the chief import of Yorktown was slaves and the chief export the tobacco they grew. Paradoxically, the acres of the Virginia landscape most associated with advances in freedom also were the scenes of slavery. Historical memory is a selective thing, however, and while the triumph of liberty was remembered the violations of it were forgotten, at least in the public culture.

Soon after the British laid down their arms, as their band perhaps played the ironically appropriate tune *The World Turned Upside Down*, Charles Willson Peale rushed from Philadelphia to record for posterity Washington and his generals at the scene of their most decisive triumph. In the resulting portrait/landscape a dismasted and half-sunken ship refers to Cornwallis's abortive attempt to escape the night before he tendered his surrender. Grouped around Washington are three French generals—Rochambeau, Lafayette, and the Marquis de Chastellux, who not long afterward would visit Natural Bridge. Of course, Cornwallis could simply have evaded Washington's trap by sailing away had the French fleet not blockaded Chesapeake Bay and beaten off a British relief expedition. The French admiral the Count de Grasse is not included in the picture.

3.60 J. J. Lankes, *Bruton Parish Church, Williamsburg, Virginia*, c. 1930, woodcut, 6 ¾ x 5 in. (Courtesy of Dr. and Mrs. Lewis Wright)

3.61 Unknown artist, *chez Mondhare*, Paris, **Yorck touwn**, c. 1782, engraving, 12½ x 20¼ in. (Virginia Historical Society)

3.62 Benjamin Henry Latrobe, **Sketch of York town, from the beach, looking to the West**, 1798, pencil, pen, and watercolor, 7⁷⁄₁₆ x 9⁵⁄₁₆ in. (Courtesy of Maryland Historical Society)

Indeed, he never set foot on the land whose independence he did much to secure. The French ships riding at anchor refer to this pivotal, if rare, French naval triumph over the British.

The French were naturally thrilled to have bested their traditional foes and wanted it celebrated in art. French printmakers were desperate to capitalize on the public's interest. Complete ignorance of how Virginia looked was insufficient to deter them. The enterprising printmakers *chez Mondhare* on the Rue St. Jean de Beauvais hastily produced a curiously distorted panoramic view of Cornwallis's surrender (fig. 3.61). The walled city in the background, seemingly impregnable behind ramparts and redoubts, was conceived as "Yorck touwn," and facing it across the ship-infested "Baye de Chesapeack" is Gloucester, a modest hill town strategically perched above the narrows. The British troops, waiting for the ceremonies to begin, are drawn up on a plain below a forbidding mountain range raised by the printmakers in the heart of Tidewater Virginia.[267]

Before the campaign of 1781, Yorktown had been a major port. It lost its commerce in the war but gained immortality. The moment of glory was brief, however, and when Benjamin Henry Latrobe visited in 1798 and drew his "Sketch of York town, from the beach, looking to the West," he noted that the place was "half deserted. Trade has almost entirely left this once flourishing place, and none of the ravages of the war have been repaired" (fig. 3.62).[268]

The bluffs featured so prominently in Latrobe's sketch drew many comments. "The banks of the river, where the town stands, are high and inaccessible," wrote Isaac Weld in the 1790s.[269] "Its position is magnificent," wrote another visitor, in 1861. "The bluffs, a hundred feet high, and being on the outer angle of the bend, it commands an open view down the York and across the Chesapeake, limited only by the blending of sky and water to the east."[270] One of the most effective depictions of these cliffs was by Virginia's native son John Gadsby Chapman in a painting unfortunately not available for this exhibition. Likewise unavailable is Chapman's oil of the actual field on which the surrender occurred. That scene, done about 1834, shows the once war-ravaged landscape as entirely domesticated, with a rider looking very much like those seen in paintings of the Roman Campagna.[271] Chapman did a third view, of the battlefield rather than the surrender field, in which an ox-drawn cart symbolizes the return of peace. It was engraved and published as a print (fig. 3.63).

Another frequently painted scene was Cornwallis's

3.63 After John Gadsby Chapman, *Yorktown Battlegrounds*, c. 1835, engraving, 4¹/₂ x 6 in., published in *Graham's Magazine*. (Courtesy of Dr. and Mrs. Lewis Wright)

3.64 Robert K. Sneden, *Panoramic View of the Lines at Yorktown*, 1862, pencil, pen, and watercolor, 1³/₄ x 9¹/₂ in. (Virginia Historical Society, gift of Floyd D. Gottwald, Jr., © 1996)

cave, where the British general supposedly took refuge from the incessant allied bombardment. A visitor in 1816 was shown the spot, but being shown two purported Cornwallis caves, a tourist in 1890 began to doubt the credibility of either.[272]

In 1862 Robert K. Sneden, a mapmaker with the 40th New York Infantry Regiment, drew what he had been told was Cornwallis's cave. He also sketched the Nelson house,

which was shelled in 1781, and the Moore house, where the surrender negotiations took place. Sneden's presence reminds us that Yorktown was the scene of another siege in 1862. The Peninsula campaign aimed at capturing Richmond by advancing up the peninsula. The Union commander, George B. McClellan, might easily have taken lightly defended Yorktown by assault but preferred the certain but slow method of a siege. For a month Sneden had

3.65 James Warwick Jones, *Hallowed Ground, Yorktown Battlefield*, 1995, acrylic on canvas, 20 x 30 in. (Courtesy of the artist)

nothing to do but churn out countless maps and views of besieged, and finally captured, Yorktown (fig. 3.64). This delay enabled the Confederates to make a more effective, and eventually successful, defense of Richmond.

In 1995 James Warwick Jones executed the acrylic "Hallowed Ground, Yorktown Battlefield" (fig. 3.65) because of the timeless quality of the scene, which "probably looked to our ancestors three hundred years ago like it does today and hopefully in another three hundred years to our descendants."[273] The title refers to the Revolutionary contest, but the term "hallowed ground" is most often used to describe Civil War sites. At Yorktown, these often are one because the siege lines of 1862 incorporated those of 1781. The earlier siege, however, was by far the more important in world history. Generations of schoolchildren who knew nothing else about the Revolution could tell you about Valley Forge and Yorktown. In 1816 a visitor to Yorktown noted its "appearance of desolation and decay, which, being so seldom seen in our country, is the more apt to excite the notice of a stranger." "But whether flourishing or in ruins," he concluded, "York-Town will ever be an object of peculiar interest, as the scene where the progress of European arms terminated."[274]

4.41 Edward Beyer, ***Buchanan***, 1855, oil on canvas, 25½ x 53½ in.
(Courtesy of Town Improvement Society, Buchanan)

IV

LIVING ON THE LAND, 1750–2000

"But Mount Vernon and Arlington, shrines of unnumbered pilgrims, the matchless Shenandoah, the numerous crystal caves, the magnificence of fertile farm lands, the great army and navy posts, the teeming commerce of Richmond and Norfolk, these have their appeals to one individual or another till one may say Virginia sits securely by her sea and mountains, certain of capturing the admiration of all American generations."

—Wallace Nutting, *Virginia Beautiful*, 1930

Countryseats and Market Towns

By the time landscape painting reached Virginia in the middle of the eighteenth century, this most populous of Britain's mainland colonies was also the wealthiest. Virginia was at the height of its golden age of tobacco prosperity. The crop that saved Virginia was not indigenous but was a West Indian strain introduced into the colony about 1615 by John Rolfe, who is remembered by history, if at all, as Mr. Pocahontas.

Historians are fascinated by the interplay of culture and environment. In Virginia, the fact that the economy came to be dominated by tobacco was principally determined by environment. The climate and soil suited cultivation of tobacco. There would have been no demand for the crop, however, and no salvation for the colony, had not there been in Europe at that time a cultural change in the growing popularity of smoking. Once Virginia's economy became dominated by tobacco—to the point that it was the currency used in most financial transactions—the shape of the colony was determined for generations to come. Virginia would be overwhelmingly rural. As mentioned in the introduction, this was the reason that Virginia did not produce landscape art as early as several of the other, less populous and wealthy American colonies.

The profits from tobacco did not go into the pockets of the actual producers. In the Virginia climate, labor by slaves imported from the equatorial regions of Africa proved far more profitable than fields worked by whites, either free or bonded, and because it was profitable it flourished. The tobacco wealth was generated by a vast number of slaves—forty percent of the population in 1776—who did not even own themselves. The profits went to a gentry elite.

These Virginia gentlemen built quite imposing "seats," or houses, on their plantations. In 1732 William Hugh Grove wrote of going "Up the York River, which has pleasant Seats on the Bank which shew like little villages."[1] Each plantation was a largely self-sufficient community. To the extent that it was not, direct communication with England was possible by ships that sailed well up the James, York, Rappahannock, and Potomac Rivers to inland plantations. Towns were superfluous.

The Marquis de Chastellux approached Westover on the James River, seat of the Byrd family, "by a very agreeable road, with magnificent houses in view at every instant; for the banks of the James form the garden of Virginia. . . . That of Mrs. Bird, to which I was going, surpasses all of them in the magnificence of the buildings, the beauty of its situation, and the pleasures of society."[2] Westover then was occupied by the widow of William Byrd III, who had committed suicide on New Year's Day, 1777, being ruined by gambling debts. In his heyday, however, Byrd had lived in great ostentation, not only at Westover but also at Belvidere, a house he built about 1750 on a hill across from what now is called Belle Isle in Richmond. The city had been founded by Byrd's father at the falls of the James River, the most inland point of navigation, in order to capture the tobacco trade of the rapidly growing Piedmont between the falls and the mountains to the west. The Reverend Andrew Burnaby called Belvidere "as romantic and elegant as any-thing I have ever seen."[3] Benjamin Henry Latrobe painted the estate in watercolors between 1796 and 1798 (fig. 4.1). It had been sold by the estate of the bankrupted William Byrd III and bought by "Light-Horse Harry" Lee, who himself was to die bankrupt.

Bushrod Washington bought it from Lee in 1795 but would in turn sell it in February 1798.[4]

Belvidere sat atop a hill, and a New England traveler observed with bemusement, "Almost every gentleman's seat, even if not presidential, has some romantic appellation, as—Farmer's Hill, Hunter's Hill, Mount-Pleasant; but you need not suppose all these swells to be mountains."[5] By the word "presidential" he was, of course, alluding to Mount Vernon, Monticello, and Montpelier, the homes of Washington, Jefferson, and Madison. The latter two also died bankrupt or nearly so. By 1800 the land of eastern Virginia

had been farmed, mostly for tobacco by short-sighted methods, for more than 150 years. It was worn out in Tidewater and severely gullied in Piedmont.

Some Virginians believed that the problem lay not only in the land, but also in the system of labor. They blamed slavery as well as tobacco culture. Thomas Jefferson agreed, but felt too old to tackle the problem, and wished the next generation well. One of the second-generation Jeffersonians was John Hartwell Cocke of Fluvanna County. He became an early supporter of the American Colonization Society, which repatriated African Americans to Africa. On his Virginia and Alabama plantations he educated slaves—contrary to law—and trained them to be independent. Those who passed his rigorous test were emancipated and sent to Liberia.

Cocke's seat was called Bremo. Deeply influenced by Jefferson in matters architectural as well as constitutional, Cocke himself designed Bremo as a Jeffersonian house. Perhaps in the late 1830s Bremo was depicted on canvas by Edward Troye, who was in Virginia to paint gentlemen's horses, not their houses, but who nonetheless consented to execute this estate portrait in the English tradition (fig. 4.2). The artist took delight in painting the details of the

4.1 Benjamin Henry Latrobe, *View of the North front of Belvidere, Richmond*, 1796–98, pencil, pen, and watercolor, 6 15/16 x 10 15/16 in. (Courtesy of Maryland Historical Society)

4.2 Edward Troye, *Bremo*, c. 1830s, oil on canvas, 18 1/4 x 24 3/8 in. (Private collection)

4.3 Edward Beyer, *Bellevue, The Lewis Homestead, Salem, Virginia*, 1855, oil on canvas, 36 x 50 in. (Private collection)

landscape and the play of sunlight on them. Views like this were painted throughout the nineteenth and into the twentieth century. The frequency of their appearance seems to relate to the serendipitous availability of visiting artists, like Troye.

Col. William Lewis took advantage of the presence of the German artist Edward Beyer to paint his seat, Bellevue (fig. 4.3). While in western Virginia, Beyer painted five scenes known by the name of a house and two known as "farm."[6] Unlike Troye's landscape of Bremo, Beyer's painting of Bellevue clearly depicts the slave workforce in the foreground. He offers no criticism of the use of slaves, which his patron would have found objectionable, but in a brochure to accompany a panorama he exhibited after returning to Germany, it is clear that he accepted the Virginia line on race completely. A section of the brochure about Salem states that "Every time negroes have a get-together, a white man must be present to keep them in line."[7] Colonel Lewis, too, seems to have been unembarrassed about slavery. He may have consoled himself with Biblical precedents and with the conviction that he was a benevolent patriarch to his "slave family," a term often used in apologies for slavery. In truth, Beyer portrays Bellevue as Arcadia. Lewis's agricultural operation seems prosperous, man is in harmony with nature, the scene is sheltered by distant mountains, and a tiny train alludes to

progress without significantly compromising the environment. The description of a plantation by Arthur Singleton in 1824 seems to capture in words what Beyer put on canvas:

> If you visit a plantation, you strike off the main road. . . . You feel a solitary emotion, as you find a house and out-buildings, on a spot cleared in the middle of the woods, and surrounded by broad wheat and corn fields; not fifteen or twenty acres of arable land, but from one to five hundred; not tilled by five or six hired men, but from thirty to one or two hundred slaves.[8]

Plantations like Bellevue provided the economic underpinning for the market town of Salem, which Colonel Lewis had founded, and which appears in the far distance. Produce from nearby plantations was sold in the town, and with the income from the sales planters bought hard and soft goods of every description as well as farm equipment, seed, and feed. Beyer was commissioned to paint a panorama of Salem by some twenty gentlemen of the town. He called it "Churches, Blacksmith Shop, and College: A View of Salem of Virginia in 1855" (fig. 4.4). In it we see the buildings and their positions in the landscape, and how people dressed, worked, and traveled in this setting. A comparison of Beyer's view of Salem with nineteenth-century maps, photographs, and written accounts that describe the town is revealing about the artist's methods. Typically with such

4.4 Edward Beyer, *Churches, Blacksmith Shop and College: A View of Salem of Virginia in 1855*, oil on canvas, 29 x 48 in. (Virginia Historical Society, gift of Lora Robins, E. Claiborne Robins, Jr., Bruce C. Gottwald, Paul Mellon, D. Tennant Bryan, Henry F. Stern, Mrs. E. Schneider, and Thomas Towers)

towns, he positioned himself at a high vantage point where he could take in the breadth of the town and most of the key buildings, which he plotted on his canvas with the accuracy of a geographer. Some near and far buildings inevitably were juxtaposed by his line of sight, so Beyer varied the value of his colors to suggest their spatial relationships. Near buildings are more intensely colored than distant ones. Then the artist proceeded to paint microscopic details that, in the field, cannot be perceived at such a distance by the human eye. He must have had a telescope for distant details and may have used a camera obscura for nearer ones.

Both before and after visiting Virginia, Beyer was involved in producing large narrative panoramas, turned on revolving drums, which viewers paid to watch. Although the Salem view is static, Beyer approaches it in much the same way as a moving panorama. We enter the town on Main Street, like the foreground couple on horseback, and then we proceed to tour Salem, at least visually. We have passed F. Johnston's terraced garden on the right. We approach the brown sheds that are Mr. Day's blacksmith shop. Two doors down is Joshua Brown's brick house. We encounter townspeople as we proceed. At the other end of

Main Street is the white steeple of the Presbyterian church. Halfway there—where two wagons have driven—is the Lutheran church, recognizable by its cupola. Turning right at that church, we proceed up a hill, past the porticoed courthouse to the white-steepled Methodist church, near the center of the picture. Beyond and distant is the classical main building of Roanoke College, dedicated seven years earlier.

Thirty years later a visitor still seems to describe what Beyer saw:

> Seven miles from Roanoke stands the old town of Salem, the bulk of which is a mile or so distant. What one can see tempts us to alight and discover more. The village lies in a broad valley, is surrounded by large estates, and an air of prosperity and pleasant home-life pervades the whole scene. One of the oldest and most prominent communities in this part of the state, Salem long ago became noted for its highly educated and religious society, which was partly a cause, partly a result, of the location there of two academies of high repute—Roanoke College for boys, and the Hollins Institute for girls.[9]

Lexington in Rockbridge County was another market

town blessed by two institutions of higher learning—Washington College (now Washington and Lee University) and the Virginia Military Institute. Travelers' opinions of Lexington were uniformly favorable. "Entered Lexington, quite a handsome little town"—the view of Thomas W. Claybrook in 1832—was typical.[10] The military college, however, was not founded until 1839. From the hill it occupies, Seth Eastman drew a pencil sketch of the town on 1 December 1849 (fig. 4.5). Then he turned around and sketched House Mountain (fig. 4.6). From the same vantage point he drew the west side of the original 1816 building at the Lexington arsenal and, behind it, the arsenal barracks with a cupola (fig. 4.7). These buildings were used by Virginia Military Institute until the 1850s, when special-purpose buildings designed by Andrew Jackson Davis were completed.

Based in New York City, Davis was a leading national exponent of the Gothic revival movement. A fascination with all things medieval grew out of the romantic movement in England and was popularized in Virginia by the enormous vogue for Sir Walter Scott's medieval romances, such as *Ivanhoe*. In the 1840s and 1850s jousting tournaments were popular social events throughout the commonwealth. The Gothic style was considered especially suitable for a fortified place. The resulting battlements of the new Virginia Military Institute buildings are shown in a watercolor of 1853 by Sir William Fox of New Zealand (fig. 4.8). They still are in evidence today, the school having been rebuilt in the same style after being burned down by Union general David Hunter in 1864. Despite the deliberately anachronistic style of the buildings, they were quite modern in their appointments. One cadet said, "After we moved into the new barracks we had steam heat and gas."[11]

Near Lexington lay the smaller community of Fairfield. In 1851 Mary Jane Boggs from Spotsylvania wrote, "About four miles from Mr. Bell's we passed through a village called Fairfield. I never in my life, saw such pastures, such cows, nor such springhouses as the people have over here. I wish I could live over here."[12] Half a century later the village looked much the same in an oil

4.5 Seth Eastman, *Lexington, Virginia*, 1849, pencil, 6½ x 9⅞ in. (Courtesy of Peabody Museum of Archaeology and Ethnology, Harvard University)

painting by self-taught artist Bessie Patton (fig. 4.9).

Another market town with an academic air was Charlottesville, where Thomas Jefferson situated the University of Virginia. Miss Boggs did "not think Charlottesville a very pretty place, though the scenery around it & the University are certainly beautiful."[13] The scenery seems also to have captivated the artist Russell Smith, in whose "View of [the] University of Virginia and Monticello Mountain, taken from back and to the left," those two places are reduced to tiny specks in the landscape (fig. 4.10).

Those who viewed the school closer up generally had favorable things to say about it. An exception was John Robert Godley, an Englishman who in 1844 called the university "grotesque."[14] At the other extreme was Margaret Bayard Smith, a friend of Jefferson's who came to Charlottesville two years after his death. She wrote that

Never have I beheld a more imposing work of Art— On a commanding height, surround[ed] by mountains, lies the Rotunda, or central building. . . . The whole impression on my mind—was delightful—elevating!—for the objects both of nature & art by which I was surrounded, are equally sublime and beautiful. . . . It has a most imposing effect—In a city, or land cultivated country, it would not be so impressive—But on a noble height—embosomed in mountains—surrounded with a landscape so rich, varied & beautiful—so remote from any city—There was something novel, as well as grand in its locality, that certainly had a strong effect on the imagination.[15]

4.6 Seth Eastman, **House Mountain**, 1849, pencil, 6 1/2 x 9 7/8 in. (Courtesy of Calder Loth)

4.7 Seth Eastman, **Virginia Military Institute**, 1849, pencil, 6 1/2 x 9 1/8 in. (Courtesy of Peabody Museum of Archaeology and Ethnology, Harvard University)

Lynchburg was larger than Salem, Lexington, and Charlottesville, but not quite in a category with Richmond and Norfolk. Nor would it be especially associated in the public mind with higher education until well into the twentieth century. The city's topography evoked mostly favorable comment among early visitors. "In point of scenery, it is far beyond Richmond," wrote Mrs. Anne Royall. She went on to explain its charm in terms that will sound familiar by now:

4.8 Sir William Fox, *Military College, W. Lexington V.*, 1853, watercolor, 9¹/₂ x 13⁴/₅ in. (Courtesy of National Library of New Zealand)

> What distinguishes the scenery of Lynchburg, from any I have met with is, that such a number of images are drawn within so narrow a compass. The rough, the smooth, the sublime, and the beautiful are thickly mingled, and combines every catalogue for the picturesque and the fanciful.[16]

Another Englishwoman, Marianne Finch, wrote in 1853 that "Lynchburg is pleasantly situated, and very convenient—for the manufacture and transfer of tobacco, which is its principal trade." Just a few years earlier, in June 1845, the German-born artist Augustus Köllner made a

delicate wash drawing of the town with the pencil inscription "Lynchburg on the James River, Virginia. The great staple for Tobacco" (fig. 4.11). When preparing the drawing for exhibition he added a new, bolder title in ink, "Lynchburg on the James River, Va." This double-page illustration seems to have been at the center of Köllner's sketchbook, which also included views of Richmond and Jamestown.[17]

4.9 Bessie Anderson Patton, *Fairfield*, c. 1900, oil on canvas, 30 x 55 in. (Private collection)

Forty years after Köllner, Ernest Ingersoll wrote:

Lynchburg is well worth seeing . . . The James River passes through a group of hills at this point, which begrudge it room and rise steeply from its edge. It would be hard to find a more unsuitable place to set a town; yet here has grown up a city of between fifteen and twenty thousand people, half of whom can look down their neighbors' chimneys. The railways and a few mills, by the help of excavations and bridges, have made room enough to lay their tracks and build a station down near the river level, but all the rest of the town clings precariously to some steep hill-side. If you walk up from the station, you climb a series of staircases; if you ride, your omnibus is drawn by four or six horses. When you leave your hotel and walk abroad you must choose between going up hill or down. . . .[18]

By 1916, Lynchburg had become considerably more industrial, losing some of its earlier charm. A New York visitor regretted the change but sensed that few inhabitants of the city agreed with her:

I don't know as Lynchburg felt as I did about the disfigurement, for the city has become, in proportion to its size, one of the richest in America. If one sees a green hill from the rear of the Carroll House, one finds at the front window a sky scraper quite as soaring.[19]

The smaller market towns of the

Jeffersonian and antebellum eras also survived into the twentieth century, although not all were attended by the same level of prosperity as Lynchburg. Gari Melchers, a native of Detroit who had a distinguished career of international renown, settled in 1916 at the Belmont estate in Falmouth, a town overlooking the falls of the Rappahannock River. From 1916 until his death in 1932, Melchers painted a number of Virginia landscapes, some in a realistic manner, and others with a warm, reassuring, Impressionistic style and palette adopted late in his life. Among the latter group is "Stafford Heights" (fig. 4.12), one of several panoramic views he painted of the quiet and even stagnant area around Falmouth. He had a proprietary attitude toward what he regarded as his turf. He scared off one rival artist by saying, "Do you know that you're

4.10 Russell Smith, *View of [the] University of Virginia and Monticello Mountain, taken from back and to the left*, c. 1844, ink, 12 x 16 ½ in. (Courtesy of Library of Virginia)

4.11 Augustus Köllner, *Lynchburg on the James River, Va.*, 1845, wash, 7 ¼ x 18 ¾ in.
(Courtesy of Maier Museum of Art, Randolph-Macon Woman's College, Lynchburg, Virginia)

4.12 Gari Melchers, **Stafford Heights**, c. 1920, oil on canvas, 30¼ x 40 in. (Courtesy of Belmont, the Gari Melchers Estate and Memorial Gallery, Mary Washington College, Fredericksburg, Virginia)

4.13 Ed Bordett, **Blue Ridge Steeples**, 1991, oil on canvas, 8 x 15 in. (Courtesy of Roddy Moore)

poaching on another artist's territory?"[20]

To view Ed Bordett's "Blue Ridge Steeples" (fig. 4.13), a study for a large oil painting of the town of Fincastle, is almost to revisit Edward Beyer.[21] In fact, it is a deliberate evocation of Beyer's work. The technique is almost photo-realistic and clearly of the twentieth century, but all the technologies that have revolutionized the small town of Fincastle since Beyer's day are absent; there are no automobiles, power or telephone lines. The composition cleverly omits them without denying their presence. If one

did not know the picture's date of execution, one might suppose that beyond the trees are horses and buggies.

A Landscape for Sport

With the wealth and population of the state centered in the countryside, and with the gentry class freed by slave labor to enjoy leisure time, Virginians for more than three centuries were active on the land. They were routinely engaged in sport of one type or another, in contrast to some of their northern counterparts. In 1851 a contributor to the *New-York Home Journal* commented about the latter, "we are less in the habit of luxuriating in the beauties of nature than any other pretending to civilization. We neither hunt, fish, ride on horseback, indulge in rural sports or athletic exercises." He added that because his neighbors were not outdoors people, they paid too little attention to the beauty of nature; in the outskirts of New York City he "scarcely met a soul susceptible to the genial influence of the American landscape."[22]

The Virginia landscape became known at an early date as a setting for sport. A 1618 engraving in Theodor de Bry's *America* is captioned as "What the Gentry and others in Virginia Do for their Entertainment" (fig. 4.14). As mentioned in the introduction, this engraving may be based on eyewitness testimony from the New World, but probably it is purely fanciful as a landscape. The text explaining this image reads in part:

> For gentlemen, what exercise should more delight them than ranging daily these unknown parts for fowling, fishing, and hawking. . . . For hunting, also, the woods, lakes and rivers afford not only sufficient chase for those who enjoy such pleasure, but such beasts as not only are their bodies delicate food but also their skins are so rich that they will recompense a day's work with a captain's pay.

To be sure, this was part of the paradisal literature of the period, and not to be taken literally in all respects. The various pursuits depicted, however, were real enough. While fowling or bird shooting was difficult with the slow and inaccurate firearms of the 1600s, it waxed in popularity as firearms improved in speed and accuracy. Falconry waned.

In Virginia, bird shooting became popular among people of widely varying backgrounds, but the commissioning of paintings of it remained a prerogative of the upper classes, and the pictures "remain household treasures of the foremost shooting families of America," according to a New York City gallery catalogue from the 1930s. In that catalogue "Quail Shooting on the St. James River, Va." was illustrated. (Much as King James might have wished to be canonized for giving us the Authorized Version of the Bible in 1611, we must overlook this slight error in the title.) The picture illustrated in the 1930s catalogue bears a striking compositional likeness to the oil reproduced here, John Martin Tracy's "A Field Trial—The Point" (fig. 4.15), and it is on this basis that the scene is believed to be a Virginia one. A description by southern art historian Estill Curtis Pennington cannot be improved upon:

> In both works, black men wait patiently in the background while members of the

so-called "foremost shooting families" pursue their sport. The black presence is a jarring punctuation of the composition, a reminder of social function and social role during the heyday of Robber Baron English affectation. From a formalist standpoint, the work itself is at once very painterly and redolent of the warm color harmonics of early fall.[23]

Bird hunting today is not much changed from what it was centuries ago, except that there are better guns but fewer birds and fewer wild settings in which to find them. Those landscapes either are held by individuals or they are nature preserves that are owned by private groups or government agencies. Once in the field, however, the modern wildlife artist encounters the same conditions that were known to his predecessors, although he may be more appreciative of the setting because it is so diminished. He also may be more concerned about the quarry than his forebears because the animal population is much depleted. In "Elegance in Gold" (fig. 4.16), by Guy Crittenden, a Richmond artist who paints in the Tidewater region, Canada geese pass in flight across the line of sight of the viewer, who somehow senses that a hunter is present and will fire at these inviting targets. The landscape is still and bathed in the first golden light of dawn. The artist addresses a strange dichotomy that he says troubles him and many hunters today—he appreciates the beauty of the bird yet also wants

4.14 Unknown artist, ***What the Gentry and others in Virginia Do for their Entertainment***, 1618, engraving, 5¹⁄₈ x 6⁷⁄₈ in., published in Theodore de Bry's German *America*. (Virginia Historical Society)

4.15 John Martin Tracy, *A Field Trial—The Point*, c. 1885, oil on canvas, 30 x 50 in.
(Courtesy of Morris Museum of Art, Augusta, Georgia)

4.16 Guy Crittenden, *Elegance in Gold*, 1999, oil on canvas, 24 x 48 in. (Courtesy of the artist)

to "bring it down." It is his lifelong love of hunting that has made him love the landscape, particularly under special conditions of lighting and atmosphere that change quickly, and these loves lure him to the field. In *Landscape into Art*, Kenneth Clark points out that this paradox has a long history. It is chiefly through the instinct to kill, argues Clark, that man achieves intimacy with the life of nature.[24]

As shown in de Bry's engraving of 1618, hunting with horses and hounds goes back to the beginnings of recorded history in Virginia. In the 1780s Luigi Castiglioni observed that "Hunting is done on horseback, and not without danger, since they pursue the deer through the woods and over places where the terrain is very rough."[25] Stags are no longer pursued by hounds, but foxes are. In 1730 eight tobacco planters imported English foxes "to secure the same sport that many of them had enjoyed in

England." In 1739 John Clayton wrote from Gloucester, "Some here hunt foxes with hounds as you do in England." Lord Fairfax, proprietor of Virginia's Northern Neck, settled in Virginia permanently in 1747 and introduced the sport to his young surveyor George Washington.[26]

The firmer footing and fewer waterways of the Piedmont made it more hospitable to fox hunting than the Tidewater. A sign from the early 1800s for Shelton's Inn in Hanover County may be the earliest depiction of a fox hunting scene in Virginia (fig. 4.17). Or, two famous paintings from Selma, the Truehart seat in Powhatan County, may be. Informally entitled "Start of the Hunt" and "End of the Hunt" (fig. 4.18), they were commissioned by Bartholomew Truehart (1770–1834) about 1800. If they

portray him they are among the first Virginia landscapes. Or, they may have been based on English sporting prints, although no exact prototypes have been located. Certain features of these landscapes are believably Virginian, among them the architecture and especially the zigzag fences called "Virginia Fences," of a type not generally found in England. In New England, a drunkard was said to be "walking Virginia fences." The mountains visible from Powhatan, however, are problematic.

In the 1800s packs of hounds owned by individual grandees gave way to organized clubs. The first in the United States was the Piedmont Foxhounds in 1840. A year later came the Albemarle County Hunt. It is not clear whether John J. Porter's "Fox Hunting in Culpeper" from the 1850s represents a formally organized hunt (fig. 4.19). A native of Pennsylvania, he twice married women from Culpeper and spent his artistic career there. This picture descended in a Culpeper family. Porter studied in Italy for two years, and on his return "He often stated that he drew his highest inspiration for landscapes from the Blue Ridge Mountains."[27] The mountains

4.17 Unknown artist, ***E. Shelton's Inn***, probably 1820s, oil on wood, 20 ⅛ x 45 ¾ in. (Courtesy of the High Museum of Art, Atlanta, bequest of Edgar William and Bernice Chrysler Garbisch, 1981.47)

4.18 Unknown artist, ***The End of the Hunt***, c. 1800, oil on canvas, 30 x 45 in. (Courtesy of National Gallery of Art, Washington, gift of Edgar William and Bernice Chrysler Garbisch)

4.19 John J. Porter, *Fox Hunting in Culpeper*, 1855–60, oil on canvas, 16 ⅛ x 30 ⅛ in. (Courtesy of Vernon Grizzard)

4.20 Jean Bowman, *A Scurry—The Orange County Hunt in 1988*, 1988, oil on canvas, 31 x 65 in. (Courtesy of the Westmoreland Davis Memorial Foundation, Inc.)

appear in the background of "Fox Hunting in Culpeper," a painting that also shows the artist's familiarity with English sporting prints in the elongated forms of the hounds and the extreme horizontal composition.[28] Another of Porter's known works, "Presentation of the Charger Coquette to Colonel John Singleton Mosby by the Men of His Command, December 1864," shows the presentation in a panoramic landscape typical of the northern Piedmont known during the Civil War as "Mosby's Confederacy."[29]

Fox hunting is on the verge of being outlawed by the Labour government in Great Britain. It is less likely to be abolished in Virginia, where the American fox hound is the official state dog. The tradition of painting hunts continues as well. A recent example is "A Scurry—The Orange County Hunt in 1988" by Jean Bowman (fig. 4.20). The reference is not to Orange County, Virginia, but to the hunt of Orange County, New York, which relocated to Fauquier County, Virginia, early in the twentieth century. By the 1930s, fourteen of the most famous pack hounds in the United States were concentrated in Virginia's northern Piedmont.[30] This is the only known American scurry, a popular form of English painting in the early 1800s. The characteristic of the scurry is that all the horses, hounds, and people are represented by actual portraits. Virginia hunt scenes of a more generic and less demanding nature are more common.

Thomas Anburey, who had the misfortune to be in Virginia as a captive from the army surrendered at Saratoga by British general John Burgoyne in 1777, observed that "Colonel Randolph possesses that fondness for horses which I observed was peculiar to the Virginians of all stations, sparing no trouble, pains, or expense in importing the best stock and improving the breed." Besides fox hunting, Virginians were mad for racing, and horse breeding became an important part of plantation life. Planters took as much pride in their horses' bloodlines as in their own, and they commissioned portraits of their horses as well as of their families. Many of these portraits show the plantation house in the far distance; the horse was more important. One example is a painting of Argyle, a horse belonging to "the Napoleon of the Turf," William Ransom Johnson (1782–1849), in which the owner's Chesterfield County estate, Oaklands, is minutely painted in the background. Half Sink, the Henrico County estate of John Minor Botts, is shown in the background of Edward Troye's 1833 portrait of the horse Rolla.[31]

A horse portrait in which the landscape background is especially important is that of "Fly by Night" by artist Jesse Atwood (fig. 4.21). Painted for Col. William Townes of Occoneechee plantation in Mecklenburg County, it contains the earliest pictorial representation of the Roanoke River Valley. In the background the Dan and Staunton Rivers come together to form the Roanoke at Occoneechee Island. It also is rare in being a landscape of Southside Virginia. The region was settled relatively late because the rivers flowed away from the Chesapeake Bay and Atlantic Ocean. It remained remote until after 1800, when improvements in overland transport made it more accessible. Then it developed rapidly. A traveler in 1885 had a low opinion of its landscape, however, writing, "Well, south-eastern Virginia is flat, truly, and less entertaining than the mountain country; and if one has to travel through its pines and scrub oaks for several days in succession . . . he gets extremely tired of it."[32] Thirty years later another northerner had a quite different perspective:

> The landscape had many of the elements which one must see before leaving Virginia: fine farms worked by negroes, real swamps, and patches of magnificent pine. The cultivated fields would be entirely surrounding these forests, and they stood like soldiers of

4.21 Jesse Atwood, *Fly by Night*, c. 1838, oil on canvas, 26 x 36 in. (Courtesy of the Prestwould Foundation)

4.22 Frank Buchser, ***Noosing the Trout***, 1867, oil on canvas, 20 x 31 in. (Courtesy of Kunsthaus, Zürich)

a lost legion making their last stand against the encroachment of an insidious little enemy which walked toward them like relentless headmen, axe in hand.[33]

Angling or fishing also is shown in the 1618 engraving. Of course, fishing for food was important to the native people of Virginia as it would be to the European colonists. It remains a significant industry today. No one can know when the first Virginian fished purely for pleasure, however, but the late 1800s marks its emergence as a truly popular sport. In 1897 the English traveler A. G. Bradley published a fictionalized account of an 1870s fly fishing adventure in the "Windy Gap" section of the Blue Ridge Mountains, boasting that this was "the very first invasion of the Alleghenies south of the Potomac ever undertaken with fly-rod and tackle." According to this account, a new sport had been introduced and "The news spread up the valley like wildfire, that there were strange fishermen below and that 'one big man in gum pants was trompin' up the middle o' the crick with a dip net, flickin' a silver pole about like a buggy whip, and rakin' out the fish like old Scrat.' Many a mountaineer that day left his corn-row unhoed and his tobacco-hills half finished upon distant heights."[34] Perhaps the earliest painting of sport fishing in Virginia is "Noosing the Trout," painted by Frank Buchser in 1867 (fig. 4.22). He was a Swiss artist who came to Lexington to paint a portrait of Robert E. Lee, then president of Washington College, but he stopped on numerous occasions to paint the Virginia landscape, which he found alluring.

Landscapes of Progress

To some Virginians progress meant something entirely different than large countryseats and small market towns of the Jeffersonian ideal. To these people, who in the thirty years before the Civil War tended to be Whig in their politics, progress was to be measured not by rural settlements but rather by urban growth and advances in industry and transportation.

Of course, Thomas Jefferson himself had not been entirely averse to cities. He loved Paris, and he embellished Richmond with a capitol that was the first classical "temple of liberty" in America. Jacques-Pierre Brissot de Warville viewed the capitol when it was but midway through its construction, from 1785 to 1796, but nevertheless remarked that "This capitol turns the heads of Virginians; they imagine, that from this, like the old Romans, they shall one day give law to the whole north."[35]

The several hills upon which Richmond was situated, overlooking the falls of the James River, deeply impressed many writers and painters. In 1816 James Kirke Paulding wrote that "Richmond deserves to have a song written about it." Another visitor was reminded of Edinburgh, yet another of Richmond, Surrey, from whence the Virginia city got its name.[36] In 1842 Charles Dickens found Richmond to be "delightfully situated on eight hills overhanging the James River."[37] Author and attorney William Wirt wrote that

Richmond occupies a very picturesque and most beautiful situation. I have never met with such an assemblage of striking and interesting objects. The town, dispersed over hills of various shapes; the river descending from west to east, and obstructed by a multitude of small islands, clumps of trees, and myriads of rocks; among which it tumbles, foams, and roars, constituting what are called the falls. . . . the white sails of approaching and departing vessels exhibit a curious and interesting appearance. . . . all these objects, falling at once under the eye, constitute, by far, the most finely varied and most animated landscape that I have ever seen.[38]

Among the first artists to paint Richmond was Benjamin Henry Latrobe, whose watercolor "View of the City of Richmond from the Bank of James River" was drawn in 1798 (fig. 4.23). Latrobe records the new city as it was being developed east of the capitol. The capitol also

4.23 Benjamin Henry Latrobe, *View of the City of Richmond from the Bank of James River*, 1798, pencil, pen, and watercolor, 7 x 10¼ in. (Courtesy of Maryland Historical Society)

4.24 J. L. Bouqueta de Woiseri, *View of Richmond*, c. 1822, watercolor, 35 x 23 in. (Virginia Historical Society)

4.25 Jane P. Braddick, *Richmond: Panorama*, c. 1822, oil on canvas, 21½ x 28½ in. (Courtesy of Valentine Museum)

dominates in an etching by the French artist Charles-Balthasar-Julien Fevrét de Saint-Mémin in 1805 taken from the south side of the James below Mayo's bridge. In the foreground Saint-Mémin takes care to maintain the rustic republican environment from which the city sprang.[39] Another French artist, J. L. Bouqueta de Woiseri, proved capable of capturing the picturesque beauty of Richmond in a topographically correct manner in a watercolor panorama dated about 1822 (fig. 4.24). The twin toll houses of Mayo's bridge lead the viewer's eye into the fledgling town. He also did an earlier view of Richmond. Since 1797 he had been doing sketches for a print entitled "First Cities of the United States." The six-section print issued in 1810 included Richmond.[40] On both occasions when he visited Richmond the city was growing rapidly and roughly. Jane P. Braddick's "Richmond: Panorama," also from 1822, suggests that she believed Jefferson's imposing and inspira-

tional capitol was seen to best advantage from the undeveloped land to its west rather than from the happenstance city developing to the east (fig. 4.25). She seems to have had an interest in things Jeffersonian for she also painted a rare watercolor view of Monticello in the 1820s.

In 1847 John William Hill painted a watercolor view of Richmond (fig. 4.26). From the late 1840s until about 1855 he was employed by Smith Brothers to paint watercolors of North American cities from Halifax, Nova Scotia, to Havana, Cuba, to be issued as a series of engraved or lithographed views. In 1853 they published Hill's "A View of Richmond in 1852 from Manchester" on the south side of the James looking north. It was lithographed by Fanny Palmer, best known for her later work for Currier and Ives. Hill's 1852 watercolor has a more elevated vantage point than the 1847 work and was painted from a spot farther upstream. The 1847 view is farther downstream, obscuring

4.26 John William Hill, *View of Richmond*, 1847, watercolor, 8 x 26 ½ in.
(Virginia Historical Society)

4.27 James Mooney, *Richmond from Hollywood Cemetery*, 1908, oil on canvas, 24 x 40 in. (Virginia Historical Society, gift of Heth and Margery Owen)

Mayo's bridge, so prominent in the 1852 view. The town is so far in the distance, and consequently so small, that it might not be recognized at once by viewers. The presence of the African-American woman and children, however, would instantly have identified the scene to contemporaries as one of a southern slave society.[41]

One of the best-known views of Richmond in the 1800s, and one widely reproduced in books in the 1900s, is that painted in a now lost original by George Cooke, but engraved and published in 1834 (see fig 2.17, above). The site on which Cooke stood would less than twenty years later become part of Richmond's renowned Hollywood Cemetery, one of the first and best examples of the "rural" cemetery movement in this country. Seventy-four years after George Cooke, James Mooney stood at approximately

the same spot and painted Richmond in oils (fig. 4.27). Mooney had been a soldier in the Civil War and knew its devastation. After the war, Richmond embraced the economic development themes of the New South movement. Industrialization brought great mills and factories to the banks of the James River, which linked the city to ocean trade and, by its canal, to markets in the western counties. Writing in *Picturesque America* in 1872, J. R. Thompson described "the forges of the Tredegar Iron-works, the fiery chimneys of which at night belch forth flames that sent their sparkle into a thousand windows, and make pictures in the rippling waters" as well as "the gigantic [Gallego] flour-mill for which Richmond is justly famous, it being claimed that these buildings are the largest of the kind in the world."[42] These additions were not seen as detriments to the land-

scape but as welcome evidence of recovery. Tall smokestacks and high-rise buildings punctuate the skyline of Mooney's panorama. They speak of progress and modernity in this first twentieth-century landscape of Richmond, yet they do so within a still-pleasing landscape setting.

During the early twentieth century Richmond ceased to be a large town and became, finally, a city. Authors and artists were sensitive to the transformation. A small booklet was issued, pairing reproductions of works by local artists with appropriate quotations. A drawing of downtown Richmond by Adèle Clark appeared with Henry Sydnor Harris's observation that "It isn't every generation that can watch its old town change into a metropolis right under its eyes."[43] Whatever others thought of the change, artists had reason to be thankful. Only in a metropolis would there be the critical mass of galleries, museums, art schools, and patronage needed for art to thrive.

The nineteenth century had been a bleak period for landscape painters in Richmond. Portraits were almost the only saleable paintings for most of the century. For this study, a systematic search of newspapers could be done only for Richmond, but it seems logical that the few references to landscape art in the newspapers of the state's capital and largest city throughout the 1800s would hold true for the rest of the state as well. In 1786 the Chevalier Marie de Quesnay de Beaurepaire laid the foundation stone for an Academy of Sciences and the Fine Arts, but he was detained by the Revolutionary authorities in Paris, and the building burned down in 1798. James Warrell's Virginia Museum opened in 1817. It had copies of landscapes by Claude and Rubens, which artists could study, but it closed by 1836. The Mechanic's Institute, founded in 1854, sponsored exhibitions until taken over by the Confederate government in 1861. As for teachers, in 1814 Thaddeus Sobieske offered to teach "landscape & figure drawing."[44] One Signor Louis Paduane briefly advertised in 1821 that he painted "Landscapes and Miniatures."[45] J. E. Warfel, a pupil of Thomas Sully's and John Neagle's in Philadelphia, announced his intention of offering instruction to young ladies in "FANCY PORTRAIT and LANDSCAPE painting" in 1846.[46]

Among the few artists offering to paint landscapes were Lewis P. Clover, Sr., whom we met when he owned Jacob Ward's painting of Natural Bridge, who advertised in 1850 as a "portrait and landscape painter."[47] In 1859 "Mr. John Grant, a skillful draftsman and architect as well as a landscape painter" was noticed in the public prints.[48] There are thirty or more notices of portrait painters for each of these examples.

Mention of individual landscape paintings were likewise few. In 1857 a newspaper reported that Alexander Davidson's oil paintings of Richmond and the James River were for sale. In 1859 the estate of W. Rosier included Davidson's "View of Richmond from Church Hill," valued at $225.[49] A Richmond newspaper on 16 December 1865 reported that Harry A. McCardle had two pastels on exhibition "representing two plantations owned by Mr. J. B. Davis, Esq., of this city, of Springfield in King William County, and the other of Corottoman in Lancaster County."[50] In 1881 Carter Nelson Berkeley drew landscape views for lithographs that appeared in Mayo Tobacco Company's calendar for that year, an indication of the low status of landscape painters.[51] That same year Thomas Ellis wrote an extensive letter to the editor that recapitulated the art scene in Richmond and Virginia since about the 1820s. Although he lists who owned many different works of art, not one was a Virginia, or even an American, landscape.[52] Owning them did not yet convey status, an important and sometimes underappreciated aspect of collecting. Also, while portraits usually were commissioned, landscapes more often were painted on speculation, and there were few outlets for showing art other than the front window of a rented studio, if it had one, or at one of the succession of short-lived art academies.

The late nineteenth century inaugurated a period of increased institutional support for artists. The Richmond Art Association held exhibitions from 1878 to 1888. The Richmond Art Club had annual exhibitions from 1895 until 1917.[53] The Valentine Museum, founded in 1898, sometimes showed art. It was not, however, until well into the twentieth century that such support became substantial. The Virginia Museum of Fine Arts, founded in 1936, regularly showed the work of local artists in the 1930s and 1940s. In 1927 Theresa Pollak founded the art school at Richmond Profes-

4.28 Frank Hobbs, *Richmond Riverfront—Early Evening*, 1999, oil on canvas, 18 x 24 in. (Private collection)

sional Institute (now Virginia Commonwealth University), which grew into one of the largest in the United States. As mentioned in chapter one, the role of colleges and universities in fostering the explosion of landscape art in Virginia in the second half of the twentieth century, contrasted to the paucity of it in the nineteenth century, cannot be overstated.

Today artists still paint the city of Richmond, but its progress is seldom their theme. However, the engineering feats that built elevated highways and bridges are impressive, and these structures can have dynamism, beauty, and a power of attraction not unlike that which Mayo's bridge had for Bouqueta de Woiseri in 1822. Frank Hobbs's "Richmond Riverfront—Early Evening" of 1999 is more reductive in what he chooses to show and bolder in his elements of composition than the Frenchman, however, and his rough style suggests vitality rather than the serenity of the picturesque (fig. 4.28).

"Richmond and Norfolk," wrote James Kirke Paulding in 1816, "are the belles of 'Old Virginia'; the one being the beauty of the region of river alluvious, the other of the region of sea sand."[54] The two cities could not be more different, however, in how the American Revolution affected them. The capital was moved from Williamsburg to Richmond in 1780 because the latter was thought safer from depredations by British ships. Norfolk was burned by the British in 1776. One of the incendiaries exulted that "The detested town of Norfolk is no more! Its destruction happened on new year's day! . . . but no more remains than about twelve houses, which have escaped the flames!"[55] Francis Baily, who visited in 1796–97, called it "a poor-looking place," noting that most of the burned places had not been replaced.[56] Ruins always had a perverse appeal to artists, however, and Benjamin Henry Latrobe included a "View of part of the ruins of Norfolk" among the sketches of the city he made in 1796 (fig. 4.29). By 1810 another traveler still found that "The town is an irregular, dirty, ill-built group of wooden houses, chiefly surrounded by unwholesome swamps." On the other hand, she wrote with approval of "the little town of Portsmouth, on the opposite shore, the great number of ships, some at anchor, some at the wharves, some repairing, and others building; which enliven the scene, and render it agreeable."[57] A French naturalist, Auguste Plée, sketched "Entrance to the Elizabeth River at Norfolk" in 1821, but it was drawn at such a distance that the port's condition is unclear.[58] Two years later, however, a visitor from Bermuda had no doubts. He

4.29 Benjamin Henry Latrobe, *View of part of the ruins of Norfolk*, 1796, pencil, pen, and watercolor, 6¹⁵⁄₁₆ x 10⁵⁄₁₆ in. (Courtesy of Maryland Historical Society)

4.30 E. A. Christie, **Old Fortress Monroe, Virginia**, c. 1860s, oil on canvas, 23³/₄ x 33 in. (Courtesy of The Mariners' Museum)

found "that general air of dulness which is so distressing in a sea-port town."[59] Norfolk did improve in the ensuing decades, only to suffer yet another setback in the Civil War.

A picture that may or may not relate to the war is E. A. Christie's painting "Old Fortress Monroe" (fig. 4.30). The darkest of clouds approach the venerable fort, and the figures in the foreground are busily preparing for the storm, but they do so apparently convinced that they will endure its fury. Great military events did unfold at Fortress Monroe, built between 1819 and 1834 to command the entrance to the Chesapeake Bay from its position on Old Point Comfort, north of the body of water called Hampton Roads, and across it from Norfolk. It was occupied and held by Union forces throughout the war. It witnessed the revolutionary first battle of ironclads, between the *Monitor* and the *Virginia* (named *Merrimack* in the pre-war Union navy). It welcomed the first "contrabands," escaped slaves from nearby plantations. It incarcerated Confederate president Jefferson Davis from 1865 to 1867. Regardless of whether or not this painting makes reference to any of those events—and no evidence is known about this undated

4.31 George Cook, **Norfolk Harbor**, late 1870s, gelatin silver print from original glass plate. (Courtesy of Valentine Museum)

picture that will answer that question—it is an image about stability and endurance in the face of the threat of change.

The Union endured, but so did defeated Norfolk. Few places, however, would be so constantly a vortex of rapid change. The city's unfulfilled promise lay in its superb location. Perhaps because Virginia was a slave state, it had not developed as a major port for the hundreds of thousands of immigrants from Germany and Ireland who poured into Boston and New York in the 1840s and 1850s. After the war, recovery was rather swift, and in George Cook's photograph of the 1870s Norfolk harbor has an air of prosperity (fig. 4.31). River boats, wooden and steel sailing vessels, and

4.32 Edward Biedermann, ***300th Anniversary Celebration of the Founding of Jamestown***, 1907, gouache, watercolor, and pencil, 18 3/4 x 29 1/4 in. (Virginia Historical Society, Battle Abbey Council purchase)

freighters line the harbor. The domed building at the left is the courthouse. Just right of center is the customs house. The capitalists of the New South, and in New York, were not unaware of Norfolk's potential. Emory Allen wrote in 1891:

> Talk about natural advantages! Do you know that right before us is the ideal natural harbor of North America? Yes, sir; Hampton Roads is only just beginning to be shown at its true worth. The waters are deep enough for the largest ship afloat, and the harbor is so large that if the navies of the world were gathered here they would fill only a part of it.[60]

Sixteen years after Allen wrote this, the fleets of the world did congregate in Hampton Roads. The occasion was the three hundredth anniversary of the founding of Jamestown. Jamestown had no facilities to host a major international exposition, so Norfolk was chosen instead. Fifty ships from eight major powers responded to the invitation of President Theodore Roosevelt. Normally, they stretched out in line from Old Point Comfort to Newport News, but on special days they weighed anchor and sailed

on parade past the exposition grounds. One such occasion was Virginia Day, perhaps the one depicted here by Edward Biedermann, who specialized in scenes of world's fairs (fig. 4.32). There was some criticism of the martial aspect of the exposition, but it was prophetic of the dominant role that the navy would play in the region in the twentieth century. When the United States needed to build a major naval base during World War I, the old exposition grounds were chosen. Today the Norfolk Naval Base is the largest in the world.

The fair's civic organizers had viewed it as "an advertising opportunity unsurpassed in history." It would "give Norfolk an impetus such as she had never known."[61] Perhaps the slights Norfolk had suffered through the years, the setbacks of wars, and the large transient population inevitable in a navy town disposed the city leadership to embrace the future without much nostalgia for the past. In the twentieth century, old neighborhoods were demolished wholesale. There were some protests, but a visitor who commiserated with the people of Norfolk's vision of progress wrote in 1917, "the modernness on which Norfolk evidently prides herself is not to be lightly valued. Fine schools, fine churches and miles of pleasant, recently built homes are things for any American city to rejoice in."[62]

The pace of change accelerated in 1940 when the Norfolk Housing and Redevelopment Authority began the largest demolition project of any in the country. The rapidly changing urban landscape provided a wealth of material for the artist. One who dedicated himself to recording it was Kenneth Harris, a native of Pennsylvania who came to Norfolk in 1949. Both the "slums and grandeur in the old port city" appealed to him. He "worked at his easel in streets and parks, and on decaying wharves, producing two watercolors daily, many of scenes that were soon obliterated by urban renewal bulldozers."[63] His talent and enthusiasm soon were recognized, and in 1951 he was commissioned by the Norfolk Newspapers' Art Trust Fund to do a series of watercolors for the city documenting the world we have lost. One of them, "East Main Street Looking West," depicts the eastward continuation of Main Street, which had deteriorated from a splendid residential district to what in 1951 was considered Norfolk's "Bowery" (fig. 4.33).

Another of Kenneth Harris's images, "Virginia Coal Pier No. 2," reminds us that the discovery in 1873 of high-grade coal in southwest Virginia did much to contribute to the growth of both Norfolk and Newport News (fig. 4.34).

Trains of seemingly endless length brought the coal from the mines to the two cities, which became among the world's largest coal ports, shipping it across the globe to fuel the world's ships, factories, and homes. Harris portrays one of the enormous structures needed to handle coal in such volume.

Of course, this discovery transformed southwest Virginia, too, from a land of hardscrabble farmers to the most industrialized section of Virginia, with lumbering, timber mills, the extraction of various minerals, and train after train to transport everything out to the wider world. The village of Big Lick became the city of Roanoke. "We all know the stories of wondrous development of towns in the New South," wrote Emory Allen in 1891, "The tide seems to be turning in the direction of old Virginia now. . . . Vast manufacturing plants, representing a capital of many hundred thousand dollars, are to be found where but a short time previously there was a wilderness."[64] How different is this description of Roanoke in 1885 from most of the preceding passages about Virginia's towns and cities:

> The city of Roanoke blazes up ahead like an illumination; red-mouthed furnace chimneys light like giant torches above the plain; the roar of machinery, the whistle of engines, the ceaseless hum of labor and of life in the very heart of a quiet, mountain locked valley! We roll into the finest depot in the state, and are escorted to a hotel that would do credit to the proudest city. We tourists go to bed dumbfounded![65]

The ruthless exploitation of natural resources in southwest Virginia in the late nineteenth and early twentieth centuries took a terrible toll on the environment. Few artists pointed to this evil, as they would do nowadays, probably because the general standard of living was so dramatically improved in what had been a backward area. In one view that does depict mining in Page County, an unidentified

4.33 Kenneth Harris, *East Main Street Looking West*, 1951, watercolor, 22 1/4 x 30 1/2 in. (Courtesy of Chrysler Museum of Art, Norfolk, purchased through Norfolk Newspapers' Art Trust Fund)

4.34 Kenneth Harris, *Virginia Coal Pier No. 2*, 1951, watercolor, 22 x 30 in. (Courtesy of Chrysler Museum of Art, Norfolk, purchased through Norfolk Newspapers' Art Trust Fund)

4.35 Unknown artist, *Mining, Page County*, early 20th century, gelatin silver print. (Virginia Historical Society)

photographer is uncritical of the destruction of the landscape; instead he manages to compose a scene that appeals to the eye (fig. 4.35).

In the fifty years that followed the attack on Pearl Harbor in 1941, northern Virginia was changed utterly, as much as southwest Virginia had in the half century after coal was discovered. It is ironic that George Washington, who loved the natural beauty of the region that was his home, caused it to be dramatically altered when he placed the nation's capital on the Potomac. Indeed, Arlington and Alexandria were part of the District of Columbia until 1846, when they were ceded back to Virginia. Arlington House, which was owned by George Washington Parke Custis and then by his daughter and her husband, Robert E. Lee, elicited many golden opinions in the early 1800s. Augusta Blanche Berard wrote in 1856 that, on the river route to Mount Vernon, "The most beautiful object I saw was Arlington which shows strikingly for miles."[66] The Potomac had long impressed travelers. "There are rivers such as we have never seen," wrote Charles Maurice de Talleyrand-Périgord, in exile during the French Revolution. "The Potomac, for instance, nothing more beautiful than the Potomac!"[67]

In 1860 William MacLeod, whose view of the falls of the Potomac we encountered earlier, painted a luscious

4.36 William MacLeod, *Bridge over Hunting Lake Near Alexandria, Virginia*, 1860, oil on canvas, 26 ½ x 36 in. (Courtesy of Mrs. Harry K. Fowle and Ann Fowle Rumble)

scene, "Bridge over Hunting Lake Near Alexandria, Virginia" (fig. 4.36). Alexandria itself was equally picturesque, being called "one of the neatest towns in the United States" in the 1790s.[68] A century later, however, it seemed to be in a land that time had forgotten. "Its buildings are antique," wrote the Reverend S. L. M. Conser in 1891. "It is a dilapidated town," he continued, "no manufactures, no commerce, no enterprise. How 8,000 or 10,000 inhabitants manage to live is a mystery."[69] In 1910 northern Virginia had but seventy-eight thousand people, and seventy-seven percent of the population lived in rural areas. That same year John Ross Key painted "Potomac River above Washington," in which the landscape seems idyllic because it is completely uninhabited (fig. 4.37).

The transforming events for northern Virginia were the New Deal and especially World War II. As the federal government mushroomed, the explosion of administrative activity caused a spillover of government offices from crowded Washington to areas across the Potomac. War contracts led to the creation of industries such as Alexandria's torpedo factory. In sixteen months in 1941–42, the world's largest office building, the Pentagon, was hastily and shoddily constructed in Arlington on the site of an old contraband camp from Civil War times that had become a shanty town. Fort Myer and Fort Belvoir ballooned. Schools were taken over by the Army Signal Corps's intelligence branch. Thousands of new jobs attracted people from other parts of the country, and housing had to be thrown up. From 1930–60 Arlington grew from twenty-four thousand inhabitants to more than ninety thousand, and Fairfax went from twenty-five thousand to more than two hundred thousand.

With Arlington almost full, Fairfax County became the focus of growth and development as the Cold War extended for half a century the federal spending that revolutionized northern Virginia. Those who think the

4.38 Gladys Nelson Smith, ***Georgetown from Rosslyn***, 1924, oil on canvas, 29¾ x 24⅝ in. (Virginia Historical Society, Lora Robins Collection of Virginia Art)

twentieth-century flood of outsiders into Fairfax has made it un-Virginian would do well to contemplate this observation from 1852: "Here more than in any other Virginia county, the present is forgetting the past . . . Ancient Fairfax, like a man waxing wealthy, does not wish to see herself as other than she is now—Northern."[70] "Progress" has turned out to be a particularly uncomfortable process for Fairfax, a county with more than four times the population of the city of Richmond, but an area that developed without the benefit either of an initial design or subsequent urban planning.

An interesting case study of transition is Rosslyn, on the Potomac River opposite Georgetown. It was initially a farm at the end of a ferry crossing. A village developed there that following the Civil War housed saloons, race tracks, and gambling establishments that lured the worst residents of the federal city to its riverfront. Those businesses were expelled by 1910, but by then the open landscape was gone. In 1924, when Gladys Nelson Smith painted "Georgetown from Rosslyn" (fig. 4.38), the hills of Rosslyn were spotted with randomly placed buildings that survived from its tawdry past. Unable to anticipate any promising future for

4.39 Prentiss Taylor, *From Rosslyn to Georgetown*, 1955, lithograph, 12 ¹/₅ x 17 ⁹/₁₀ in. (Virginia Historical Society, Frank G. Byram Fund purchase)

this already congested landscape, Smith could only retreat into the world of art. Her method of idealizing the scene was to transform the buildings before her into Cézannesque geometry using a palette of grays, salmon, and mauves. In 1955 Prentiss Taylor produced the lithograph "From Rosslyn to Georgetown" (fig. 4.39). Housing is gone altogether and the landscape is purely industrial. This, however, would not be the end of the story. Northern Virginia would become a leader in information technology. Half the world's Internet traffic passes through it. America Online, start-up software companies, and high-paying federal agencies such as the Central Intelligence Agency at Langley have made Fairfax the richest county in the country. But a landscape of sprawl has reached its limits, and among American urban areas traffic congestion is worse only in Los Angeles. Fear of sprawl was a leading factor in the successful fight by citizens in several northern Piedmont counties against the proposed Disney Corporation American history theme park at Haymarket, Prince William County, in 1995. In the aftermath of victory, the Piedmont Environmental Council organized a traveling photographic exhibition extolling the region called "Hallowed Ground."

Apart from urban growth, many Virginians in the 1800s apparently measured progress in terms of significant developments in industry and transportation. Edward Beyer suggests as much in his title page to the *Album of Virginia*, where railroads, steamboats, and factories belching smoke share pride of place with Mount Vernon and Monticello (fig. 4.40). Among Beyer's oil paintings is a view of Buchanan, which was invigorated when the James River and Kanawha Canal was extended to it in 1851 (fig. 4.41, p. 102). Canal boats could reach the town through a slack-water finger lake. The docks and warehouses shown in the painting were used to unload and store the goods transported on the canal. Thirty years after Beyer painted the scene, Ernest Ingersoll described a visit:

> As we approach Buchanan, the hills grow even steeper, and crowd upon the river so closely that its current is greatly deepened and confined, and rushes with noisy turbulence along a lane of gigantic sycamores, willows, and other water-loving trees, toward the gap where the James bursts its way through the lofty cross-range of Purgatory Mountain. This gap is one which will especially interest not only the scenery hunter but the geologist.[71]

Almost from the first appearance of the railroads in the 1830s, it was evident that the canals that had trans-

4.40 Edward Beyer, title page to *Album of Virginia*, 1855, lithograph, 15 x 20 in. (Courtesy of Chiles Lawson)

1858–59 of construction on "the Lynchburg Extension" of the Orange and Alexandria Railroad (fig. 4.42).[72]

The coming of the railroad would affect the well-being of vast numbers of communities in Virginia, as did its disappearance a century later. O. Winston Link decided to record America's last steam railroad, the Norfolk and Western Railway, between 1955 and 1960. The distinguishing characteristic of Link's work is the dramatic effect produced by photographing at night. In a work such as "Hawksbill Creek Swimming Hole, Luray, Virginia," "the timeless character of the rural community coincides with the momentary, fleeting passage of the steam trains to produce an often startling incongruity" (fig. 4.43).[73] The No. 96 lets off steam as a safety measure, as in another sense do the children at the swimming hole on a hot summer night. The northbound train heads for Hagerstown, Maryland, passing over elevated highway U.S. 340.

Well before the discovery of high-grade coal in southwest Virginia, the commonwealth had a variety of mines that attracted the attention of artists. In 1844 Russell Smith drew an ink sketch of "Mass[anutten] Mountain from Miller's Iron Works near cave" (fig. 4.44). In 1848 a color lithograph appeared of "Vaucluse Goldmine, Property of the Orange Grove Mining Company of Virginia" (fig. 4.45). That same year, however, gold would be discovered in California, in the presence of a Virginian, and at a time

formed towns like Buchanan would be doomed by this new competition. Artists found the new technology to be a worthy subject, an unmistakable sign of progress. Alfred Brown Peticolas, the scion of a gifted artistic family, recorded in a series of twenty-four sketches the progress in

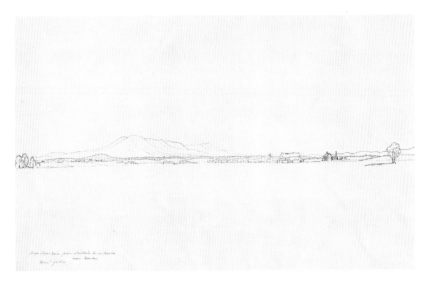

4.44 Russell Smith, *Mass[anutten] Mountain from Miller's Iron Works near cave*, c. 1844, ink, 12 x 16 ½ in. (Courtesy of Library of Virginia)

4.45 J. Stuz (?) for Thomas Sinclair lithography, *Vaucluse Goldmine, Property of the Orange Grove Mining Company [of] Virginia*, c. 1848, lithograph, 5 ⅞ x 9 ½ in. (Virginia Historical Society)

when a Virginian was mayor of San Francisco. In 1849 hundreds of ambitious and largely impecunious young Virginians would become forty-niners, heading by ship around treacherous Cape Horn to California for $300. The Old Dominion's treasure would be the black gold of coal.

The Wilderness

Progress, paradoxically, brought about an interest in the wilderness. Over several generations we have been conditioned to think of wilderness as good, to agree with Henry David Thoreau, who wrote that "In wildness is the preservation of the World." Of mountains James Kirke Paulding wrote, "I never see one that does not conjure up a hundred pleasing associations."[74] Prior to the onset of the

romantic movement, this was not the traditional view. The Puritans spoke of "the howling wilderness," and Virginians used the same language to describe their county of Kentucky before (and yes, after) it achieved separate statehood in 1792.

By the mid-nineteenth century, improved roads and the coming of railroads to the Shenandoah Valley made the remote landscapes farther west reachable, although still not with ease. The difficulties, however, were well worth the effort according to David Hunter Strother: "Far beyond the range of pleasure-seeking tourists, he will be often surprised with scenes whose beauty would charm an artist into ecstasies, whose sublimity might awe a poet into silence."[75] As it happens, Strother portrayed himself in ecstacy as "The Rapt Artist," an ink and wash drawing of about 1852 (fig. 4.46). For this image he must have posed before a mirror and then integrated into the background details from his drawings of Blackwater Falls, now in a state park in West Virginia.[76]

The railroads that brought artists to the wilderness also brought danger—the threat of excessive exploitation—and it might be argued that the wilderness was not appreciated by artists until its spoilation became thinkable.[77] Unspoiled, untouched nature kindled in Americans thoughts about God's plans for the nation. Wilderness was not only a place of spiritual redemption, but the quintessen-

4.46 David Hunter Strother, *The Rapt Artist*, c. 1852, pencil, ink, wash, white, 9 ⅝ x 12 ⅜ in. (Courtesy of West Virginia and Regional History Collection, West Virginia University Libraries)

tial environment in which to develop as an American. An early instance of this in literature is the character of Leatherstocking in James Fenimore Cooper's novels, such as *Last of the Mohicans*. In 1890 historian Frederick

Jackson Turner would argue that the frontier experience, taming a wild continent, was what defined America, distinguished it from Europe, and determined its free institutions.

Thomas Cole in New York had (excuse the expression) pioneered this theme in art in the Hudson River Valley. Russell Smith carried it forward in Virginia. Smith worked his sketches from nature into finished oils that followed the themes that were fashionable and appropriate. Jackson River is west of Warm Springs and Hot Springs in Bath County, near what would become the border with West Virginia. It was wilderness when Smith viewed it in the 1840s while on the Rogers geological expedition. The painter later transformed what he saw into art (fig. 4.47). In the manner of Cole, he inserted the figure of an Indian to signal the march of progress through a region lost to the native people, while working the composition into one that exemplifies the Picturesque. By these means Smith has it both ways. He portrays an unspoiled environment, yet he tames it and makes it seem more accessible to eastern viewers.

Smith also produced a picturesque scene of an outdoor baptism in Virginia (fig. 4.48). In 1835–36 Francis C. Wemyss of Philadelphia asked Smith to do scenery painting for the old Washington Theatre. While in Washington, Smith was asked to keep the famous actor Junius Brutus Booth "away from barrooms and other temptations."

4.47 Russell Smith, *Jackson River, Virginia*, 1848, oil on canvas, 24 x 20 in. (Courtesy of the Executive Mansion, Commonwealth of Virginia)

4.48 Russell Smith, *Baptism in Virginia*, 1836, oil on canvas, 19 1/4 x 28 1/4 in. (Courtesy of Morris Museum of Art, Augusta, Georgia)

4.49 Edward Beyer, *Elk River*, 1855, oil on canvas, 20 ¼ x 30 in.
(Private collection)

Accordingly, Booth accompanied Smith, who perhaps thought witnessing the baptism might do some good to the old reprobate.[78]

A decade after Smith, Edward Beyer turned his attention briefly from his depiction of plantations and market towns to paint a rare wilderness view, "Elk River" (fig. 4.49). This actually is a scene showing the beginning of settlement in the wild reaches of what would become West Virginia. Beyer depicts logging. For decades, some northerners who had seen too much progress unfold too quickly had had reservations about the unlimited manipulation of the environment by man. Because Virginia remained an overwhelmingly rural society, these doubts were rarely shared in the Old Dominion. In "Elk River" Beyer reflects the Virginian perspective that there is only good in the march of progress.

It was William Louis Sonntag, however, who produced the grandest views of the Virginia mountains. He applied the Hudson River School formula to both the Blue Ridge Mountains and the Alleghenies. After training in Europe, he made several southern excursions from his home in New York City. Scholars and amateurs alike often struggle to pinpoint Sonntag's locations, but usually in vain because mostly his works are composites of mountain scenery, rather than actual views of a single spot, forming an idealized wilderness scene of the type his patrons in eastern cities would buy because it fit their idea of what wilderness should look like and reminded them of a perfect past and a promised future. In Europe, too, he would have learned the conventions of the French Salon that encouraged one to paint the ideal, not the real. Both "Shenandoah Valley" (fig. 4.50) and "Blue Ridge Mountains, River View" (fig. 4.51) are from Sonntag's earlier period and brighter palette. Later in the century he would adopt the tonal palette of the French Barbizon school.[79]

Sonntag's positive interpretation of the wilderness as landscape that Americans were destined to develop into a great nation was stated in the clearest terms early in his career, in 1847, when he produced a now lost series of four paintings entitled "Progress of Civilization." The first

canvas was described by one writer as "Nature in her primitive grandeur" and by another as a "dismal waste." Indians were shown in the second, pioneers in the third, and in the fourth he pictured "a palatial private residence, in the suburbs of a great city, teeming with manyhanded activity, and sending out on all sides streams of trade and travel." This was an obvious reference to, and an abrupt shift from, Thomas Cole's earlier and pessimistic cycle of four paintings entitled "The Course of Empire," which saw the dissolution of civilization as the end product. Sonntag was

one of several northern artists at mid-century who reversed Cole's vision of American destiny, rewriting it with a better ending, one that Virginians had always believed in, and now one that suited the agenda of the northeastern school of landscape philosophers as well.[80]

One of the areas Sonntag frequented was the Cheat River and Cheat Mountain in what would become West Virginia. Just a year before fifty of Virginia's western counties were admitted to the Union as West Virginia, William Sheridan Young painted "View on Cheat River,

Western Virginia" (fig. 4.52). The Troy Run Viaduct that the Baltimore & Ohio Railroad built over the Cheat River was considered such an engineering marvel that Edward Beyer pictured it in his *Album of Virginia* in 1857. Unlike Beyer, Young makes no references to progress, or even to man's presence. Instead, he conveys the profound silence that precedes civilization. Forty-five years earlier, writing of mountains farther east, James Kirke Paulding noted that

> one of the first things that struck me was the solemn, severe silence which prevailed everywhere, and only broken, at distant intervals, by the note of the cock-of-the-wood; the chirping of a ground-squirrel; the crash of a falling tree; or the long echoes of the fowler's gun, which render the silence, thus broken for a moment, still more striking.[81]

Another New York writer, Charles Fenno Hoffman, discovered a "wild delight" in being so alone in the Virginia mountains:

> There is a singular joyousness in a wilderness; a vague feeling of solitude, and a vivid sense of the primal freshness which breathes around you, that mingle most strangely together, and make you own at the time that the subduing hand of cultivation and the golden embellishments of art, could add nothing here; while the sympathy of companionship, however desirable in a crowd, would but divide the full impression of the hour.[82]

A decade after Young's picture, David Hunter

4.52 William Sheridan Young, *View on Cheat River, Western Virginia*, 1862, oil on canvas, 14 x 20 in. (Courtesy of West Virginia and Regional History Collection, West Virginia University Libraries)

Strother, taking pride in his new state of West Virginia, implored his fellow artists to visit the region: "Will not some of our famous masters of landscape-art who have buried the Hudson and White Hills under mountains of canvas, and venturously plucked the mighty hearts out of the distant Andes and Rocky Mountains, condescend to accept this challenge from the virgin wilderness of West Virginia?" In general, the answer was no. Thomas Cole's nationalistic agenda was played out. The Civil War had cost America its innocence. Once again, artists would look to Europe for inspiration.

The Crisis of the Civil War

In the early stages of the Civil War it seemed merely a great adventure. William D. Washington created several romantic images of the war such as "Confederates Observing a Union Encampment" on the Gauley River in what soon would be recognized as West Virginia (fig. 4.53). The solidity of the rock formation that shelters the Confederate lookouts may be a convenient symbol of the strength of Confederate resolve. In 1861 Sanford Gifford painted a bloodless scene that one journalist called a "picturesque bivouac" of New York's Seventh Regiment at Arlington Heights. Albert Bierstadt's "Guerrilla Warfare (Picket Duty in Virginia)" also shows a beautiful panoramic landscape but hints at the irony that what then was called God's "great book of nature" was the stage for fratricide (fig. 4.54).

Bierstadt presents magnificent trees like the giants that appear in forest scenes by Asher B. Durand; beneath these the human figures at war seem insignificant, their purposes fleeting.

The first well-illustrated military campaign in American history was the Peninsula Campaign of 1862. After the battle at Williamsburg, the bucolic campus of the College of William and Mary became an outdoor surgery. A Confederate soldier wrote, "And what a strange metamorphosis was this of the peaceful abode of science and learning into a veritable chamber of horrors, where every turn of the eye remembered some shocking spectacle of human misery or human destruction!"[83] In the opposing camp, Robert K. Sneden, a Union topographical draftsman whom we met at Yorktown in the previous chapter, drew more than one hundred watercolors of McClellan's slow advance up the Middle Peninsula. Sneden's "View of the Battle of Malvern Hill" shows the site of one of the Seven Days' Battles where the Union army's progress was checked (fig. 4.55). Although his subject is battle, Sneden nonetheless presents a beautiful panorama of the Tidewater landscape.

Most surviving Civil War art is from the Union side; a rare exception is "Drewry's Bluff" by Conrad Wise Chapman, who painted the scene while in Confederate service (fig. 4.56).[84] It was the war that brought Chapman to Virginia. He was the son of the Alexandria-born artist John Gadsby Chapman, who had immigrated to Italy in search of patronage. There his son was born, and raised to love Virginia, so that at the outbreak of war he enlisted as a Confederate, although he had never set foot in America before. The elder Chapman had been an outstanding engraver before moving to Italy, and he taught his son how to paint on a

4.53 William D. Washington, ***Confederates Observing a Union Encampment***, c. 1862, oil on canvas, 40 x 48 in. (Courtesy of The Museum of the Confederacy, Richmond, Virginia)

4.54 Albert Bierstadt, ***Guerrilla Warfare (Picket Duty in Virginia)***, 1862, oil on canvas, 15^1/$_2$ x 18^5/$_8$ in. (Courtesy of The Century Association, New York)

4.55 Robert K. Sneden, *View of the Battle of Malvern Hill*, 1862, pencil, pen, and watercolor, 2⅞ x 8½ in. (Virginia Historical Society, gift of Floyd D. Gottwald, Jr., © 1996)

4.56 Conrad Wise Chapman, *Drewry's Bluff*, 1863, oil on board, 8½ x 10⅝ in. (Virginia Historical Society, Lora Robins Collection of Virginia Art)

small scale with remarkable detail.

In his painting of Drewry's Bluff, the younger Chapman tells the story of a Confederate victory. With the fall of Norfolk, the Confederates burned their only ironclad, the *Virginia* (formerly *Merrimack*), giving Union forces complete naval supremacy on both the seas and rivers. President Lincoln ordered his apparently unstoppable ships to Richmond to "shell the city to surrender." It was at Drewry's Bluff, a few miles below Richmond, that this fleet was turned back. The defenders drove pilings into the river bed and, just hours before the Union ships arrived, sank several stone-filled canal boats and three ships, including two steamers. The invading fleet retreated when it could

advance no farther and came under heavy shelling from the bluffs. In the year between the battle of 15 May 1862 and Chapman's depiction of it, the Confederate complex on the bluff was enlarged, and it became a principal post for the Confederate navy without ships. The steeple of the post's new chapel is at the center of the canvas. The pilings, paddlewheel of a steamer, and rigging of a ship were still visible to Chapman as reminders of the humble ingredients of the Confederate victory.[85]

The Shenandoah Valley was another important theater of war, not only in 1862 with Stonewall Jackson's Valley Campaign, but also in 1864 when Jubal Early opposed Philip Sheridan. The axis of the valley from northeast to southwest was of great advantage to the Confederates. Each of their successes there brought them closer to the Union capital at Washington, whereas Union victories only drew them farther way from Richmond. By 1864 there had been so many battles in the valley that Currier and Ives felt obliged to issue a print, "The Valley of the Shenandoah," in which the military presence has equal billing with the landscape (fig. 4.57).

Various "special artists," representing northern newspapers, traveled with Union forces and sent sketches back to be engraved for publication. One such sketch, which appeared in *Harper's Weekly* in 1863, portrayed the ruins of the Fauquier White Sulphur Springs. Writing to his father on 29 December 1864, Henry Chester Parry, an assistant surgeon in the U.S. army, described the scene:

It was a handsome structure in its time built of brick covered with yellow plaster—ten doric columns stood among the ruins like great sentinels keeping their watch. I felt like restoring the place as the wind and rain howled through the grounds and made leafles[s] trees sigh for the departed glory of the place.[86]

There was but one newspaper artist active among the Confederate forces, Frank Vizetelly. Having just completed reporting on Garibaldi's campaign to unify Italy, in 1861 the *Illustrated London News* sent him to cover the war in America. His unsparing illustrations of the Union retreat after First Manassas so infuriated Union officialdom that he was expelled. Thereafter he followed the war in the train of

4.59 Andrew J. Russell, ***Battery of thirty-two pounders, Fredericksburg, May 3, 1863***, 1863, albumen print. (Courtesy of Morgan Library)

4.57 Currier and Ives, ***The Valley of the Shenandoah***, 1864, lithograph, 14 ³/₄ x 20 in. (Virginia Historical Society)

the Confederate forces, which made him a captain. One of the more than 130 drawings by Vizetelly published in the *Illustrated London News* (on 4 April 1863) was "Confederate Encampment on the Shenandoah" (fig. 4.58). It is inscribed on the reverse:

> Encampment of a portion of the Confederate Army, between Winchester & Martinsburg. In this illustration I have endeavored to give your readers an idea of an encampment of southern troops in front of the enemy. Far away are seen the mountains of the Blue Ridge while in the middle distance the eye stretches over a portion of the lovely valley of the Shenandoah unfolding its beauties like a casket of jewels opened in the golden sunshine of autumn. Every tree has donned its gala costume robing itself in its brightest

4.58 Frank Vizetelly, ***Confederate Encampment on the Shenandoah***, 1862, pencil and Chinese white, 6 ⁷/₈ x 18 ³/₈ in. (Courtesy of Houghton Library of the Harvard College Library)

garments to say good bye until another year comes round. But one is scarcely permitted to indulge in the reveries that such peaceful scenes suggest for on all sides are heard the harsh sounds of war and the bright face of nature is distorted by man's evil purpose.[87]

By 1863, many photographers were in the field, among them Andrew J. Russell. In "Battery of thirty-two pounders, Fredericksburg, May 3, 1863" he gives us not only the great spectacle of war, but also the beauty of the setting at Fredericksburg (fig. 4.59). The

4.60 Edward Lamson Henry, *Westover*, 1864, pencil and pastel, 17 x 24 in. (Courtesy of New York State Museum)

splendors of the Virginia landscape made the events unfolding on it seem even more tragic. Using the imagery of the landscape, the poet Walt Whitman defined the magnitude of what Virginians had lost in perhaps a more vivid way than did the painters and photographers. Whitman left Brooklyn in 1862 to find his brother George, who had been wounded at Fredericksburg. The poet then served as a volunteer nurse in Washington. In 1864, near the battlefront at Culpeper, he wrote this passage, which was published later in *Memoranda during the War* (1874):

> Dilapidated, fenceless, and trodden with war as Virginia is, wherever I move across her surface, I find myself rous'd to surprise and admiration. What capacity for products, improvements, human life, nourishment and expansion. Everywhere that I have been in the Old Dominion, (the subtle mockery of that title now!) such thoughts have fill'd me. And how full of breadth is the scenery, everywhere with distant mountains, everywhere convenient rivers. . . . Last evening (Feb. 8) I saw the first of the new moon, the old moon clear along with it; the sky and air so clear, such transparent hues of color, it seem'd to me I had never really seen the new moon before. It was the thinnest cut crescent possible. It hung delicate just above the sulky shadow of the Blue mountains. Ah, if it might prove an omen and good prophecy for this unhappy State.[88]

By 1864 defeat of the Confederacy seemed inevitable unless Lincoln was not re-elected. In the decisive month of November, Edward Lamson Henry sketched the venerable old Byrd family seat at Westover (fig. 4.60), then a head-

quarters for a division of the Army of the James. After the war, in a letter to sculptor Edward V. Valentine of Richmond, Henry explained that

> I have painted & sold some of these gorgeous old Manors on the James River. . . . Old Westover is one, that place set me nearly crazy. I was there Nov. 1864 on a U. S. transport just to see what I could see & though I longed to see Richmond you fellows wouldn't let any one, you were so selfish, but I made a number of sketches up & down the River & on the Potomac & in Alexandria, so my trip was very profitable though I had to be so "loyal", so I could see all these things you know.[89]

Although the twenty-three-year-old Henry served in the Union army in 1864, he was a native of Charleston, South Carolina, and either was not as loyal to the United States as he seemed, or at least he wanted Valentine to think that.

Henry was a captain's commissary clerk on a federal transport charged with supplying General Grant's forces on the James, which were investing Petersburg. When Lincoln was re-elected, Grant's ultimate victory was assured. His army was profusely supplied from City Point, where the Appomattox meets the James River. It is depicted in Henry's own "City Point, Virginia, Headquarters of General Grant," a painting completed by 1872 from eyewitness sketches (fig. 4.61). In this autumn landscape the numerous ships, the wharves and wagons, give some hint that this was, briefly, one of the world's busiest ports. The Union's overwhelming advantage in matériel and supplies was an

4.61 Edward Lamson Henry, *City Point, Virginia, Headquarters of General Grant*, 1865–72, oil on canvas, 29¾ x 61 in. (Courtesy of Addison Gallery of American Art, Phillips Academy, Andover, Massachusetts, ©, all rights reserved)

important element in the subjugation of an agricultural society by an industrial one and, in a sense, was yet another triumph of man over the land.

Mostly Henry sketched from his transport vessel. When he ill-advisedly stepped ashore to sketch, one sentry mistook him for a spy and threatened to shoot him. According to Henry's notes the picture shows (left to right):

> Transport disembarking troops/horses/Mail dock/Adams Exp. Barge. Embalmed bodies being sent north. Andy Hepburn's barge. Head sutler. Captain's gig./Grant's Hd Qts/Gen. Ingall's Hd. Qts/15-inch Mortar & 2 Hundred Pound parrots [a species of ordnance] on platform cars. Mouth of Appomatx./Schooners with stores, forage & lumber swinging to the current Monitor [ironclad] in the distance, Bermuda Hundreds [a neck of land between the Appomattox and James Rivers].[90]

Photographers were more attuned than painters to depicting war's obliteration of the landscape, partly because there would have been no market for such paintings. "Inside the Fort Mahone cheval-de-frise; April 1865" by Andrew J. Russell shows a landscape as ravaged as Verdun's would later be (fig. 4.62). Fort Mahone was part of the forty miles of trenches that the Confederates built around Richmond

4.62 Andrew J. Russell, *Inside the Fort Mahone cheval-de-frise; April 1865*, 1865, albumen print, 6⁵⁄₁₆ x 10¼ in. (Virginia Historical Society)

and Petersburg and that held the numerically superior Union army at bay for nine months. The devastation of the urban landscape is most effectively shown in another of Russell's photographs, "Richmond from Oregon Hill, April 1865" (fig. 4.63). The magnitude of the destruction can be measured by comparing it to Edward Beyer's prewar lithograph, "View from Gambles Hill" (fig. 4.64). The Virginia armory at the left of Beyer's print is at the right in Russell's photograph. A few days after the evacuation fire, Edward Moseley wrote, "The scene of ruin and devastation presented on entering the place is beyond description."[91]

Some Virginia artists, like Flavius Fisher, spent the war abroad. Those who remained found little interest in commissioning pictures during the war. A few landscapes, however, are mentioned in newspapers. The Richmond *Daily Examiner* of 30 July 1862 reported that Mr. Torsch and Mr. King of the city had returned from the battlefield of Seven Pines with sketches "soon to be elaborated as engravings." The same paper on 5 January 1864 reported that Lee Mallory was sketching in crayon the "most celebrated battlefields of Virginia as they appeared at the time the battles were fought." He had then completed scenes of Fredericksburg and Stafford Heights. It was further reported that he intended to apply to the legislature for a waiver of the tax usually levied on exhibitions. Three weeks later the same newspaper reported that Mallory had done a painting of the naval battle of the C.S.S. *Virginia* and the U.S.S. *Cumberland* and *Congress* that measured three by seven feet. A painting called "Yankee Battery at Chancellorsville and the Confederate Charge" was said to be three by five feet in size and was to be displayed at the Virginia State Library. It was written of Mallory that "He

will continue the production of the series until all the prominent battles are conveyed to canvas."[92] None of these pictures is now known. They, too, may have perished in the fires that consumed downtown Richmond.

Nostalgia

Nostalgia has a long history in Virginia. The Virginia Historical Society was founded in 1831 to collect materials from Virginia's golden age of political hegemony, already past and presumed lost forever. In 1848 Branch Tanner Archer, an expatriate Virginian living in Texas, tried to induce his uncle to move there, "where he will find what he found in Virginia forty years past, in her halcyon days of Liberty, quiet, and defiance."[93] Archer's uncle stayed put, but hundreds of thousands of others did leave the commonwealth. A formal literature of decline developed. In Nathaniel Beverly Tucker's novel *George Balcombe*, the owner of Raby Hall, Essex County, lives in poverty on his dilapidated plantation. In George Tucker's *Valley of the Shenandoah*, Edward Grayson returns to the ancestral home in Charles City County, where "the sight of this venerable seat of his ancestors, reminded him of the fall of his family from their former opulence and consequence to the most absolute poverty."[94]

About 1841 Albert C. Pleasants executed an oil painting depicting Richmond as it looked about 1798 (fig. 4.65). Why is not known. The existence of at least two versions of the composition argues against its being a singular, eccentric commission by someone nostalgic for yesteryear. Were

4.63 Andrew J. Russell, ***Richmond from Oregon Hill, April 1865***, 1865, albumen print, 6 ¼ x 9 ¾ in. (Virginia Historical Society)

4.64 Edward Beyer, ***View from Gambles Hill***, 1858, lithograph, 10 ¼ x 18 ¼ in. (Courtesy of Chiles Lawson)

Richmonders of the 1840s already nostalgic for the picturesque beauty of their city, compromised by later additions? Or did they perhaps long for the city's former political importance, when Virginia was the most populous and powerful state? It may be instructive that in 1996 John Stobart painted "Richmond, A View of the City from the Banks of the River James in 1858." Prints based on the painting have sold well (fig. 4.66). Today, John Barber paints commercially successful views of life in the waters of eastern Virginia in bygone days. Perhaps Albert Pleasants likewise thought there was a market for nostalgia.[95]

Artists who visited Virginia during its steep decline for some fifty years after about 1790 often gravitated toward historic subjects, to the glorious past rather than the troubled present. In 1841 Seth Eastman sketched a "View from Mr. Williamson's House at Norfolk, Virginia, Showing Old Fort Norfolk," a War of 1812 fort (fig. 4.67). Three years later Russell Smith sketched a panorama "From the house of Col. Jef. Randolph. Edgehill." A key to the drawing at its lower left locates sites in the vista associated with Thomas Jefferson—Monticello, Shadwell Hill, Rivanna River, and the birthplace of the patriot (fig. 4.68). The artist's vantage point, Edgehill, was the home of the former president's

4.69 Sir William Fox, **The Stone on Which Captn. Smith's Head Was Laid**, 1853, watercolor, 9½ x 13⅘ in. (Courtesy of National Library of New Zealand)

favorite grandson, Thomas Jefferson Randolph. There were also sites fancifully connected with the past. In the 1850s Sir William Fox sketched the purported "Stone on Which Captn. Smith's Head Was Laid" when he was rescued from death by Pocahontas's intervention (fig. 4.69). A skeptical author in 1859 called it "another fugitive stone, more imaginatively termed Captain Smith's Rock." Another local attraction near Gloucester was "Powhatan's Chimney. It is all that is left of the house which [Capt. John] Smith built as a residence for this savage King," wrote an author who went on to observe that "Another house is now attached to

this chimney."[96] The English artist Lefevre Cranstone chose to draw the landscape at "Porto Bello nr. Williamsburg, Virginia," the former seat of Lord Dunmore, Virginia's last royal governor, as it appeared in 1859, when the house was already gone (fig. 4.70).

Dunmore fled in the excitement engendered by Patrick Henry's famous speech ending in the peroration "give me liberty or give me death!" The speech was given, not in Williamsburg, but at St. John's Church in Richmond on 23 March 1775. Several of Virginia's revolutionary conventions were held there. The building did not immediately become a hallowed site, but by the late nineteenth century an artist named J. C.

4.70 Lefevre Cranstone, **Porto Bello nr. Williamsburg, Virginia**, 1859, watercolor, 4¼ x 7½ in. (Courtesy of The Lilly Library, Indiana University, Bloomington, Indiana)

4.71 J. C. Bridgewood, *St. John's Church, Richmond*, after 1879, oil on canvas, 16 x 26 in. (Courtesy of Valentine Museum)

4.72 C. R. Rees, *Petersburg, Va.* (The Crater), c. 1887, albumen print, 7⅝ x 9½ in. (Virginia Historical Society)

Bridgewood found a market for at least two paintings of it (fig. 4.71). By then, however, the church's most prominent feature was a bell tower on the north front that had not been erected until 1830.

The Civil War created a vast new category of historic places in Virginia. A brochure promoting railroad tourism read: "From Manassas to Gordonsville every foot of the way was a camp, a battlefield, or ground over which the contending armies marched, and for much of the distance it was all of these." "Passing over the Shenandoah," it continued, "there again, for the veterans, or those interested in what they did, is classic ground on every side."[97] "War has transformed the 'Garden of the South' into the 'Graveyard of the South,'" wrote Russell Conwell of Philadelphia in 1869, "and Prince de Joinville used apt words when he said, 'Virginia should be enclosed with a high fence and kept sacred as the Cemetery of the War.'"[98] Nostalgia took another turn as Virginians felt obligated to defend the Old South and to memorialize the recent defeat as "the Lost Cause."

The places where Confederate soldiers had fought were considered sacred sites, but compromises had to be made; people had to eat. An example is the place on the Petersburg siege lines where Pennsylvania miners tried to blast a hole through Confederate defenses. The Union forces were surprised by their success, did not take immediate advantage of it, and only too late sent in troops. The Confederates were ready. Sir George Campbell, who visited in 1879, wrote, "There is a famous place—a sort of hole or small crater—where a large number of black Federal soldiers were surrounded and, I am afraid I must almost say, massacred." In 1867 another foreign visitor was disappointed to find that "The 'Crater' and the mine are now partly surrounded by a fence; and are shown at twenty-five cents a head, by one Griffiths,

4.73 Currier and Ives, *Old Blandford Church, Petersburg, Virginia*, n.d., lithograph, 6¹⁄₂ x 9¹⁄₂ in. (Virginia Historical Society)

who farmed the land before the siege and now makes a living as a showman."[99] About 1887 C. R. Rees of Worcester, Massachusetts, photographed the Crater (fig. 4.72). By then it was "covered with a rank growth of underbrush and small trees." According to Louise Smith Squier, "The owner of the old Griffiths Farm, the old battled ground, derives a good revenue by an exhibition of relics." By 1916 a visitor could write that "The Crater is now softly covered with green, Time's healing hand for the torn earth."[100]

A foreign visitor wrote that "By the end of the war, most of the fences in Virginia had been burnt in camp fires." It is not surprising, therefore, to learn from Russell Conwell that "The cheveaux-de-frise by which Forts Davis and Steadman were surrounded has now become the insurmountable fence of a peaceful Negro farmer."[101] At Cold Harbor Conwell pointed out yet another way in which Virginians were making the best of miserable conditions. "The earthworks are fast disappearing under the hands of diligent lead searchers," he wrote, "who are found everywhere along the line. A profitable business they make of it, too. Tons of old iron and lead are carted into Richmond from this field, for which a round price is paid." He also met "several Negroes, with large sacks, collecting the bones of dead horses which they sold to the bone grinders in Richmond."[102]

In 1867 the Reverend S. L. M. Conser wrote of the terrain around Manassas that "The vegetation, although

sparse and scanty in this section, was sufficient to mercifully hide all traces of the dreadful battles." Two years later, Russell Conwell noted that the earthworks at Manassas, Ball's Bluff, Winchester, and Cedar Mountain, as well as the battlefields near Washington, were "nearly obliterated." At Petersburg, Henry Latham found the trenches largely intact in 1867. "To-day the snow was playing winding-sheet over all the battlefields," he wrote on 14 January, "but in Spring there are said to be fields along the line where graves are visible, and rifle-pits not yet filled up."[103]

By natural and artificial means, the Virginia landscape recovered. In 1879 Sir George Campbell found Petersburg rebuilt and thriving, observing that "There is only one ruin, and that is the English church of the early days of the colony." This was Old Blandford Church. Its picturesque charm was captured in a drawing by Fanny Palmer published as a color lithograph by Currier and Ives (fig. 4.73). As the church's fame spread, a new purpose was adopted for it, one connected with the nostalgia of the Lost Cause. In 1916 Louise Hale wrote that "Old Blandford, gleamingly restored, is now serving as a Confederate Memorial Chapel." Its highlight was windows by Louis Comfort Tiffany.[104]

Undoubtedly, the prominent position given in *Picturesque America* to William Ludwell Sheppard's "Chickahominy" was because of that river's many associations with the recently fought Civil War (fig. 4.74). Another of the artists for *Picturesque America*, Harry Fenn, later

4.74 William Ludwell Sheppard, *The Chickahominy*, 1872, engraving, 12 x 9¹/₁₆ in. (Virginia Historical Society)

4.75 Harry Fenn, *The James R[iver] from Malvern Hill looking south west shewing extreem left of Union positions*, 1887, pencil, wash, and chalk, 9 x 10³/₄ in. (Courtesy of Margaret T. Mayo)

made a beautiful pencil drawing of the battlefield at Malvern Hill in 1887 for an unknown publication (fig. 4.75). Although he visited the site two decades earlier, Russell Conwell seems to describe what Fenn drew:

> Without a doubt the battle-field is one of the most beautiful spots in Virginia. At the time your correspondent visited the place green acres of wheat were waving before the wind. The buds were appearing on the trees, the apricots, cherries, and peaches were in full bloom. . . . Far away the James River glittered in the sun. How strange to think that these high bluffs were the scene of such a conflict.[105]

Virginia's Civil War sites continue to interest both painters and photographers. In the 1950s, Aubrey Bodine, a photographer for the *Baltimore Sun*, made a series of photographs documenting the current appearance of Virginia's Civil War battlefields. In 1997 Norfolk's Chrysler Museum held an exhibition called *Sacred Sites* that juxtaposed not only vintage and modern photographs of Civil War battlefield but also contemporary paintings from the war itself with modern multi-media works inspired by or evocative of Virginia's "hallowed ground."

In the aftermath of the centennial of American independence in 1876, the inherently nostalgic Colonial Revival movement grew in strength, and inevitably Virginia was a focus of its attention. The old Anglican churches became increasingly popular subjects for art. About 1900 the Canadian-born watercolorist Thomas Harrison Wilkinson painted Blandford and Bruton, St. John's in Richmond, and St. Luke's in Smithfield. Eva LeConte painted in oils the ruins of the Presbyterian church, built in the 1790s, at Opequon. In the 1930s Theodore Ballou White was but one of several Virginia artists to issue a series of lithographs or wood or linoleum block prints of old churches in Virginia, including St. John's in Hampton.

"Old Virginia" was seen by northern artists as an antidote to the rampant urbanization of their own section.

4.76 Gari Melchers, *In Old Virginia, Belmont*, c. 1918, oil on canvas, 32 x 40 in. (Courtesy of Belmont, The Gari Melchers Estate and Memorial Gallery, Mary Washington College, Fredericksburg, Virginia)

The exaltation of the supposed superiority of agricultural society would find its ultimate expression in a manifesto by southern writers in 1930 called *I'll Take My Stand*. A few years later the philosopher Arnold Toynbee said that Virginia seemed a place where time stood still, not a good thing for most of its inhabitants to be sure, but with compensations for the artist. Gari Melchers, who settled at Falmouth to be near the rural subject matter he loved, called one of his local scenes "In Old Virginia, Belmont" (fig. 4.76).

Not everyone approved of Virginia's obsession with the past. In 1940 *Life* magazine published an article on Virginia art that reproduced "First Robin," a painting by Marion Junkin, then associate director of the Richmond School of Art. Painted thinly with oils, it has the freedom and spontaneity of a watercolor (fig. 4.77). A bird rests on the tail of J. E. B. Stuart's statue on Richmond's Monument Avenue, and according to the artist, he first called his work "Giving Our Past the Bird" because "it's time our section forgot some of its yesterdays and thought of tomorrow."[106]

In the 1990s Claiborne Gregory drew and painted that onetime wonder, the James River Canal (fig. 4.78). Marion Junkin would find it not nostalgic but ironic that Richmond looks to the restoration of its portion of the nineteenth-century canal as the salvation of its downtown in the twenty-first century. In Virginia, not only is the past not past, as William Faulkner once said; it is the hope of the future.

4.77 Marion Junkin, *First Robin*, 1941, oil on canvas, 25¾ x 35½ in. (Courtesy of Washington and Lee University)

Sally Mann is the most famous contemporary Virginia photographer. "Untitled" from 1993 is from her portfolio "Virginia," executed between 1992 and 1996 (fig. 4.79). Through deliberate blurring of distinctions and manipulating light leaks, imperfections, and distortions, she creates a lush, atmospheric, abstracted landscape that brings to mind those who trod this ground before. Beside these photographs hung a quote from Shelby Foote's *Shiloh*: "We were in love with the past . . . in love with death."[107] In her preface Sally Mann writes, "Our history of defeat and loss sets us apart from other Americans and because of it, we embrace the Proustian concept that the only true paradise is a paradise lost. But we know that love emerges from this loss, becomes memory, and that memory becomes art."[108]

Renewal from the Land

"Land's the *only* thing that matters—because it's the only thing that lasts," says Gerald O'Hara to his daughter Scarlett in the motion picture *Gone with the Wind*.[109] During the decades that followed the Civil War there was considerable truth to those words. It was the land, the only constant after Appomattox, that allowed life to continue in Virginia with some normalcy. Thomas Nelson Page explained this phenomenon in an 1893 article in *Harper's New Monthly Magazine*:

> The fact that the land had survived gave it a peculiar if not a fictitious value. It was estimated and appraised highly. Money was borrowed on it to restock and plant it, and the old life went on for awhile almost as before, like a wheel that continues to turn with its own propulsion even after the motive power is removed.[110]

4.78 Claiborne Gregory, *Canal Culvert near Confluence of the James and Hardware Rivers*, 1994, watercolor and white charcoal, 6 x 7 in. (Courtesy of Mr. and Mrs. Martin Brill)

The Virginia landscape played a crucial role in both the material and spiritual recovery of its inhabitants. Because the population was still overwhelmingly rural, economic recovery was possible at least for those who lived on the land. Nature also inspired a sense of renewal by its beauty and its cyclical patterns. For those in the expanding urban areas, artists produced a sizable body of paintings, prints, and photographs of the landscape that suggested revival, stability, and hope. Many of the prints also

4.79 Sally Mann, *Untitled*, 1993, photograph, 30 x 38 in. (© Sally Mann, courtesy of Edwynn Houk Gallery, New York)

4.80 Alfred Wordsworth Thompson, *Road Out of Norfolk*, 1888, oil on canvas, 18 x 30 in.
(Courtesy of Chrysler Museum of Art, Norfolk, purchased through Norfolk Newspapers' Art Trust Fund)

reached and comforted northern viewers who longed for national reconciliation.

One of the artists who worked in eastern Virginia during this period was the New Yorker Alfred Wordsworth Thompson. He may have had a special interest in the South because he had been born and raised in nearby Baltimore. In 1888 Thompson was at Norfolk, where he encountered the characteristic Tidewater landscape made up of flat scenery with broad vistas that evoke serenity and timelessness. A traveler in 1879 called this "a very poor country," but Thompson found stability and order in this environment; it became the subject of his painting entitled "Road Out of Norfolk" (fig. 4.80).[111] The road carries little traffic and that at a slow pace. Norfolk itself had recently changed; the city is visible in the background as a bleak industrial center that one would readily leave by any route. But grinding rural poverty led people to flock to the city by this very road; even the principal figure in Thompson's scene must carry his produce there. He and the other black people who move along the road out of Norfolk are presented like the peasants in Barbizon landscape paintings that Thompson had seen when studying in Paris in 1861–68. Figures in the French paintings are shown to work hard, but accordingly they

enjoy an honest and uncomplicated life. The Barbizon artists had looked to peasant life in their search for meaningful values that seemed to them endangered by the changes brought about in Paris by the Industrial Revolution and rapid urban growth. In the same way, Thompson responded in Virginia to a yearning for continuity from an earlier time. The Norfolk road, once it left the city, ran through a rural landscape that was unchanged, peaceful, and ordered, like the forests of Barbizon. Even though living conditions there were in fact so difficult as to be far from idyllic, this landscape made an appealing image in 1888.

The Richmond photographer Huestis Cook, who also was active in these years of recovery, recorded figures busily cultivating the crops that grew on this same Virginia landscape (figs. 4.81 and 4.82). The productivity of their fields stands as evidence of economic recovery; some farmers even reap the benefits of new mechanized harvesting. At the same time, these photographs are visions of a return to order in that the laborers are shown to be back in their place in the fields as before the war. The workers are both black and white. Cook proves that the old social ranking had in fact survived the war and the Emancipation Proclamation. Some local viewers of Cook's photographs,

4.81 Huestis Cook, ***Tending the [Tobacco] Crop***, c. 1890s, gelatin silver print from original glass plate. (Courtesy of Valentine Museum)

4.82 Huestis Cook, ***Wheat Harvest at Curles on the James River***, 1890s, gelatin silver print from original glass plate. (Courtesy of Valentine Museum)

which tend to be masterful compositions, no doubt felt more renewed by the social evidence that he presented than by his imagery of peaceful landscapes.

A painting that addressed the same subject of laborers returned to the fields attracted considerable attention in 1880 in both Richmond and New York newspapers.[112] This was "A Old Virginia Tobacco Farm," a large canvas, now lost, that was painted by Edgar Melville Ward, the younger brother of the better-known sculptor John Quincy Adams

Ward. Like Thompson, Ward had studied in Paris; he produced a number of paintings of peasants on the French coast in Brittany and Normandy that he exhibited regularly at the National Academy of Design in New York City. According to the newspaper accounts, his Virginia landscape, apparently the same canvas that he exhibited at the academy in 1881 as "Tobacco Field-'Old Virginny,'" pictured five African-American figures at Bizarre, the Prince Edward County plantation that had been owned by John Randolph of Roanoke. Presumably Ward selected this setting because it evoked memories of the Old South. The reference in the title to "old" Virginia, and the prominent inclusion of black laborers as New World peasants, shows the determination of another artist to remember the state as it had been.

Near the turn of the century, Max Weyl, a Washington-based artist, painted a view of marshland along the Potomac River that, like Thompson's Norfolk landscape, is an image about constancy and renewal (fig. 4.83). Again, the horizon is set low and the vista is wide. Scenes of marshes had been painted in the North by Martin Johnson Heade both during and following the war years, in wistful canvases that present a quiet, peaceful setting where man learns from and lives with nature. No farmers worked the Potomac marsh for Weyl to paint, but the absence of man in this landscape served only to enhance the reality of its permanence and peacefulness. The setting was in fact unchanged since the colonial era, when George Mason developed this region into his plantation Gunston Hall; it remains today virtually the same as Weyl saw it. This landscape is now Mason Neck State Park and Mason Neck National Wildlife Refuge, a habitat for more than two hundred species of birds and waterfowl.

Today the visitor approaches this setting with the same need for renewal, but following an environmental rather than a social crisis—the near loss of this landscape to development in the 1960s. "The animal and plant kingdoms

4.83 Max Weyl, *Potomac Marsh*, c. 1890–1900, oil on canvas, 28½ x 43¾ in. (Virginia Historical Society, Lora Robins Collection of Virginia Art)

are indeed the living Word that can never be written down. Once they are gone, they are gone, and their wisdom is forever lost to the Earth and to human consciousness," wrote essayist Judith Kahn after visiting this site in 1999. "Soul needs plants and animals to grow and mature," she added. "Soul feeds on wildness." She found these "acres of water and grass" to be "soothing to the eye and mind, food to the spirit." Kahn explained that when she reached the marsh "there was no where else [she] wanted to be" and that she "felt grateful and privileged to be there."[113]

Even the burned city of Richmond was a landscape of recovery that artists and writers recorded. Harry Fenn, an English artist, sketched a new railroad bridge that carried freight across the James River to and from the rebuilt capital; he composed the scene in such a way as to suggest that a sense of vitality had returned to this once defeated political and commercial center (fig. 4.84). Fenn's drawing was engraved to provide visual evidence for readers of *Picturesque America*, a publication that surveyed not only natural landmarks but also "places which attract curiosity." J. R. Thompson's text accompanying Fenn's illustration

stated that "Richmond has nearly recovered from her misfortune, and there are now visible but few traces of the great conflagration" that destroyed much of the city.[114]

It was in the western reaches of Virginia, however, that the spirit of renewal following the Civil War was most often and most vividly recorded. The Valley had become famous during the war, its beauty recognized. If its farm buildings were burned and its livestock killed, the fecundity of the soil and the work ethic of its inhabitants ensured renewal. The western lands offered elements of both wilderness and beauty.

In a sketch of the Roanoke Valley drawn shortly after the war (fig. 4.85), James Wells Champney of Boston presents a pastoral landscape that is intersected by the path of a train. The railroad encouraged development of the Valley, particularly the town of Roanoke, while at the same time allowing not only artists but even tourists to enjoy parts of the landscape that hitherto had been less accessible. One visitor to Roanoke in 1885, Ernest Ingersoll, described the Valley in idyllic terms that complement Champney's vision of it: the "rich fields and pasture lands" made "scenes of surpassing beauty," where "the sheep-bells tinkle on the hills [and] aeolian winds ring among the dusky trees."[115] For many Americans, such inviting landscapes were still intertwined with ideas about the future and national destiny.

Fenn's sketch of Richmond was one of many that appeared in *Picturesque America*, a massive two-volume travel account that appeared in 1872. Champney was on assignment in the Roanoke Valley for Edward King, who in 1875 issued *The Great South*. Both publications were commercially successful ventures, evidence of public interest in southern scenery. Arguments had been made before the war that painters of the national landscape should

4.84 Harry Fenn, ***Richmond from the James***, 1870–72, transparent and opaque watercolor over graphite pencil, 10 5/8 x 18 1/2 in. (Courtesy of Museum of Fine Arts, Boston, M. and M. Karolik Collection of American Watercolors and Drawings, 1800–1875, © 1999)

4.85 James Wells Champney, ***Roanoke Valley***, c. 1873, pen and ink, 6 1/4 x 9 1/4 in. (Virginia Historical Society)

4.86 Harry Fenn, ***Cumberland Gap***, 1872, engraving, 5⁵/₁₆ x 8 in.
(Virginia Historical Society)

picture the entire nation. The editor of the *Cosmopolitan Art Journal* reasoned in 1858 that "we shall not know our country until these recognized interpreters [the northern landscapists] reveal to us the excellence of our native possessions."[116] In his *Romance of the American Landscape* (1854), Thomas Richards questioned why Virginia "has won so little of the attention of our landscapists"; he concluded that it was largely a matter of difficulty of access. No doubt he frightened readers he might otherwise have lured to the state when he reported that throughout the South "the by-ways are miserable, the people ignorant, the fare scant and wretched, the expense of travel disproportionately great."[117] Not surprisingly, relatively few of the established painters made the effort to travel to Virginia in those years. This left a rich vein to be mined following Appomattox.

The landscapes in both *Picturesque America* and *The Great South* can be viewed as a late flowering of the prevailing pre-war philosophy, developed along the Hudson River, that saw the nation as favored by God and the land as a convenient symbol of its extraordinary potential and destiny. The Hudson River movement was actually in decline in the 1870s, not only because the nation's destiny had been compromised by the Civil War, but also because of the not unrelated vogue then for new European paintings of the Barbizon school, the Munich school, the French academic tradition, and the British Aesthetic movement. In fact, it was in this decade that the term "Hudson River School" was conferred in disdain.[118] Nonetheless, the old

vision seemed plausible enough when applied to landscapes like those in Virginia west of the Blue Ridge. True to their titles and to the earlier landscape movement, both *Picturesque America* and *The Great South* did not look beyond what was beautiful in either nature or the urban landscape; in that way they conveyed an upbeat and mythologized vision of the newly reunited nation.[119]

Both publications set out to reclaim the culture of the South that seemed lost to their northern readers and to show them the landscapes that they never had seen; it was for those reasons that they devoted ample attention to Virginia. George W. Bagby, author of a section in *Picturesque America* that is titled "Scenes in Virginia," justified the inclusion of so much landscape from this state in a book that purported to survey the entire nation without regional emphasis:

> From Harper's Ferry to the farthest southwest corner of the State there is literally a world of scenic beauties, ravishing to the artist, and inviting to even the dullest traveller or sight-seer. . . . Other scenes . . . are almost as remarkable as the better-known features of the State.[120]

Oliver Bell Bunce, the actual editor of *Picturesque America*, agreed, selecting Harry Fenn's "Cascade in Virginia" to illustrate the title page of Volume I (see above, fig. 3.27). Fenn had found in the western wilderness of the state one of those "glens murmuring with water-falls which the ear has never heard" that William Cullen Bryant, who was the nominal editor, pointed to in his preface to the book.

The landscape of the western counties of Virginia constituted one of the "new realms" where art was to be carried, according to Bryant. He argued there that while "in the Old World every spot remarkable . . . has been visited by the artist; studied and sketched again and again," America was different: "our country abounds with scenery new to the artist's pencil." In *The Great South*, Edward King boasted in his preface of having "penetrated into mountain regions heretofore rarely visited by northern men" and that "the

4.87 William Ludwell Sheppard, ***Natural Tunnel***, 1872, wood engraving, 9 x 6 ⅛ in. (Courtesy of Dr. and Mrs. Lewis Wright)

unaltered: "In short, it is an old, old region, covered with the time of centuries, and but slightly changed by the progress of events."[123]

Not far from the Cumberland Gap is Natural Tunnel, probably once a subterranean cave like Natural Bridge. It is 150 yards in length and seventy to eighty feet to its roof. William Ludwell Sheppard, a Richmond artist, presented this landscape to the readers of *Picturesque America* with the fresh light and air that follow a storm, so that a sense of beginning is suggested; only a rainbow could have conveyed that message more emphatically (fig. 4.87). George W. Bagby, who provided the accompanying text, argued that the tunnel is, "after the Natural Bridge, . . . undoubtedly the most imposing *lusus naturae* east of the Mississippi River." He thought it comparable to the Natural Bridge in several respects: they are "similar formations," both excite a sense of "surprise" when seen, and both are sublime.[124]

Like Natural Bridge, the tunnel was internationally known. It was one of the few landmarks pictured in *Etwas Über Die Natür Wünder in Nord Amerika*, which was published in St. Petersburg in 1837. An American engraving of it that appeared in 1830 captures the same sense of primeval beauty that Sheppard recognized and that apparently pervaded the spot throughout the nineteenth century.[125]

dawn of a better day is breaking" in the South. This idea that wilderness scenery could still renew man's spirit would be given pronounced visual expression in sunbursts and rainbows that artists in Virginia for the next half century would not infrequently add to their drawings and canvases.

The remotest landscapes of the southwest counties received considerable attention in *Picturesque America*. One was the Cumberland Gap, which Harry Fenn sketched with a freshness that must have matched the vision of early explorers and settlers like Daniel Boone as they traveled through this spectacular passage (fig. 4.86).[121] The Cumberland Gap was not what Bryant could call a "new realm," since many Americans were familiar with its history, but Fenn made it seem that this region was still the wilderness that gave the name to the road that leads through it.[122] In the foreground is a tiny covered wagon that serves to recall the earlier, glorious period. The accompanying text described mountain ridges "in the skies." The writer even imagined the sound of "a warhoop" and the answer of "the rifle-shot of a pioneer." He concluded that the gap stands

4.88 William Ludwell Sheppard, ***Great Falls, New River***, 1872, wood engraving, 6 ½ x 6 in. (Virginia Historical Society)

Thus, Sheppard offered a pair of views from perspectives that had never before been seen.

In depicting the Great Falls of the New River, which is located farther north, Sheppard showed mists hanging in the air above a primeval landscape (fig. 4.88). In the accompanying text for the readers of *Picturesque America*, George Bagby painted an even more vivid and dramatic picture of an Edenic landscape:

> Civilization is far behind us. Mountains tower on every hand; there is seemingly no escape for the imprisoned waters, lake-like here, still as death, enchanted and asleep. The solitude and grandeur of the scene become oppressive; respiration is almost impeded. We push on. A murmur is heard, it becomes a roar; we turn a corner, and behold—the Great Falls![126]

New River was in fact a "new realm" of picturesque scenery, little known to Americans, and was and remains a special place. It runs not east to the Atlantic Ocean but north and west; it is an ancient drainage that has existed for 250 million years and was never submerged when the ice caps flooded most of the surrounding continent, and even today the region is so remote that its fauna and flora have been little damaged by man, as nature writer Bruce Stutz explained in his essay "Ridge, Valley, and River: A Journey to the New" (1994). Stutz gives validity to the seemingly exaggerated vision of the New River that was projected by Sheppard and Bagby:

> During the comings and goings of the glaciers, the place served as a refuge for northern animals fleeing the cold and others fleeing the rising waters. The most ancient species—dragonflies and millipedes, for instance—remained where they were. So, a millipede man tells me, there is hardly anywhere better to go, anywhere in the world so rife with millipedes as these mountains. . . . The Appalachians here form the eastern continental divide; species from as far north as Canada can survive on their cool ridges, and southern species live in the warmer valleys.[127]

For *Picturesque America*, Sheppard also sketched Rainbow Arch, another unique natural formation in western

4.89 William Ludwell Sheppard, *Rainbow Arch*, 1872, wood engraving, 6 1/4 x 9 in. (Virginia Historical Society)

4.90 William Ludwell Sheppard, *Goshen Pass, Virginia*, 1871, wood engraving, 8 3/4 x 11 5/8 in. (Virginia Historical Society)

Virginia that, like Natural Tunnel, had attracted attention earlier in the century (fig. 4.89). It is located west of Natural Bridge at the headwaters of the James River. In 1807 the English artist William Constable produced a wash drawing of the site, but it seems tame and topographical compared to Sheppard's handling.[128] Rainbow Arch had in fact long been a settled landscape; by 1872 a furnace built there had been abandoned. The arch also was on the projected path of the James River and Kanawha Canal, though the canal would never reach this far west owing to the advent of the railroad. Because of its history, Sheppard inserted multiple figures into a partly cultivated landscape (one man is shown to sketch a dam that survived from the days of the forge);

Bagby wrote about the "natural picturesqueness of the place" and "the grandeur and loveliness of the picture."[129] Despite man's presence at Rainbow Arch, the artist manages to suggest that there was a wildness about this setting, where rocks rise high on a hillside, as if God had carved a message there about renewal by building a permanent sign out of stone. Rainbow Arch is shown to be an invigorating apparition in a lush natural landscape.

A final example of Sheppard's vision of western Virginia is his view of Goshen Pass from the periodical *Every Saturday*. The pass is located just west of Lexington and carries the Maury River through a range of mountains into the Valley. For *Picturesque America*, Sheppard showed the pass from below, in a fairly subdued depiction, choosing not to frighten viewers with an image that evokes the Sublime, despite Bagby's warning about "overhanging crags, the high, naked summits, the black masses of foliage" that rise beside a "gigantic and horrible chasm," where "monstrous rocks threaten to topple and crush the foolhardy wayfarer who ventures" into this "wild" scene.[130] Sheppard saw only the grandeur of nature at Goshen. For *Every Saturday*, he stepped back from the gorge to render a spectacular view of a landscape that rivals in grandeur any setting along the Hudson River or in New England (fig. 4.90). This is a continental panorama in that the waves of mountains are magnificent and inspiring in their majesty, they stretch beyond the horizon, and they invite man to venture into a wilderness that awaits him, which God alone placed there for him. Man does not feel humiliated in this environment, as Bagby would suggest, only invigorated.

John Douglas Woodward, who spent some of his later years in Philadelphia and New York, was another prolific Richmond artist active in the Valley. He sometimes used light as the principal narrative element in a landscape.[131] One example is his wood engraving of a peaceful setting entitled "Moonlight on the Shenandoah," which speaks in a quiet way about the role of nature as a regenerative force. His depiction of "Balcony Falls, James River, Virginia" (fig. 4.91) makes the same statement in a more dramatic fashion.

In this wet, lush setting Woodward inserts a rainbow as evidence that God intends the spectacular landscape of this continent as a place where man can learn and live and in which Americans are destined to develop a great nation. Amid scenery like this, the memory of the tragic Civil War can be almost entirely forgotten.

Woodward in fact suggests that the Balcony Falls landscape was essentially unchanged from what it was before the war.[132] His view is little different from one composed three decades earlier, in 1845, by the German artist Augustus Köllner (fig. 4.92). Köllner had pictured this region as a magnificent landscape that awaits the pioneer; light shines from beyond rugged mountains, beckoning the

4.91 John Douglas Woodward, *Balcony Falls, James River, Virginia*, c. 1871, wood engraving, 10 x 15 in. (Virginia Historical Society)

4.92 Augustus Köllner, *Balcony Falls, James River, Virg. at the Blue Ridge Mountains*, 1845, watercolor, 14 3/4 x 20 in. (Virginia Historical Society)

4.93 John R. Johnston, *Scene in the Blue Ridge*, 1877, oil on canvas, 20 x 36 in. (Virginia Historical Society, Lora Robins Collection of Virginia Art)

settler westward. Köllner's biographer describes the artist as an admirer of "the disordered aspects of nature—tumbling rocks, tangled trees, [and] rushing rivers"; at Balcony Falls there was much for him to celebrate.[133]

One artist whose work seems linked to these prints is John R. Johnston, like Worthington Whittredge and William Louis Sonntag a Cincinnati painter attracted to the wilderness scenery of western Virginia. The precision that he gives to the treatment of foreground details is common to the engravings and woodcuts of this period. Johnston's "Scene in the Blue Ridge" of 1877 depicts a setting enveloped in mists (fig. 4.93). This is a landscape so primeval that God's hand seems still visible in it. The canvas is not a topographical view but a vision of an almost tropical wilderness, so lush that it seems untouched. The clearing of the morning atmosphere gives emphasis to the theme of beginning. In the foreground of this mountainous Arcadia, cattle drivers set out, inspired by their natural setting. Johnston's painting is admittedly a late example of the Hudson River style that was so popular with the Cincinnati artists, but masters like Albert Bierstadt and William Trost Richards were also perpetuating the style long after the war.[134]

Dramatic mists do engulf the Valley landscape at times; James Kirke Paulding described such a moment in 1816:

> The vapours of the night had settled in the wide valley, at the foot of the hill, and enveloped it in one unbroken sheet of mist, that in the grey obscurity of the morning, looked like a boundless ocean. But as the sun rose, a gentle breeze sprung up, and the vapours began to be in motion. As they lifted themselves lazily from the ground, and rolled in closer masses towards the mountains, the face of nature gradually disclosed itself in all its varied and enchanting beauty. The imaginary sea became a fertile valley, extending up and down, as far as the eye could reach.[135]

As the tide of settlement and the traffic of tourists inevitably made the wilderness theme untenable, that idea gave way to visions of tranquility, order, and promise that were set in a tamer, more developed landscape. This was the type of scenery that artists like Sonntag and Johnston had envisioned as a stage in man's progress through the wilderness; this was a part of his reward. This second phase of painting the scenery of western Virginia persisted for decades. The setting was narrowed to the Valley itself, particularly the northern half where it runs parallel to the Shenandoah River.

4.94 John Douglas Woodward, *Luray, Va. July 1870*, oil on board, 6 ¾ x 11 ⅞ in. (Courtesy of the Episcopal Diocese of Virginia, Shrine Mont)

John Douglas Woodward's view entitled "Luray, Va. July 1870" is an example of the new subject matter for landscape painting (fig. 4.94). In his engravings, Woodward looked at the wilder scenery of the Valley; here he turns to its settled landscape. This view of an Arcadia of tidy farms and well-ordered fields under cultivation actually could have been recorded at any time in the preceding hundred years. In 1760 the later vicar of Greenwich, England, Andrew Burnaby, had described such scenery as he traveled alongside the Shenandoah River:

> The low grounds upon the banks of this river are very rich and fertile; they are chiefly settled by Germans. . . . I could not but reflect with pleasure on the situation of these people; and think if there is such a thing as happiness in this life, that they enjoy it. Far from the bustle of the world, they live in the most delightful climate, and richest soil imaginable.[136]

The rainbow and other conditions of light and atmosphere, which were a mainstay of expression for the printmakers, also appear in this period in paintings of the settled landscape. Andrew Melrose, a New Jersey artist who traveled extensively, produced two canvases that function as a pair and are titled "Valley of the Shenandoah, Va." (figs. 4.95 and 4.96). One is set early in the day and the other at sunset; they are composed as almost mirror images that balance each other. In both there is abundant evidence of bountiful harvests and the wagons, boats, barges, and rafts that carry the produce away; there are domesticated animals and wildlife that are shown to be as healthy as the people

who enjoy this Arcadia. The ideal weather contributes to the sense of tranquility. If the settings of these canvases are picturesque and bear a resemblance to those of the Old World, it is because Melrose had recently painted the landscapes of Cornwall in England and Lake Killarney in Ireland. In the second painting, the one that is at sunset, Melrose utilizes to the fullest the power of light to evoke mood. He shows what Kenneth Clark has called the poignant light of twilight, when the landscape seems to give back the light that it has absorbed all day.[137]

In 1854 William Gilmore Simms had viewed the Valley landscape as no less idyllic than Andrew Melrose's vision of it. It is almost as if both had been reading Virgil or looking at Claude's canvases of the Roman Campagna, so picturesque is the scene that they describe:

> The Valley of the Shenandoah might realize to the youthful romancer his most perfect idea of Arcadia. Reposing cosily in the bosom of protecting mountains, she unfolds to the embrace of the sun the most prolific beauties. Her charms are of a sort to inspire the most perfect idylls, and to mature the mind for contemplation, and enliven the affections for enjoyment. A dream of peace, sheltered by the wings of security, seems to hallow her loveliness in the sight of blue mountains, and the smiling heavens. On every hand spread out favorite places for retreat and pleasure, the most grateful of all, in which life suffers no provocations inconsistent with mental revery, and where the daily necessities harmonize pleasantly with the most nutritious fancies. Here the farmer may become the poet; here solitude may yield proper occasion for thought: and thought, enlivened by the picturesque, may rise to a constant enjoyment of imagination. There is no scene so uniform as to induce monotony or weariness. . . . [Here] life may pass away as a long and grateful sunny day, lapsing sweetly into sleep at last . . . under a sky of blue, draped with the loveliest hues and colors of a peaceful sunset.[138]

Simms said that in time, when the Valley was more developed, "as the means of life increase, and as prosperity leads to leisure," this region would "be justly known, in all its

4.95 Andrew Melrose, *Valley of the Shenandoah, Va.* (morning), 1887, oil on canvas, 22 x 36 in. (Courtesy of the Executive Mansion, Commonwealth of Virginia)

4.96 Andrew Melrose, *Valley of the Shenandoah, Va.* (sunset), 1887, oil on canvas, 22 x 36 in. (Courtesy of the Executive Mansion, Commonwealth of Virginia)

charms and treasures." That time had come in the decades following the war. Still, lacking urban centers and patronage, yet another century would pass before the region attracted a resident population of artists who in the 1980s and 1990s would paint it again and again. For the immediate future, there would be only the occasional canvases by visitors.

The inclusion of animals in a bucolic scene, which Melrose was quick to do, follows the tradition of earlier Dutch and French artists, who were particularly fond of the cow, a placid animal that seems to understand the tranquility of nature. It is not surprising to find cows in a view by Hubert Vos of "Mossy Creek," at Mount Solon near Harrisonburg, probably painted at the turn of the century (fig. 4.97). Vos was an accomplished Dutch artist who came to this country in 1893 to serve as an art commissioner at the Columbian Exposition in Chicago; afterwards he settled in New York City. He had been trained in Brussels and Paris, winning exhibition medals there and in Amsterdam, Munich, and Dresden, but he was best known as a portraitist.

4.97 Hubert Vos, *Mossy Creek*, c. 1900, oil on canvas, 40 x 30 in. (Virginia Historical Society, Lora Robins Collection of Virginia Art)

"Mossy Creek" is the work of an artist rooted in Holland. It was there in the seventeenth century, when the telescope and the microscope were developed, that painters learned to record the features and details of the landscape rationally and lovingly. They found delight in the perception of fact and in the rightness of nature. Much of the canvas would be given to broad expanses of the sky, because cloud patterns control the moving light and shadow that determine the mood of a landscape. Vos brought Dutch traditions to the Valley of Virginia, where a pastoral vision of peaceful and simple rusticity fit well. This is a quieter and more subtle image than what was produced in the 1870s, but

like that earlier work it is one that offers spiritual renewal.

Several prominent American artists preceded Vos to Virginia in these years. Their visits celebrated national reconciliation; their paintings can be seen as "visions of order" in a time of renewed peace and serenity.[139] George Inness was the leading landscapist in America when he traveled to Goochland County in 1884. His scene there seems to transcend time, carrying the viewer from the present to the past (fig. 4.98).[140] Inness was influenced by the theories of the Swedish philosopher and religious writer Emanuel Swedenborg to look for spiritual meaning in the natural world, and by the Barbizon artists to paint quiet views of the settled countryside. He preferred a landscape that was imbued with history, such as scenery that he had discovered in Italy. Perhaps more than any other reason that was why he came to Virginia. In Goochland County, particularly in those landscapes where slaves had lived and endured, Inness saw evidence of what he called "the sentiment of humanity." He had explained the term in an interview six years earlier:

> Some persons suppose landscape has no power of communicating human sentiment. But this is a great mistake. The civilized landscape peculiarly can; and therefore I love it more and think it more worthy of reproduction than that which is savage and untamed. It is more significant. Every act of man, every thing of labor, suffering, want, anxiety, necessity, love,

4.98 George Inness, *Gray Day, Goochland*, 1884, oil on plywood panel, 18 1/8 x 24 in. (Courtesy of The Phillips Collection, Washington, D.C.)

marks itself wherever it has been. In Italy I remember frequently noticing the peculiar ideas that came to me from seeing odd-looking trees that had been used, or tortured, or twisted—all telling something about humanity.[141]

In the Virginia landscape, Inness envisioned ideas about human labor, suffering, and love that seemed to him to linger on the land. His Goochland views serve to acknowledge the presence of Virginia's past.

One of Theodore Robinson's several landscapes that

4.99 John Ross Key, **Afternoon, Hawksbill River, Blue Ridge Mountains**, c. 1908, oil on canvas, 28 x 40 in. (Virginia Historical Society, Lora Robins Collection of Virginia Art)

he painted in northwestern Virginia in 1893 pictures a red-brick, classical mansion nestled under tall trees; the image evokes thoughts of the English gentry tradition in rural Virginia that dates back to a quieter period.[142] John Ross Key's view painted along the upper Potomac River about 1910 remembers the landscape in northern Virginia before man changed it (see above, fig. 4.37). These artists were looking to turn back the clock to a simpler time, before the nation had become industrialized and before the rapid growth of the post-war period. Through these images they could use America's past to help bring order to the present.

Key was a northern artist who had studied abroad and divided his time mostly between Boston, New York, and Baltimore. In his view near Hawksbill Mountain, a region that in 1935 would become part of the Shenandoah National Park, he was happy to avoid any reference to settlement (fig. 4.99). Here he had found another landscape that was bucolic and a setting where man could be rejuvenated by nature. Tourists today still value the Hawksbill Mountain setting in this way when they visit the park. It is perhaps surprising that the 190,000 acres of that reserve are mostly recycled land that had been lived on for two centuries, because today the whole

4.100 Alexis Fournier, **The Passing Storm, Shenandoah Valley**, 1924, oil on cardboard, 24³/₄ x 36 in. (Virginia Historical Society, Lora Robins Collection of Virginia Art)

4.101 Gari Melchers, *Rainbow*, c. 1925, oil on canvas, 27½ x 30 in. (Courtesy of Morris Museum of Art, Augusta, Georgia)

region looks like the scenery that Key depicted. The recovery of this land is remarkable, as naturalist Eileen Lambert explained in "A Walk in the Forest Primeval" (1984): "After nearly five decades as a national park, the forest again covers almost all the land. Shenandoah clearly demonstrates that nature can recreate wilderness."[143] Naturalists appreciate this landscape because of the special botanical and zoological life that it supports; Napier Shelton wrote in *The Nature of the Shenandoah* (1975), "here on Hawksbill, at 4,050 feet the park's highest peak, lower temperatures and abundant moisture make a home for numerous forms of northern plant and animal life" that are not usually found in Virginia.[144] By celebrating on canvas the beauty of a remarkable region that was fast disappearing, Key actually helped to provide the impetus for its preservation.

As late as the 1920s, painters were still following the lead of that post–Civil War generation that looked to find picturesque, timeless scenery in the Valley. In "The Passing Storm, Shenandoah Valley" (fig. 4.100), painted in 1924, Alexis Fournier shows that nature is always renewing itself, and in turn the spirit of those who depend upon the land for

their well-being. Fournier was a Minnesota painter who eventually settled in New York State and exhibited regularly in New York City. In 1893 he had traveled to Paris for academic training, but there he found inspiration instead from the avant-garde Impressionists.

Working on site in the Valley, probably in Rockingham County or farther north, Fournier adapted French Impressionism to an idyllic setting where so many styles of landscape painting have been tried and seem to work well. He was sensitive to the atmosphere that envelops a setting and gives it a mood; he painted a number of scenes of the changing conditions that follow a storm. How was an artist to capture the moisture lingering in the air and on the ground, the fleeting effects of light, and the rapidly moving and transitory cloud formations? Of course the French masters had answered that the painter can only give an impression. Fournier paints with a delicate pastel palette, recording not the solidity and precision of objects, but instead the shimmering sensation of light and his feelings about nature. Both are transformed into color. Color replicates the tonality of outdoor light, so that a sense of truth to nature is conveyed. Color conveys as well the artist's joy in the visible world.

The rainbow that extends across the panorama of Fournier's canvas was by the time of his visit an old symbol of renewal in New South landscapes; it appears again and again in these "visions of order." A painting by Gari Melchers of c. 1925 even carries the title "Rainbow" (fig. 4.101). By the time that Melchers settled near Fredericksburg in 1916, on a rural estate of twenty acres where the landscape would sustain his spirit and his art, he was an experienced master who had enjoyed an illustrious career winning innumerable medals and public mural commissions. He had come to work in a style in which the loose brushwork of Impressionism is applied over traditional, academic drawing of the type that he learned years earlier as a student at the academies in Düsseldorf and Paris. This reluctance to use a spontaneous technique without the structure of an underlying armature was typical of the conservative American approach to art; we saw that Adele Williams was adapting Impressionism in the same way in Richmond at this same time (see above, fig. 2.38). While the landscapes of both artists resemble those of the American Impressionist Childe Hassam, who worked in New England, they differ by responding to the mood of the South, where the population was still physically and more emotionally attached to the land.

In Melchers's view set at Falmouth, he is sensitive to the Stafford County landscape in spring, when fruit trees blossom and the Rappahannock River is the clearest from new rain, some of which still lingers in the moist air. The painting is a remarkably fresh vision of nature, in part no doubt because Melchers recorded the landscape in all of its seasons and was alert to its changes. He seems to suggest by the fecundity of this setting and the tasteful architecture on it that the recovery from the changes of the late nineteenth century has by now been fully accomplished. The renewal must be complete because this region of north-central Virginia that had been trampled by Union and Confederate troops has become an Arcadia. As in the earlier post-war landscapes by Thompson, Ward, and Huestis Cook, peasants are still present on the land; now they are white figures like those whom Melchers had painted decades earlier in Brittany and Normandy in the Barbizon tradition of reverence for rural simplicity. And, as in those earlier images, Melchers suggests order, renewal, and promise. The black

population in rural Virginia had by no means vanished, however, as Robert Gwathmey would be quick to point out two decades later during the period of Regionalism.

Regionalism and the Post–World War II Era

Rejecting the spirit of internationalism that had drawn the nation into World War I, and later in reaction also to the stock market crash of 1929 and the Great Depression, many American artists of the period that began in the 1920s turned to local themes and were inclined to render them in a simple, straightforward manner, rejecting the styles of those avant-garde Europeans who had moved in the direction of abstraction. The term Regionalism is generally used to describe this work, which was part of a national self-investigation that directed attention back to rural life and values. The most recognized artists of this movement were the Midwestern painters Thomas Hart Benton, John Steuart Curry, and Grant Wood. Many writers of this period also were isolationist and attuned to the same subjects. In Virginia there was little need for redirection away from urban problems, because the state had remained predominantly rural following the Civil War.

Nonetheless, the Regionalist period in Virginia was one of dramatic transition, as the state moved from its agrarian past into the modern era. It is perhaps inevitable that in a period of rapid change different philosophies will coexist and find expression in art. In the environment of rural Virginia in the 1930s, when a legacy from the past survived alongside beautiful settings, social problems, and the advent of modernism, the impulse to celebrate American values yielded a set of varied approaches to the landscape. At least one generalization can be made about them: there were artists who were inclined to mythologize about the landscape and others who tried to look realistically at their subject and with an eye to the future. Some of the former pursued the "picturesque" (meaning quaint) subject, which, ironically, could even be an urban scene. Others envisioned as idyllic the rural settings in which most Virginians still lived. The opposing philosophy guided those photographers and artists who rejected pretentiousness and sentimentality; they were determined to picture instead the reality of life on Virginia soil, where social commentary was long overdue and where evidence of a new, modern world was emerging.

4.102 J. J. Lankes, *Worn Road*, c. 1930, woodcut, 8¼ x 6¾ in. (Virginia Historical Society)

The American belief in the land was shaken by the Great Depression but survived through the 1930s. Even Benton, Curry, and Wood, who worked in the region of the Dust Bowl, continued to paint the landscape. Virginia artists of the Regionalist era shared a fundamental but tempered philosophy about the importance of nature; this was given expression by Franklin D. Roosevelt when he dedicated the Shenandoah National Park in 1936. The president confirmed that man can be "invigorated" from "great natural beauty." "There is merit for all of us," he said, "in the ancient tale of the giant Antaeus, who, every time he touched his Mother Earth, arose with strength renewed a hundredfold." Roosevelt pointed to the advantage of "lay[ing] hold of the perspective that comes to men and women who every morning and every night can lift up their eyes to Mother Nature."[145]

In his "Essay on Virginia" written

in 1932, William Carlos Williams put into writing a widely held perception of Tidewater Virginia as slow paced and picturesque: "The opalescent, sluggish rivers wander indeterminately about the plain. Africans, corn, tobacco, bull-bats, buzzards, rabbits, figs, persimmons are the common accompaniments of these waters."[146] Williams was not eager to criticize the conditions of social, racial, and economic inequality that had always characterized life in Tidewater Virginia; in fact he tried to detach himself from this subject by means of his style of writing, which he later described as "automatic." However, a school of artists emerged in eastern Virginia in the 1930s to celebrate this unhurried lifestyle. They saw in the land an evocation of the Old South, which they remembered fondly. The best known of these artists was J. J. Lankes, whose Virginia woodcuts were then so celebrated that they were recognized by the *New York Times* (fig. 4.102).[147]

A more academic artist who worked in the same manner was Eliot Clark, whose painting of a "Mill at Logan, Albemarle County, Virginia" also depicts with sentiment the evidence of an earlier period (fig. 4.103). Clark taught at the University of Virginia at the end of a long career as both a painter and an author. He wrote monographs on Alexander Wyant, J. Francis Murphy, John Twachtman, and Theodore Robinson. They were Tonalists

4.103 Eliot Clark, *Mill at Logan, Albemarle County, Virginia*, c. 1935, oil on canvas, 32 x 40 in. (Virginia Historical Society, Lora Robins Collection of Virginia Art)

and Impressionists, thus the dusky palette and loose brush-work of Clark's own paintings. Clark reasoned that if old masters could paint simple rural subjects, then the mills of the Piedmont that surrounded him in the rolling hills outside of Charlottesville were fitting subjects. Edith Kimball, who traveled through much of Virginia around 1920, held the same viewpoint. She noted the grist, flour, and saw mills that she thought gave the landscape a settled, peaceful, and rustic appearance: "Some of these mills, with their pictur-esque surroundings of tangled vines and lacy willows, look as if they had been taken directly out of a familiar old-world painting."[148] In selecting the subject matter of, say, John Constable, Clark created an anachronistic image. Appar-ently that was his intention.

An urban scene that also seemed picturesque was painted in this period by James F. Banks and titled "Old Richmond" because it depicts decrepit wooden structures in a bleak setting. Presumably this image was meant to represent a black neighborhood, which might have been one reason that the painting "provoked a storm of criticism" in 1938 when it was selected by a Virginia Museum jury for inclusion in an exhibition of contemporary American paintings and in turn was purchased for the museum by a trustee.[149] Another reason was that the canvas is so crudely painted that it has little artistic merit. Nonetheless, "Old

Richmond" was pictured in 1941 in *Life* magazine, with the commentary that "its dilapidated houses bathed in a mellow glow and its red-shirted loafer sitting on [the] curb, conveys a mood of lyric laziness." This was the same southern sluggishness that William Carlos Williams had celebrated. The fact that Banks "completed [his] canvas by candlelight after his house burned down" only added to its picturesque aura; perhaps it should be viewed under candlelight.

Another urban scene that was conceived as a pictur-esque landscape is Cordray Simmons's "Fishing in Virginia" (fig. 4.104). Simmons was a New York artist who had studied there at the Art Students' League with such notable realist artists as George Bellows and Robert Henri, who directed him to paint the urban scene. In Virginia, where he traveled on the eve of World War II, African Americans were still viewed almost like the French peasants of the nineteenth century, whose lifestyle attracted interest because of its simplicity and slow pace, which survived from an earlier time. African-American fishermen are the subject of Simmons's view set on the Potomac River at Alexandria; they are what made the landscape seem picturesque.

Many Virginians of the Regionalist period saw the land as idyllic, yet in a way that was independent of any legacy from the past. Earl Hamner, the novelist who was born in Nelson County, said that "when I was growing up in the foothills of Virginia's Blue Ridge Moun-tains in the thirties, I was certain that no one on earth had quite so good a life."[150] Hamner perpetuated that sentimental view of rural life in *Spencer's Mountain* (1961) and *The Homecoming* (1970), on which the popular television series *The Waltons* was based. One painter who pictured the setting that Hamner knew, in terms that he would have understood, was Georgia Morgan. Her painting of a mountain landscape (fig. 4.105) depicts the very scenery that nurtured the young Hamner; she was a Lynchburg painter who taught at Lynchburg College from 1915 to 1945. Morgan painted in a simplified style that was derived from European Expressionism. Forms and colors are so simplified that the landscape assumes almost a quality of fantasy.

A similar vision of an idyllic landscape

4.104 Cordray Simmons, ***Fishing in Virginia***, c. 1938–39, oil on canvas, 23 ¼ x 29 ½ in. (Virginia Historical Society, Lora Robins Collection of Virginia Art)

4.105 Georgia Morgan, *Mountain Landscape*, c. 1930–40, oil on canvas, 34 x 40 in. (Courtesy of Lynchburg College)

was conceived by the Richmond artist Nora Houston, whose depiction of a fall field with a harvest of hay shows nature to be both beautiful and productive (fig. 4.106). Houston would abandon Richmond to travel to actual sites in the Blue Ridge and as far west as White Sulphur Springs, where she could experience the serenity of bucolic mountain scenery. Although these were the years of the Great Depression, when poverty gripped the rural counties through which Houston traveled, she, like Georgia Morgan, made no reference to it in her landscapes. Instead, she would observe nature carefully, with sensitivity to the seasons, sometimes entitling a scene with the name of the month in which she painted it. Nature to Houston was a manifestation of God's goodness; to prove the point she gave to one of her landscapes a title taken from the 99th Psalm, "Jubilate Deo Omnis Terra" ("Shout with joy to God, All the Earth"). As with Hamner, the landscape served to remind her of the goodness of life.

A landscape close in theme and location to Nora Houston's was painted by an itinerant artist in southwest Virginia named W. C. Coleman, who for each of his

canvases would carve a simple frame that is as charming as the scenes that he conceived (fig. 4.107). During the Depression Coleman survived day to day by painting landscapes like this in exchange for meals. His patrons, understandably, wished to be reminded of happier times rather than view evidence of rural poverty, so Coleman

4.106 Nora Houston, *Fall Landscape*, c. 1930–40, oil on board, 15 x 24 in. (Virginia Historical Society)

produced idyllic scenery. He offers not the slightest suggestion of the hardships that he and so many others encountered in that difficult period.

A contemporary and friend of Nora Houston's was Adèle Clark, who also was an advocate for the arts in Richmond (and like Houston a pioneer for women's causes). Reversing the injunction that gentle folk discuss things while only servants talk about people, Clark said that she would always prefer to draw pictures of people rather than things. But she did paint landscapes, of which she thought the best was her "Cherry Tree" (fig. 4.108). This is an Impressionist rendering of the view from her Richmond

house and studio: the tree "was out in the yard, and it was in bloom and it looked so lovely with the cherries all over it that I painted a picture of it."[151] The landscape is once again beneficent.

Adèle Clark, however, also painted scenery in which figures are shown, accurately, involved in the daily chores of their lives, such as washing clothes or cutting wood. In these scenes the artist aligned herself with yet another creative and accomplished woman of this period, Ellen Glasgow, who described her novels as a "revolt against the formal, the false and affected, the sentimental, and the pretentious, in Southern writing." Glasgow's *Vein of Iron*

4.107 W. C. Coleman, *Landscape*, c. 1930–40, oil on canvas, 10 x 33 in. (Virginia Historical Society)

4.108 Adèle Clark, *The Cherry Tree*, mid-20th century, oil on canvas, 30 x 24 ½ in. (Courtesy of Virginia Museum of Fine Arts)

(1935), for example, which was so popular as to enjoy a print run of one hundred thousand copies in its first year of publication, realistically tells the story of life for a poor Scots-Presbyterian family in western Virginia that demonstrates the sort of fortitude that is alluded to in the book's title.[152] Several landscape photographers and painters active in Virginia during this period would in the same way reject those idealizations that ignored the havoc of the Great Depression, the social injustice of segregation, and the problem of transforming a rural society into an increasingly modern and urbanized one.

A principal subject of the photographer was the Virginia farmer, whose recovery from the economic setback of the Depression was accomplished at least partly through the aid of federal programs. President Franklin Roosevelt was determined to conserve both human and natural resources. "We have seen," the president said at Big Meadows in 1936, "the tragedy of waste—waste of our people, waste of our land. It was neither the will nor the destiny of our Nation that this waste of human and material resources should continue any longer."[153] From 1935 to 1943 the Farm Security Administration, or FSA (and its predecessor, the Historical Section of the Resettlement Administration), under the direction of Roy Emerson Stryker, set out to document the devastating effects of the Depression on rural America and to document the signs of recovery. FSA photographers such as Arthur Rothstein (fig. 2.40), Walker Evans (fig. 2.30), Dorothea Lange, and Marion Wolcott captured convincing pictorial evidence in Virginia.

Lange, whose compelling images of migrant families would establish her reputation as a leading photographer of the century, was in Sperryville, at the edge of the Shenandoah National Park, the same summer that Roosevelt dedicated that preserve. Her photograph of "Men Cradling Wheat" (fig. 4.109) has all of the compositional strengths of a painting of harvesting by Winslow Homer; the image is both timeless and specific, the broad expanse of landscape is stable and inviting, while figures move through it with grace. At the same time, the point is made that a healthy wheat crop has been grown and harvested.

In 1941 Marion Wolcott provided evidence of farm productivity in western Virginia that must have been assuring to those worried about the nation's progress while Europe was at war (fig. 4.110). The title identifies the site only as somewhere in the Valley; the image, because it seems to stretch for miles, suggests that much, if not all, of this region of Virginia is under cultivation. The photograph is conceived like a Pieter Bruegel landscape that acknowledges a world beyond the horizon. This is a landscape that renews man, literally feeds him, and is worth fighting for.

Despite the evidence of these photographs, the New Deal actually had less influence on Virginia than elsewhere. But the Byrd Organization did cooperate with those projects that concerned the environment: the Civilian Conservation Corps (CCC), the Shenandoah National Park, the Skyline Drive, and the Blue Ridge Parkway. The Skyline Drive had been initiated by Herbert Hoover; Roosevelt built the road and the park that surrounds it with his CCC, beginning in 1933. No doubt it was the excitement stirred by those projects that in 1935 inspired Carson Davenport of Danville to paint a view of mountain roads by using the bold colors and simplified forms of European Expressionism and Futurism (fig. 4.111). Davenport transformed a landscape that had been a formidable barrier to travel into an inviting scene that awaits the modern motorist.

4.109 Dorothea Lange, *Men Cradling Wheat near Sperryville*, 1936, gelatin silver print. (Courtesy of Library of Congress)

Although the Farm Security Administration vision of the independent farmer was upbeat, not every individual owned land, or land that was fertile, nor was everyone able to use the land to lift himself out of poverty and social discrimination. In these same years Robert Gwathmey, whose family had been rooted in the Tidewater region for generations, would periodically return to Virginia from self-exile in New York City. Back home he found a subject for his art in a landscape that in his vision of it was so stark that it seemed nearly dead. The artist told *Art News* in 1946, "I don't want to get labeled as a painter of the South. But then I go back home every summer to Virginia and I see these things—and they affect me all over again, sort of shock me—and I paint them."[154]

4.110 Marion Post Wolcott, *Planting Corn, Shenandoah Valley*, 1941, gelatin silver print. (Courtesy of Library of Congress)

The "things" that shocked Gwathmey are laid out in a painting of c. 1941 entitled "From Out of the South" (fig. 4.112). This is William Carlos Williams's Tidewater landscape that is peopled by Africans and where life, like the rivers, is sluggish. The field of play is uneven, visually as well as figuratively. Gone is the traditional composition from the Tidewater in which the horizon is set low to suggest the serenity and stability that is evoked by a flat landscape. Whites sit lazily at a gas station, while black sharecroppers and tenant farmers toil in barren fields, like French peasants of an earlier age; they were still paid as little as their ancestors, who had been pictured by Huestis Cook shortly after the Civil War (above, figs. 4.81 and 4.82). A white aristocrat is ensconced in a brick mansion that was built long ago in the age of slavery; he worships the portrait of an ancestor while poverty-stricken black men are imprisoned in a chain gang outside his door. Whites ride in cars; blacks walk. African Americans are even overtly oppressed, by Klansmen, while the outside world, in the form of a billboard advertisement, is oblivious to the situation. Only nature responds, in the dreary color of the sky. The entire scene is conceived to evoke moral indignation over the social misuse of this landscape.[155]

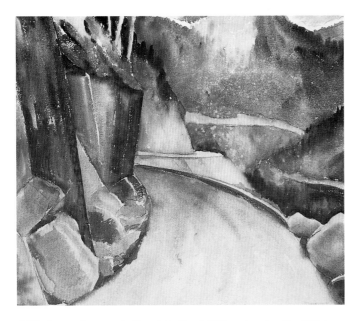

4.111 Carson Davenport, *Mountain Road*, 1935, watercolor, 19 x 22 ¹/₂ in. (Courtesy of Danville Museum of Fine Arts and History)

4.112 Robert Gwathmey, *From Out of the South*, c. 1941, oil on canvas, 39 ¹/₂ x 60 in. (Courtesy of The David and Alfred Smart Museum of Art, the University of Chicago, the Mary and Earle Ludgin Collection, © 1999)

4.113 Theresa Pollak, *Afton Country No. 4, or Mountain Landscape*, 1961, oil on canvas, 40 x 50 in. (Courtesy of Sara Pollak Gallant)

At the same time that social conditions of the nineteenth century were perpetuated on the rural landscape of eastern Virginia, the dawn of the modern age was visible in the work of Charles Sheeler, whose Precisionist style served to celebrate the mechanical progress of the twentieth century (see above, figs. 2.31 and 3.59). Modernism arrived to stay in Virginia during the years of World War II, when in serving the industrial needs of the military the state was forever transformed from a slow-paced rural economy. Local landscape artists acknowledged that their world was changed when they increasingly used a vocabulary of dynamic forms and heightened color as concessions to the new abstraction that had become the rage of the New York art world. But only very rarely did they abandon their recognizable subject matter to paint abstractly. Instead, most landscapists demonstrated an increased sensibility to

identifiable tracts of land close to where they lived and worked. Their goal was to set down on canvas their feelings about a landscape that then faced its first serious threats of destruction by development, a fact that some in America, like the architect Frank Lloyd Wright, were just beginning to realize. Among the first to foresee this future would be the naturalist writers, because they defined in clear terms the worlds of flora and fauna that would be lost by the "progress" of subdivisions and all forms of urban expansion. Both painters and writers of the 1950s and 1960s set the mood for the following generations in Virginia to rediscover the landscape.

Nowhere is the new look more visible than in Theresa Pollak's "Afton Country No. 4, or Mountain Landscape" (fig. 4.113), painted in 1961 after the artist had studied in 1958 in Provincetown with the abstract expressionist and

4.114 Theresa Pollak, *The River*, 1967, oil on canvas, 45 x 56 in. (Courtesy of Westhampton College, University of Richmond, gift of the Richmond Alumnae Club in honor of Leslie Sessons Booker, W '22)

master colorist Hans Hofmann. Pollak, who throughout her long career was continually developing and responding to new influences, had become at age sixty a great colorist herself. More important, she was able to put this new skill to use in innovative ways in her own paintings of distinctly Virginia subjects. Her view at Afton Mountain is so successful a blend of abstraction and the realist tradition as to suggest that if works like this that are now privately owned and little known were more visible, Pollak might be recognized not only as an important art teacher and administrator but also as one of the best painters that the state has produced.

In "Afton country" the sense of mountain ranges moving into space is undeniably present, as we look down at them and into the distance. Yet, while this painting replicates an actual view, it also functions like a Hofmann abstraction; advancing colors cling to the picture plane while others recede, so that a dynamic push-pull effect is put into play. The colors suggest the landscape of the Piedmont that is green, blue, and orange in the fall, while they also are the bold, modern hues of the 1950s abstractionists.

Pollak had studied at New York's Art Students' League in the 1920s, 1932, and 1941–42; in those years she painted in a predictably conservative style. In 1962, four years after she studied with Hofmann, Pollak traveled for the first time to France, where she rediscovered the work of Henri Matisse, whose work she had first encountered in a New York gallery in the 1940s. About that earlier experience she says, "I went in one where they had an exhibit of Matisse, and it was so powerful it made me dizzy. I felt like I would fall over. I loved Matisse then, and I have loved him ever since."[156] It is the influence of Matisse that invigorates her 1967 painting "The River" (fig. 4.114), which is an actual view of the James River in Richmond at the Robert E. Lee Bridge. As in a work by Matisse, the forms are light and graceful, and they bound across the canvas with energy; the colors are rich, resonant, and strategically placed, so that they invigorate the image. As with the Afton view, this painting is both a landscape and an appealing arrangement of colors on a two-dimensional surface.

A student and colleague of Pollak's, and like Pollak a teacher for decades, is Jeanne Begien Campbell, who also studied with Henry Varnum Poor. Her painting "James River

with Tugboat" (fig. 4.115) actually preceded Pollak's
treatment of the same Richmond landmark and in the same
way calls attention to scenery that seems invigorating.
When Campbell's work was first exhibited at the Virginia
Museum in 1941, its director, Thomas Colt, wrote, "Her
work . . . indicates to the viewer the essential pleasure that
she finds in putting paint on canvas. She subscribes to no
'isms' and, a competent craftsman, she concerns herself
largely in the production of beautiful and sound painting."[157] By "sound painting," Colt was referring in part to
the solid structure of her scenes. In the view along the
James the pilings are strong visual elements that take on the
energy of abstract forms.

An artist who had learned the same stylistic lessons
in Paris that Theresa Pollak did, and much earlier, was
Pierre Daura, the Spaniard who had relocated to the
Rockbridge County home of his American wife at the
outbreak of World War II. His depiction of "Milking,
Rockbridge Baths" (fig. 4.116) records an actual setting that
is brought to life by his vivid yet also delicate use of color
and form. This artist was acutely appreciative of the
characteristics of the landscape of the Valley, its overall
beauty, and the atmospheric conditions of America that
were new to his eyes (see also fig. 2.41, above).

The views shown here by Pollak, Campbell, and
Daura, like Rockwell Kent's painting of "Oak Ridge" that
was painted in the same period (see above, fig. 2.32), all

depict actual places that are identified by the artists, unlike
the scenes by Georgia Morgan or J. J. Lankes that are
located imprecisely only in one region or another of the
state. Perhaps by mid-century the time had arrived when
artists and the citizenry in general were ready once again to

look more seriously and more closely at specific landscapes.

Daura was one of several artists in the Valley at mid-century who directed a new wave of attention to its scenery. His closest neighbor was Marion Junkin, who had taught art at Richmond Professional Institute with Theresa Pollak (see above, fig. 4.77) and then at Vanderbilt University before he established an art department at Washington and Lee University in 1949, a century after his great-uncle in 1848 assumed the presidency of then Washington College. Junkin lived much of his life in Lexington and painted the countryside there. His view of nearby Goshen Pass probably dates to the 1950s (fig. 4.117). Junkin was trained in New York at the Art Students' League to work in an essentially realistic style, but in the late 1940s, in response to New York abstraction, the artist introduced into his work the earlier idea that the Cubists had developed of fragmenting form and space to evoke the sense of modern life. Junkin said in 1947, "What I am trying to do now is work abstractly, but superimpose realistic bits," defending his decision with the explanation that "art is not, never has been, and never will be a matter of imitating nature."[158]

As a resident of Lexington, Junkin valued Goshen Pass in the same manner as did Katie Letcher Lyle, a neighbor, who wrote about this landscape in an essay titled "Only in the Land of Goshen."[159] Lyle values the pass as "the jewel of Rockbridge County" and "my favorite playground most of my life." She remembers it partly for its rocks. It is "a boulder-choked five-mile gorge," she writes; boulders "as big as houses loomed above us, jutting out of the cliffs overhead," and boulders bigger than a car might even block the road through the pass. In this setting she would splash, jump, and swim as a child, she would flirt as a teenager, and college students would socialize and court there. It was a place that spawned big stories about big rattlesnakes, wolves, panthers, and bobcats. It was a landscape where birds could be watched. On canvas Junkin gives us the rocks, he suggests the memories, and he paints at least one of the birds. Unlike William Ludwell Sheppard in 1871 (above, fig. 4.90), he does not step back to picture the great chasm through the mountains; no artists in the 1950s saw nature in such grandiose terms. Nor did artists then think of ecology; Lyle said that "we'd never heard of pollution." Instead, Junkin simply states that Goshen is a place that is worthy of celebration, because it is a sanctuary for humans as well as birds. The pass was in fact an early success for the conservation movement. Lyle spells out a series of threats that "the formidable Hydra of the local citizenry rose up" against and defeated: the 1929 plan by the

4.117 Marion Junkin, *Landscape at Goshen Pass*, c. 1950–60, oil on canvas, 49 x 71 in. (Courtesy of Washington and Lee University)

power company to dam the upper end of the pass, the 1938 state proposal to modernize the road, the 1954 timber cutting scare, and the 1972 state plan to develop riding trails and walks.

Horace Day taught at Mary Baldwin College in nearby Staunton when Junkin was in Lexington. Day said that he painted at least once in almost every county of Virginia. After mid-century he focused on the scenery near Staunton. West of the city is Buffalo Gap, a rustic setting that Day recorded in 1956 (fig. 4.118). He saw this region as a landscape of gentle rolling hills carpeted with broad expanses of grass and only occasional trees, all of which take on the uniform color of the season.

Janet Lembke, also a resident of Staunton and one who has known this portion of the Valley nearly all of her life, has explained in an essay about the nearby Bullpasture River that this landscape is not forested because the earlier inhabitants, the Shawnee, Cherokee, and Delaware Indians, would yearly, at the end of hunting season, "put the dry grass to the torch," so that the buffalo would return each spring to fresh meadows.[160] Ever since then its beauty has appealed to visitors. In 1775, Philip Vickers Fithian, a Presbyterian minister serving as a missionary in western Virginia, described it when he traveled very close to Buffalo Gap:

> We began to look round in the Calf-Pasture—The Country at once surprizes me—Meadow Ground of the best Quality! . . . It is exceeding rich. I see on their Farms large Quantities of Hay—Abundance of Stock—Especially Cattle & Horses . . . The Inhabitants live in great Plenty.[161]

The only threat to the ecology of this landscape has come in the 1990s from massive poultry operations, but Lembke reports that the state has regulated the turkey growers whose practices might otherwise destroy this Arcadian landscape.

4.118 Horace Day, *Buffalo Gap*, 1956, oil on canvas, 26 x 36 in. (Virginia Historical Society, Lora Robins Collection of Virginia Art)

Of those who examined the landscape at mid-century, the naturalists made the most detailed observations. They immersed themselves in their subjects, writing about species of trees and birds, about the behavior of fish and bees. For example, in *My Health Is Better in November: Thirty-Five Stories of Hunting and Fishing in the South* (1947), Havilah Babcock made the study of zoology seem not only interesting but also significant.[162] Joseph James Murray, whose *Checklist of the Birds of Virginia* (1952) was a landmark publication, inspired children and adults to reconsider the world around them as relevant to their being:

> April is a good time to be alive. It is the adolescence of the year. The earth, warming to the full force of the sun's power, is fully awake. There is flooding growth in plants and trees; birds are on the move; on all sides are preparations for the mating time. Things are happening too fast outside for the lover of wild things to stay indoors.[163]

Edwin Way Teale made Virginia readers think twice about birds and the landscape they live in: "In all the United States east of the Rockies the number of full species is well under 450. So Virginia's 344 indicates the richness of bird life in that state."[164] These naturalists prepared the way for the next generation to turn to the land with enthusiasm and commitment.

The Endangered Environment: A New Worship of Nature

It is a curiosity of the American worship of nature that when civilization tames the wilderness, its scenery becomes simultaneously accessible, endangered, and revered. The so-called Hudson River School of landscape painters emerged in New York State after the opening of the Erie Canal in 1825, when travel along the Hudson to the Catskill Mountains became easy and Niagara Falls became a tourist attraction. In post–Civil War Virginia, the railroads opened the Valley to much less difficult travel and so initiated a revived interest in the landscape there. In the late twentieth century accessibility had long ceased to be an issue, but the landscape after mid-century became endangered, more seriously than ever before, so that by the 1970s nature was reevaluated and old landscape traditions that seemed defunct were revived, in a variety of guises.

Modern endangerment has come in the form of urban expansion, industrial growth, chemical contamination, and dramatic population increases. Parts of the American landscape that for eons had been green suddenly disappeared under new construction or were slowly poisoned. In Virginia this unprecedented degree of change emerged with the massive military build-up in the state during World War II. It brought urban sprawl in the form of new subdivisions for housing and the rezoning of rural land for commercial use, as well as less visible ecological problems. Through the 1950s and 1960s these conditions were only fueled by postwar prosperity. The specter of pollution became highly visible in the state in the mid-1970s when Hopewell earned dubious renown as the site of illegal dumping of the toxic chemical kepone, which contaminated the James River downstream for more than a decade.

The environmental crisis was one of several factors that contributed to the emergence of a school of landscape painters in Virginia in the 1970s. Ecology provided artists a cause that they could champion. These were painters who had developed in the 1960s, a decade when ideology was important to young people and when the literature about ecology was initiated with the publication in 1962 of Rachel Carson's *Silent Spring*, the first book to warn against the unbridled use of pesticides. Today Virginia landscapists read or at least are aware of many books written by naturalists. A few of them have been actively involved with conservation issues, though much less so than their counterparts in California and Colorado, where artists actually have raised money to protect land.[165]

A second factor that spurred the development of a Virginia landscape school has to do with art and style. In 1970, when many of these painters were beginning their careers, they were working in abstraction, then the vogue in New York City and at major art schools. Some artists chose to reject it for that very reason—it was the established style. Marjorie Portnow says that she was tired of hearing from an all-male establishment about "bigger and better" abstract paintings, which would only end up in museums and corporate collections.[166] The landscapist could pursue instead a better fusion of life and art, which is also what motivated the Pop Artists of this same period. While it would have been fairly difficult to shift from abstraction to figurative art, which demands a different training, it was an easy enough switch to step outdoors and quietly start to paint the landscape, which was the genre that was then furthest from the public eye. There the artist was free to pursue the same issues of structure and metaphorical content that he knew from abstraction, and Cézanne had given the genre the respectability of modernity. Also appealing was the fact that landscapes can project the timeless quality that is a strength of abstract imagery.

4.119 Dawn Latané, *Clearing, Westmoreland County, after a Rain*, 1992, oil on canvas, 33 x 49 in. (Private collection)

4.120 Philip Geiger,
Pavilion Upper Level, 1997,
oil on panel, 29 x 36 in.
(Collection of Harmon and
George Logan, Salem, Virginia,
courtesy of Reynolds Gallery)

The Virginia landscape school, which is sizable today, was developed and remains centered in the art departments of the colleges and universities. Of approximately thirty contemporary landscapists represented in our study, more than half are the teachers or the products of their advanced programs. By their numbers, by the support system that they have established to encourage one another, and because of the relatively high rate of survival of the Virginia scenery that is their subject, most of these artists have developed a positive viewpoint regarding nature that recalls the attitude of their nineteenth-century predecessors. This philosophy stands in contrast to that of a few of their contemporaries, mostly in other states, who approach a frail and disappearing landscape with only melancholy and anxiety.

Perils do jeopardize the modern landscape, however, and a number of recent Virginia paintings make reference to them. In some examples the evidence is subtle. For instance, in 1992 Dawn Latané, a Richmond artist who teaches at Randolph-Macon College, painted a field cleared by loggers because it is difficult today to locate a Tidewater landscape that conveys a sense of wildness, which is what she was looking for (fig. 4.119). To Latané the occasional

pine tree isolated against the sky was a striking visual motif. It was at the same time a sign of how the landscape not only was endangered but actually changed. The artist explains with optimism that this is a scene "of desolation but also of regrowth"; she chose to paint it after a rainstorm.

The landscape is most changed today in the way that man-made elements intrude upon it. For that reason we approach and perceive it differently than ever before, according to Philip Geiger, a Charlottesville artist who teaches at the University of Virginia and refers to the "strangeness of nature."[167] The world in Geiger's vision of it has been described as a vast and lonely space, where objects are only glimpsed and remembered, where the imagery does not organize into narrative, and where a certain poignancy arises from the relation of casual order and aesthetic order (fig. 4.120).[168] The artist, however, takes a positive viewpoint: "I see my work representing the beauty of the natural world that I see everyday, that is nature visibly influenced by man's buildings, roads, cars, and so on."[169] He paints with an exquisite eye for color.

Marjorie Portnow, an established New York artist who has traveled the country to paint the landscape from coast to coast, has visited Virginia on several occasions. She

4.121 Marjorie Portnow, *View of Roanoke from Mill Mountain*, 1999, oil on linen, 12 x 24 in. (Courtesy of the artist)

4.122 Richard Crozier, *Pantops Mountain, Late Afternoon*, 1999, oil on canvas, 28 x 48 in. (Courtesy of Tatistcheff and Company, Inc.)

4.123 Jack Beal, *Pulp Mill on the York River at West Point*, 1975, pastel, 48 x 52 in. (Courtesy of George Adams Gallery)

is particularly attuned to the clean, clear light that can still be found in America and which she records, in plein air, with such a gentle, assured hand that the freshness of nature is routinely suggested in her imagery. She says that she enjoys Virginia because there is so much beautiful scenery there, as well as a relatively warm climate and a strong support group of compatible landscapists. Her view of Roanoke from the mountain that carries the city's renowned star (fig. 4.121) is a record of how the scenery of that area has been changed at the end of the millennium. The land is cluttered with too many ordered buildings amidst too few fields, so that man's harmony with nature is out of balance. A century ago only the small village of Big Lick was visible nearby; the railroad that James Wells Champney pictured in the early 1870s transformed the landscape in a way that he could never have imagined. Portnow says that as she worked on this view she recognized how the rhythms in nature are now at odds with those formed by man.[170] But like most of the landscapists in Virginia, she finds and celebrates the beauty that remains.

Richard Crozier, another Charlottesville artist who teaches at the University of Virginia, has stated, "There is no truly virgin landscape to be found; the nineteenth-century concept of wilderness is neither interesting nor valid today. There is always a human presence . . . that must be dealt with."[171] The major theme of his art has been our necessary interrelatedness with nature and our lack of regard for it.[172] His views are handsomely rendered. Some show settings in the Piedmont that are cut by modern highways (fig. 4.122), clear evidence of the changed and endangered status of the Virginia landscape.

Perhaps the first artist to point to an environmental crisis in Virginia, and the one to state it in the strongest of terms, was Jack Beal, a New York painter of national prominence and a Richmond native. At the time of the American bicentennial, he was commissioned to produce six large pastels for the Corcoran Gallery's exhibition *America '76.* "Surface Coal Mining at Norton" shows the

4.124 Stephen Fox, *Meeting Ground*, 1992, oil on linen, 30 x 33 in. (Collection of CSX Corporation, Richmond, Virginia, courtesy of Reynolds Gallery)

4.125 Jan Knipe, *View of Pulaski, Virginia*, 1995, conte, 18 x 20 in. (Courtesy of the artist)

landscape as it is obliterated by heavy machinery. His view of a "Pulp Mill on the York River at West Point" (fig. 4.123) is a similar vision of a dark inferno, the actual destination for Latané's cleared pine trees.

Nearly as bleak and nightmarish is Stephen Fox's view of urban Richmond in the 1980s and early 1990s (fig. 4.124). Fox was trained in the Virginia Commonwealth University graduate art program at a time when emphasis was given to the photorealist technique. He shows the capital city, once a landscape of promise, as a place without

4.126 Lewis Miller, *The River Mountains, Lewis and Charles Miller, on Horseback*, 1856, watercolor and ink, 8⅛ x 6¾ in. (Virginia Historical Society)

4.127 Stephen Fox, *Point of Departure*, 1992, oil on panel,
14 ½ x 15 in. (Courtesy of Joan Elliott)

natural light or natural terrain, a desolate and uninviting setting that like the surface-mined landscape at Norton is past the stage of endangerment. This impersonal world might seem imaginary were it not so carefully recorded and were not the buildings and bridges such ominous and memorable forms. Jan Knipe, who lives in Radford and

teaches at Hollins College, has made less threatening but equally blatant statements about the desecration of Virginia's urban landscape. Her view of Pulaski is a scene of excessive telephone and power lines that clutter the vista (fig. 4.125).

Until recent times, those landscapes that showed roads and scenes of transportation were uplifting views that carried messages about progress and the enjoyment of nature. For example, Lewis Miller's 1856 depiction of riders (one is the artist) twelve miles from Christiansburg is a celebration of the beauty of the landscape of southwest Virginia (fig. 4.126). By the 1990s, however, travel had taken on a different and disturbing nature. Stephen Fox presents the runways of an airport as a surreal setting (fig. 4.127); the disquieting mood of his scene appropriately signals the loss of acres of farmland beneath asphalt and eerie lights veiled in mist. In a similar way, John Randall Younger, an artist resident in the Piedmont, shows a modern highway that traverses a landscape that is green under warm sunlight yet somehow a disturbing scene (fig. 4.128). Like the airport runways, Younger's highway seems to lead to nowhere, or at least the sense of adventure and opportunity that is routinely suggested in the older views is

4.128 John Randall Younger, *The Bridge*, 1994, egg-oil emulsion on board,
39 ¾ x 66 ¾ in. (Courtesy of Reynolds Gallery)

4.129 Tom Jones, *Epps Island*, 1998, oil on canvas, 33 x 60 ½ in.
(Courtesy of Sherry French Gallery)

gone. Younger's farmland is not yet lost to development or ecological unbalance; in fact this remains as idyllic a setting as one might imagine. The artist skillfully replicates the spectacular beauty of undisturbed nature. The result is that we are made to recognize the high stakes at risk. Perhaps for that reason we look at his landscapes with considerable trepidation. They may disappear, as highways move housing projects and shopping malls farther into the countryside, making the fertile soil toxic, repeating a scenario that has unfolded too many times since 1950.

There is the same uneasiness with the present and the future in Tom Jones's equally striking and beautiful view, painted in 1998, of Epps Island off the James River, near where the artist lives (fig. 4.129). This landscape is unchanged since the colonial era of the Eppses and the neighboring Carters of Shirley Plantation, Byrds of Westover, and Harrisons of Berkeley. (Epps Island is now a part of the Shirley estate.) But enough of the landscape of Charles City County has changed in modern times, from its use as dumping site for medical waste to the selling of its undersoil to land developers, that we have to wonder whether this setting will disappear in the early years of the new millennium. Is the present the last era when man will be able to enjoy this unspoiled environment? There is an

incredible stillness to Jones's scene that seems to underscore its fragility. Epps Island appears as if it is a magical land that we must preserve, like Venice or a national park, to borrow a comparison made by Robert Rosenblum.[173]

Rosenblum wrote in 1993 about a group of young romantic landscape painters who respond to the environmental crisis in unexpected ways. Because they know that the landscape is being destroyed and poisoned, they give their imagery a frail, deathbed poignancy and nostalgia. They depict it in stillness and desolation, as imagined rather than perceived. Some of the artists transport us to the ends of the earth, to the brink of nothingness. To Rosenblum they are like explorers of a lost world who examine it in a curiously retrospective way, as if from a vantage point distant in both time and space.

One artist whose work is so striking that it was singled out by Rosenblum is former Richmonder Ephraim Rubenstein, who has painted a number of views of the Virginia landscape in which cemeteries and abandoned farmhouses intrude upon the natural landscape. Even more poignant, and what attracted Rosenblum, are his veiled landscapes that were inspired by the writings of the early twentieth-century poet Rainer Maria Rilke (fig. 4.130). These views are so deftly painted that they transform into

4.130 Ephraim Rubenstein, *Be Ahead of All Parting II*, 1992–93, oil on linen, 22 x 46 in. (Courtesy of the artist)

art a commonplace setting, a stretch along the James River near the Huguenot Bridge in Richmond that Rubenstein recognized as scenery that Corot might have sketched. Two of the paintings in the artist's Rilke series take their title from a verse by the poet about the sadness of separation and the corresponding mood that can be found in nature:

> Be ahead of all parting, as though it already were behind you, like the winter that has just gone by. For among these winters there is one so endlessly winter that only by wintering through it will your heart survive.[174]

To Rubenstein the setting on the James called to mind the tenor of Rilke's verse; for that reason he painted the series. To Rosenblum a celebration of stillness and frailness is telling; he points out that a hundred years earlier an American artist would have painted instead a vision of almost supernatural sunlight. Rosenblum sees the melancholy in images like this one as evidence of our anxieties today in the face of nature.[175]

Rubenstein has cited the poet Rilke's statement that man struggles to find his place within nature and that "even for what is most delicate and inapprehensible within us, nature has sensuous equivalents that must be discoverable."[176] An artist

who has found a place in nature close to the one assumed by Rubenstein in the Rilke paintings is Richmonder Joan Elliott, who says that she, too, uses landscape imagery as a metaphor for her personal feelings (fig. 4.131).[177] These feelings remain mysterious; her titles provide only clues. ("Selah" is a Hebrew word of unknown meaning often used

4.131 Joan Elliott, *Selah*, 1989, oil on canvas, 40 x 43 in. (Courtesy of Ted and Meme Bullard)

in the Psalms to signal a pause.) Some of Elliott's canvases, in their emphasis on mood, the technique of thick paint buildup, and the long time required to produce them, recall the highly personal and visionary art of the earlier American artists Albert Pinkham Ryder and Ralph Blakelock. Those artists depicted mysterious but serene settings; Elliott instead pictures landscapes that embody tension. These paintings have been described as "enigmatic and vaguely unsettling"; adjectives like mysterious, eerie, tense, and spectral come to mind in describing them.[178] They stand apart, as signs of a changed attitude, because few landscapists of the nineteenth century or of any other era ever chose as their subject a writhing thicket of vegetation.

Although she is not in the group that was assembled by Rosenblum, one artist who has worked in a parallel direction for years is the established New York landscapist Susan Shatter. She literally travels to the ends of the earth to find stark, silent landscapes that by their geological structure inspire awe. Shatter says that "trying to paint moving water, changing light, and millions of years of geological time puts me in some accord with the mystery that informs all things."[179] She prefers to view the landscape from afar and from above, in order to show a vast space up close. Shatter's travels have included visits to southwest Virginia, which has been the subject of some of her smaller scale work (fig. 4.132). She describes the landscape differently than do most of the resident Virginians: "To me, the rawness, expansiveness and luminosity of nature have an indifferent grandeur which reminds us that we have no sure footing on this earth." When she states that "the natural world can be a capricious, menacing and untamable place," she introduces an entirely new landscape mythology that was inspired by the different conditions of the postmodern era. She may as well be saying that if the fragile landscape of flowers and fields is endangered by man, then she will turn to nature's mightier forces that are impervious to the hand of mortals. In this way she is assured that her subject matter will survive as long as the planet does.

Just as nature is cyclical, so is man's response to it. For that reason it should not be too surprising that a new Hudson River School of landscapists is active today in New York City and upstate New York, that scores of artists across the nation are now actively at work in traditional landscape modes, and that much of the landscape art that

4.132 Susan Shatter, *Travertine Falls, Ironto Barrens,* 1979, watercolor, 22 x 15 in. (Courtesy of the artist)

was painted in Virginia at the end of the twentieth century was conceived with the same approach to nature that guided poets and painters of the early romantic movement in America and England.[180] Some of the new Virginia paintings even bear a resemblance to the old ones. To understand the new worship of nature in Virginia and to measure its success, we can start by returning to the era of Wordsworth and Constable in England.

In his film series and book *Civilisation,* the cultural historian Kenneth Clark explains that in the early eighteenth century the status of Christianity weakened for the first time in a thousand years, leaving an intellectual vacuum that was filled by a belief, perhaps irrational, in the divinity of nature. He discusses how this new philosophy about the landscape was developed in England during the ensuing hundred years. Both the poet William Wordsworth and the painter John Constable concluded that if they would study with devotion the very elements of nature—from the simple flower to the tall mountain—they would discover in each of them a quality of the divine, and they would learn to recognize moral and spiritual lessons in nature. Clark used the term "Worship of Nature" to describe this approach.[181]

In the preface to his *Lyrical Ballads*, William Wordsworth explained that he studied nature because only in a rustic environment do "our elementary feelings co-exist in a state of greater simplicity, and consequently may be more accurately contemplated and more forcibly communicated" and that in the landscape "the passions of man are incorporated with the beautiful and permanent forms of nature." He put his philosophy succinctly into verse:

4.133 Sharon Yates, ***Roland Cliffs***, 1970, oil on canvas, 12 x 16 in. (Courtesy of Mr. and Mrs. Edgar L. McIntire III)

> One impulse from a vernal wood
> May teach you more of man,
> Of moral evil and of good,
> Than all the sages can.[182]

American poets and painters soon adapted at least the core of this philosophy to the landscape along the Hudson River, as we have seen. Now, close to two centuries later, this fundamental approach to nature has been revived throughout America. No evidence emerges from the landscapes that were painted in Virginia in the late twentieth century to suggest that people actually believe again that the woods can teach us moral lessons, but we have come much closer to that point than at any time in many decades. The current generation of nature writers and painters in Virginia seems to be saying that we best immerse ourselves in the landscape in order to find out just what it is that we can learn there.

The new return to nature in Virginia is anchored by an intense scrutiny of the environment, in the manner of Wordsworth, Constable, and Henry David Thoreau. The most recognized of these late-twentieth-century observers is Annie Dillard, whose writings about nature in the Roanoke Valley earned her a Pulitzer Prize, awarded in 1974 for *Pilgrim at Tinker Creek*. She describes this book as similar to what Thoreau called a "meteorological journal of the mind"; like her predecessor in the woods at Walden Pond she is a pilgrim in the Virginia landscape. Dillard is able to take careful note of the worlds of zoological and botanical life that earlier in the twentieth century were routinely overlooked by all but the naturalists and then ponder them, often in a metaphysical context. In *Pilgrim* she writes,

> I live by a creek, Tinker Creek, in a valley in Virginia's Blue Ridge. . . . It's a good place to live; there's a lot to think about. The creeks—Tinker and Carvin's—are an active mystery, fresh every minute. Theirs is the mystery of the continuous creation and all that providence implies: the uncertainty of vision, the horror of the fixed, the dissolution of the present, the intricacy of beauty, the pressure of fecundity, the elusiveness of the free, and the flawed nature of perfection.

Few easy answers are to be found, but there remains the need to observe and ask questions:

> We don't know what's going on here. . . . Our life is a faint tracing on the surface of mystery, like the idle, curved tunnels of leaf runners on the face of a leaf. We must somehow take a wider view, look at the whole landscape, really see it, and describe what's going on here. Then we can at least wail the right question into the swaddling band of darkness, or, if it comes to that, choir the proper praise.

The observation can only continue: "I am no scientist, I explore the neighborhood. . . . view the landscape to discover at least *where* it is that we have been so startlingly set down, if we can't learn why. So I think about the valley."[183]

Dillard's observations about zoology, such as her comments about her old tomcat or the frog that was crumpled by a giant water bug, create such memorable images that her attention to the larger landscape elements might be forgotten. But she carefully describes as well, for example, the fleeting conditions of wind and light:

> The wind is terrific out of the west; the sun comes and goes. I can see the shadow on the field before me deepen uniformly and spread like a plague. Everything seems so dull I am amazed I can even distinguish objects. And suddenly the light runs across the land like a comber, and up the trees, and goes again in a wink: I think I've gone blind or died. When it comes again, the light, you hold your breath, and if it stays you forget about it until it goes again.[184]

Dillard's immersion at Tinker Creek was matched in the same decade of the 1970s by the similar experience of a landscape painter, Sharon Yates, at the Fauquier County estate Roland, which is owned by a land conservatory, the America the Beautiful Fund. A grant from that organization allowed Yates to spend a summer in residence. Although her paintings stand by themselves as records of her observations of nature (fig. 4.133), the artist saw fit to keep a written journal as well; in this respect she is like Thoreau and Dillard. The entries complement her canvases and measure her efforts to become a part of nature in order to understand it:

> July 13th: Is the color of the water in that pond a non-color . . . something electric? A silent hazy blue-green gray—like a swamp—but it is not dirty. It glistens with ripples at times and I get dizzy with the optical effect. The reflection in the early morning is crystal clear with the absence of wind and the presence of a friendly rising sun. . . . The water is another sky. Some days the water and sky color are almost identical—it is that small fraction which I select for all the difference.

July 22nd: A silence is necessary so I can begin to be familiar to another world of sounds. The frogs in the Pond, the insects, the wind. Every whisper of noise in the grass would cause me to turn—I never thought I could be so sensitive to what was happening behind me as I am now while I paint. I become aware then how I belong to this earth—this tree—that sunrise.[185]

Other painters in Virginia in these years also managed to locate pockets of wilderness and unchanged farmland where they could immerse themselves and worship nature. We have already seen in Chapter Two examples by western artists Victor Huggins, Robert Stuart, Janet Niewald, William White, Maryann Harman, and Ray Kass, as well as canvases by two central Virginia painters, Isabel Bigelow and James Bradford, and the Virginia native Joellyn

4.134 Ron Boehmer, ***Sunlit Boulder, Piney River***, 1995, oil on canvas, 22 x 26 in. (Courtesy of the artist)

4.135 David Johnson, ***James River***, c. 1860, oil on canvas, 7 1/2 x 12 1/4 in. (Courtesy of the Executive Mansion, Commonwealth of Virginia)

Duesberry. Although these artists have painted in a variety of styles, they all have carried to the landscape a traditional reverence for it. So has Ron Boehmer, a Lynchburg painter. He found in the neighboring countryside geological and pastoral qualities that he felt warrant scrutiny; this is the same scenery that interested his nineteenth-century predecessors in Virginia. His view of a boulder along the Piney River (fig. 4.134) recalls the landscapes produced a century earlier by David Johnson when he traveled to Virginia to paint the Natural Bridge. In one canvas by Johnson that shows the James River (fig. 4.135), the artist focused attention on a single boulder, as if to acknowledge both its beauty and its importance to the history of the earth. Boehmer's views of pastures and cornfields record farm landscapes at harvest time, the season that Russell Smith celebrated in 1848 when he pictured "Callahan's Meadow" (fig. 4.136). Other scenes by Boehmer show cattle grazing (fig. 4.137). His images serve to suggest that the agrarian way of life that ties man close to the land and supports and rewards him should be

perpetuated into the next century because it is natural.

In these same years Frank Levering and Wanda Urbanska championed the agrarian experience much as Boehmer did. They even moved into the rural landscape. They live at Orchard Gap in the Blue Ridge Mountains and farm on a small scale. In *Simple Living: One Couple's Search for a Better Life* (1992), they reveal how nature nurtured them as much as they nurtured their crops:

4.136 Russell Smith, ***Callahan's Meadow, Virginia***, 1848, oil on canvas, 13 x 19 ½ in. (Courtesy of the Executive Mansion, Commonwealth of Virginia)

4.137 Ron Boehmer, ***Farm Lane, Marshall's Grove***, 1998, oil on paper, 15 x 22 in. (Courtesy of the artist)

4.138 Durwood Dommisse, ***Dungeness Farm Pond***, 1990, oil on canvas, 30 x 40 in. (Courtesy of Dan and Marcia Rubin)

August is the high season for vegetables. At noon the next day we peer into the haze from the front porch and thank God (and the Indians) for corn. It's not just the taste. . . . It's the beauty of corn rows a hundred feet from the kitchen stove, eight or nine feet high, leaves glistening, trapping a pool of dense emerald light in their shade. July thunderstorms made them tall.[186]

Durwood Dommisse, Raymond Berry, and Maruta Racenis are central Virginia artists who also have studied the rural landscape with reverence. They have defined the beauty of open, expansive settings in paintings that recall the earlier canvases of the English countryside by John Constable; their approach to nature even duplicates his philosophy (figs. 4.138, 4.139, and 4.140). Just as Constable said that his art could be found under every hedge and that he never saw an ugly thing in his life, these artists appreciate the unspectacular in nature.[187] They have looked long at the sky and clouds in order to understand the light and atmosphere that envelop a landscape and give it much of its feeling, which is what Constable did. He called the sky the "chief organ of sentiment" and referred to "the chiaroscuro of nature," meaning the play of light; he quipped that the best lesson on art is to remember that light and shade never stand still.[188] Dommisse says much the same: "It's the totality of the outdoor experience that informs the painting.

4.139 Raymond Berry, ***Pond at Curles Neck***, 1999, oil on canvas, 17³⁄₄ x 28 in. (Courtesy of the artist)

4.140 Maruta Racenis, ***Fire***, 1998, oil on canvas, 6 x 8 in. (Courtesy of the artist)

4.141 David Freed, *The River—One Year*, 1990, printed intaglio and relief, 30 x 60 in. (Collection of Westminster Canterbury, Richmond, Virginia, courtesy of Reynolds Gallery)

The landscape is changing continually before your eyes."[189] So does Berry, who talks about accumulated vision, and Racenis, who identifies interpretation and memory as important components of her procedure.[190] Constable would understand them. These artists have rediscovered the English painter's philosophy not by studying his art, however, which none of them has done in any systematic manner, but instead by studying nature itself. Their experiences in the field simply have repeated those of Constable.

Berry suggests that working at a setting like Curles Neck, where the land is flat and the light and sky seem almost like that of the Old World, an artist ends up with a Constable-like scene whether or not he wants it.[191] This is true if the painter is sufficiently confident that the land will survive. Tom Jones, it will be remembered, paints the same region in an entirely different way (see above, fig. 4.129). More important than the site is the vision of the artist. Like Yates and Boehmer, Dommisse, Berry, and Racenis have given new legitimacy to the approach that was championed so long ago by Wordsworth. They have demonstrated that it is still possible today to record the simplest scenery with freshness instead of banality.

For Annie Dillard water is the element of the land-scape that is a key to understanding nature: "the creeks are the world with all its stimulus and beauty; I live there. . . . If the day is fine, any walk will do; it all looks good. . . . But I go to the water." Like Dillard, printmaker David Freed also returns repeatedly to the water and observes the ways that a water landscape changes and the ways that it remains the same. His setting is an urban one, the James River in Richmond, a twenty-minute walk from his studio. The titles of the six prints that constitute his series "The River—One Year" (fig. 4.141) explain that he has studied the same landscape in rain and sunlight, under clouds, and in the summer and fall in an effort to understand its many moods. He talks about the role of memory ("visual, touch, smell and sound") as being the reference from which he develops his imagery.[192]

It is only in recent years that the James River as it passes through Richmond has been rediscovered. In the 1960s it "might as well have been the Chattahoochee" to Elizabeth Seydel Morgan, who has written an essay on the subject, so little did she notice it. The purity of the river was restored by the Clean Water Act of 1969; the James "is one of the great examples of the successes" of that legislation, writes Morgan. But in the 1970s the city warned people away out of fear for their safety, particularly where the rapids are dangerous, and out of lethargy to rethink old ideas. Others ("hundreds of dedicated people and scores of organizations") changed Morgan's perception "from indifference to love of the great natural resource in my city." Like Freed she feels compelled to return to this river to unlock its mysteries. In 1999 she wondered, "What secrets is it hiding? Where did it come from? How will it change? What next?"[193]

Frederick Nichols, who works in the Piedmont, has studied the rivers there with the same intensity expended by Freed and Morgan (fig. 4.142). Handling a traditional medium in a new way, Nichols reduces the elements of vision in the way that a camera does, so that a remarkable degree of detail is presented, somewhat out of focus, akin to what the eye sees. His goal is to evoke mood and moment, to bring the viewer closer to nature and make him more conscious of the type of wooded, sunlit landscapes that are survivors of the American wilderness. The next step for the viewer is to study the elements of such landscapes even more carefully, as a naturalist would; to look, for instance, at the surface in one of Nichols's streams with the intensity of a fisherman searching for the evidence of trout. Christopher Camuto, in *A Fly Fisherman's Blue Ridge* (1990), explains that concentration on the most minute elements of the landscape yields a higher understanding of nature:

> Each boil and pillow and funnel of moving water is a sign worth noting. Possibilities circle slowly in each eddy. Had I not spent time trying to think through the signs on the water's surface to the remote whereabouts of winter trout, I would never have learned what the river looks like.[194]

The purpose of the paintings of Freed and Nichols, and the prose of Morgan and Camuto, is to start in us the process of learning "what the river looks like."

The forest is a subject that has attracted Stephen Fisher, a product of the Virginia Commonwealth University graduate art program. He sees this landscape in the same primeval way in which Thomas Cole worshiped wilderness scenery and David Johnson admired its details. Fisher finds the forest powerful, beautiful, and a little mysterious; he utilizes its massive rocks and trees to create compositions that suggest its majesty (fig. 4.143). This strongly constructed and evocative imagery functions effectively both as art and to direct our attention to mountain scenery. As to the latter, Fisher follows in the tradition of an earlier generation of naturalists who celebrated that landscape and whose

4.142 Frederick Nichols, ***Reflections, Liberty Hill***, 1999, oil on linen, 40 x 60 in. (Courtesy of the artist)

4.143 Stephen Fisher, ***Morning Passage***, 1991, etching, 20 x 29½ in. (Collection of the artist, courtesy of Reynolds Gallery)

4.144 William Sullivan, *Aerial View of Orange County*, 1989, oil on canvas, 30 x 50 in. (Courtesy of the artist)

descriptions of the plant and animal life there also inspire us to reconsider it. For example, Donald Culross Peattie, in *The Great Smokies and the Blue Ridge* (1943), explains that the botany of these forests is extraordinary:

> Some forty-five species of trees—as many as are found in all of Great Britain—crowd into this luxuriant formation. There are at least as many shrubs and woody vines as trees, and ten times as many herbaceous plants. Probably a thousand species could be called typical members of the Appalachian forests proper.

Peattie, like Fisher, is sensitive to the changing seasonal appearance of this landscape:

> In early spring they [the hardwoods] are still naked, or tenderly budded out, for some weeks after genial weather has returned. So at the very season when sunlight is most needed, the hardwoods, no matter how tall and dense their canopy, admit light and warmth.[195]

The views from mountains also have been rediscovered in recent times. In his "Aerial View of Orange County"

(fig. 4.144), William Sullivan presents the panorama of a distant, settled landscape. This is essentially what Edward Beyer did in 1855 with his depiction of "The Peaks of Otter and the Town of Liberty" (see above, fig. 3.43), where the artist climbed up a hillside in order to depict an idyllic scene of rural settlement in the same landscape of the Piedmont. The key ingredient that makes this type of scene so appealing is the evidence, in the ordered buildings and tilled fields, of man's harmonious union with nature.[196] Sullivan has moved his observation point farther back, which he was able to do easily because he had access to an airplane. In Beyer's era people climbed to the tops of mountains in order to enjoy so distant a prospect. An account of such an experience by Henry Ruffner, the president of Washington College, at House Mountain in 1839, could be applied to Sullivan's image, so close are the two:

> The country appeared beneath and around me to the utmost extent of vision. On the diversified surface of the Great Valley, a thousand farms in every variety of situation were distinctly visible. . . . Stretching along the eastern horizon for many a league, the Blue Ridge mustered a hundred of his lofty heads, . . . When I

was able to withdraw my sight from the grand features of the prospect and to look down upon the country near the base of my observatory, I was attracted by the softer beauties of the landscape. The woody hillocks and shady glens had lost every rough and disagreeable feature; the surface looked smooth and green like a meadow and wound its curvatures, dappled with shade and sunlight, so gracefully to the elevated eye that they seemed to realize our dreamy conceptions of fairy land. The little homesteads that spotted the hills and valleys . . . relieved the mind from the almost painful sublimity of the distant prospect and prepared us, after hours of delightful contemplation, to descend from our aerial height and to return with gratified feelings to our college and our studies again.[197]

Today, in urban areas like Roanoke, this stimulating and restorative experience is no longer possible, or at least it is now compromised, as Marjorie Portnow proved with her view from Mill Mountain (above, fig. 4.121). Sullivan painted many Virginia scenes before he moved in the late 1990s from Orange County to North Carolina and then to California, in search of new landscapes. In recent years he has revived the style and material of the Hudson River School giant Frederic Church, even traveling to some of the South American sites that Church painted in the 1850s and 1860s.[198]

Marjorie Portnow is one of a number of nonresident artists who in recent years have visited Virginia, repeating a cycle that began more than two hundred years earlier when travelers like Capt. Thomas Davies and Benjamin Henry Latrobe sketched a much less settled landscape. Throughout the nineteenth century the views painted in the state were often by the hands of visitors, as we have seen. That tradition barely survived earlier in the twentieth century, when only the occasional patron brought a major artist to the state, like John D. Rockefeller, Jr., and Charles Sheeler or Joseph James Ryan and Rockwell Kent. It was revived later in a different way, when prominent out-of-state artists were invited by administrators like William White at Hollins College and Ray Kass at Virginia Tech to serve as visiting artists. In that way Portnow taught at both schools, Jack Beal taught at Hollins, and a series of artists participated in workshops and residencies sponsored by Virginia Tech at the nearby resort complex of Mountain Lake, beginning in 1981. One was Susan Shatter. Another was Wayne Thiebaud.

Thiebaud has been recognized as one of the major

4.145 Wayne Thiebaud, *Virginia Landscape*, 1981, oil on canvas, 12 x 16 in. (Courtesy of Matthew L. Bult)

4.146 John Cage, *New River Watercolor, Series II, # 11*, 1988, watercolor, 26 x 72 in. (Courtesy of Ray Kass and the Mountain Lake Workshop)

West Coast realists since the 1960s, when his lively canvases of cakes and pastries carried the still life tradition into the domain of Pop Art. He is both an important American landscapist who works in the open air and one of the great teachers of the late twentieth century. He visited Mountain Lake in 1981, thereby helping to establish the program. In residence he painted a landscape from the balcony of the hotel (fig. 4.145). Thiebaud's light and bright views of San Francisco and of the floodplain of the Sacramento River Delta start with visual fact and then turn reality into art, by tilting and balancing lines and shapes to give them abstract energy; the scenes are further invigorated by the bright, pure hues of a California palette. Thiebaud's adaptation of his very personal style to the green mountain scenery of Virginia could only be a solid demonstration of the modern and now seemingly timeless landscape tradition that originated a century ago with the Impressionists' concern about color and light. His painting also shows how to look anew at an old subject.

Just as nationally prominent as Thiebaud and also a visitor to the Mountain Lake workshops was John Cage, who was there in 1983 and again at the end of the decade. Cage is renowned for his career as a composer and for providing perhaps the greatest single influence on 1960s Pop Art, by encouraging experimentation in all the arts as a way to lessen the gap between art and life. In the early 1950s Cage introduced the element of chance to the process of composing music. In 1983 he applied the same principle to drawings that he made at a Zen-style dry-landscape rock garden in Kyoto, Japan. Later that year at Mountain Lake,

and during later visits in 1988–90, Cage repeated the same procedure with rocks from the New River. His imagery was simple, made by tracing on paper the outlines of the actual stones (fig. 4.146). A computer program determined what stones, brushes, colors, and papers would be used, as well as where the rocks would be placed on the paper. All of this ritual was inspired by the Zen-Buddhist idea that the ego is a barrier to understanding the natural world; the purpose was to move beyond self-expression and preconceived notions in order to see and experience nature in new ways. Cage had not set out to imitate the appearance of nature; he was interested instead in understanding nature's manner of

4.147 Jacob Kass, *Ellett Valley Sawmill*, 1981, acrylic on metal, 25 in. diameter. (Courtesy of Ray Kass)

operation. He could argue that the resultant images are composed with the same sense of randomness that governs nature, as seen, for example, in the placement of wildflowers in a field or trees in a forest.[199] During the era when abstraction dominated painting, Cage made his famous statement: "I have nothing to say and I'm saying it." Immersed in the Virginia landscape three decades later, he was ready to look for something to say. In that respect he was like the other landscapists in the state at the end of the twentieth century; nearly all of them worshiped nature in search of meanings, perhaps elusive, that they believed could be found there.

In the years that luminaries visited Mountain Lake, Ray Kass also lured to Virginia his father, Jacob Kass, a retired Brooklyn sign painter who at age sixty-five took up art, in the way that Grandma Moses did late in her life. Between 1977 and 1993 the elder Kass painted rural and urban scenes of the landscape on some 250 saws and other hand tools. He pictured settings of an earlier and simpler time, when he was young. The older Kass is now a nationally recognized folk artist with works exhibited at established museums. His 1981 view of the "Ellett Valley Sawmill" near Blacksburg (fig. 4.147), appropriately painted on a saw, is an Arcadian vision that matches Earl Hamner's memory of life in Virginia in the 1930s. Kass's paintings appeal to a wide spectrum; they are collected by such notables as Federal Reserve Chairman Alan Greenspan and actor Henry Winkler, evidence of a renewed interest in folk painting and that yet another cycle of art is in motion.

EPILOGUE

Peirce F. Lewis, in "Axioms for Reading the Landscape," has observed that "Our human landscape is our unwitting autobiography."[200] This is not true of landscape art. If a stranger were to study only the painted Virginia landscape, he would obtain a highly incomplete and inaccurate idea about everyday life in the region. When, for much of the past several centuries, most Virginians lived on farms, hardly anyone painted or drew ordinary farms. Some painted large plantations, often as Arcadia, but Arcadia with slaves was a lie. When increasing numbers of Virginians moved into cities, few artists portrayed cities. After World War II, the American dream became a quarter-acre plot in the suburbs with a house on it, but images of suburbs are rare although most Americans now live there. Landscape art has been a testament to an enduring love of the land, but not a document of life on it.

What landscape art does record, as cultural historian Kenneth Clark has explained, are the stages in our conception of nature. What have these stages been in Virginia? First, that nature had utility. Then, that it had intrinsic beauty and contributed to identity and reputation. Later, that man's arrangements could triumph over nature. Today, there is a new appreciation of nature, a rediscovery of its beauty and spiritual value.

One of the enduring appeals of nature's seasons and cycles is that they are metaphors for the passage of time in the lives of human beings and their institutions, nations, and even civilizations. At Battle Abbey, headquarters of the Virginia Historical Society, there is a famous mural cycle in which the rise and fall of the Confederacy is told through the artistic conceit of the seasons of the year. Landscape art in Virginia also has had its seasons. First, there was a long winter in which there was no landscape art. There followed a springtime burst of romantic appreciation of nature for its own sake. Because of the overwhelming strength of evangelical Christianity here, this worship of nature never substituted for organized religion, but it fostered a contemplation of beauty as a key to understanding both the human and the divine. Unlike the Old World, where the landscape was encumbered by history, mythology, and feudal inheritances, the New World environment seemed a blank slate on which a story of expansion, progress, and change might be written. The summer of our landscape art was one of feasting on this land, not only visually, but also physically and spiritually, when the land renewed its inhabitants following the Civil War. Now it is autumn. We have qualms about our stewardship of the land as we are "loving it to death," in words Professor James Tice Moore uses to describe our modern relationship to Chesapeake Bay.[201] We have reservations about our dominion of the earth and a growing acceptance with humility of our status as inhabitants, not conquerors, of this planet. We wonder if a long winter of environmental catastrophe awaits us, but we hope instead for a long Indian summer of harmony with and reverence for the natural world.

In the second half of the twentieth century, Virginia finally developed a school of landscape art. Much of the reason for this, as with everything, is economic. Finally Virginia became sufficiently urban and affluent to support such artists through employment in the college system and through the beginnings of significant patronage. The irony is that it comes at a time when the people of Virginia are less connected to the land than ever before. But there may be a causal relationship there, too. The "New Dominion" is a leader in the Information Age, an electronic world in which place is unimportant. Yet, even as we advance with hope into that brave new world, we feel a need for landscape art to help keep us spiritually rooted in the land, something our computers do not require, but our souls do.

NOTES

Abbreviations

VMHB   *Virginia Magazine of History and Biography*
WMQ   *William and Mary Quarterly*

Chapter I

1. Simon Schama, *Landscape and Memory* (New York, 1995), 61. See also Chris Fitter, *Poetry, Space, Landscape* (Cambridge, England, 1995), 8–9; Donald Meinig, "Foreword," in Michael Conzen, ed., *The Making of the American Landscape* (Boston, 1990), xv; J. B. Jackson, "Several American Landscapes," in Erwin H. Zube, ed., *Landscapes: Selected Writings of J. B. Jackson* (Amherst, Mass., 1970), 43; Kenneth H. Craik, "Psychological Reflections on Landscape," in Edmund C. Penning-Rowsell and David Lowenthal, *Landscape Meanings and Values* (London, 1986), 54. We are obliged to Professor Stephen Adams, University of Minnesota, for drawing our attention to these texts.

2. R. B. Beckett, *John Constable's Discourses* (Suffolk Records Soc., 1970), 72. We are obliged to Professor Stephen Adams of the University of Minnesota for drawing our attention to this text.

3. Kenneth Clark, *Landscape into Art* (London, 1953), xvii.

4. The illustration was by Karel Skreta-Šotnovsky and engraved by Melchior Kusell for Mathia Tanner's *Societas Iesu usque ad Sanguina at Profusionem Vitae Militans* [A history of the Jesuits] (Prague, 1675).

5. Samuel Eliot Morison, *The European Discovery of America: The Northern Voyages, A.D. 500–1600* (New York, 1971), 624.

6. Mary Newton Stanard, *Colonial Virginia: Its People and Customs* (Philadelphia, 1917), 314–19.

7. Ibid.

8. Ibid., 13; Robert Dowsing inventory of 16 May 1731, Box 18, York County Wills and Inventories.

9. *Virginia Gazette*, 18 April 1751, 21 Oct. 1773, 14 April 1774.

10. Illustrated in Jessie Poesch, *The Art of the Old South: Painting, Sculpture, Architecture & the Products of Craftsmen, 1560–1860* (New York, 1983), 64.

11. The overmantel is installed at the Henry Francis duPont Winterthur Museum near Wilmington, Delaware.

12. Graham Hood, *Charles Bridges and William Dering: Two Virginia Painters, 1735–50* (Williamsburg, 1978), 108. On p. 105 is pictured the portrait of George Booth, which is owned by Colonial Williamsburg.

13. Massachusetts Historical Society, comp., *Witness to America's Past: Two Centuries of Collecting at the Massachusetts Historical Society* (Boston, 1991), 79.

14. William T. Oedel, *Philadelphia Portrait, 1682–1982* (Philadelphia, 1982), 16. The original is at the Library Company of Philadelphia.

15. Illustrated in Ella-Prince Knox et al., *Painting in the South: 1564–1980* (Richmond, Va., 1983), 2. The original is at the Newberry Library, Chicago.

16. Illustrated in Poesch, *Art of the Old South*, 37. The original is at the Archives Nationale, Section Outre-Mer, Paris.

17. Massachusetts Historical Society, *Witness to America's Past*, 79.

18. Museum of Fine Arts, Boston, *Paul Revere's Boston, 1735–1818* (Boston, 1975), illustrated 66, discussed 67.

19. Knox et al., *Painting in the South*, 178. The original watercolor is owned by Colonial Williamsburg.

20. Oedel, *Philadelphia Portrait, 1682–1982*, 16.

21. Philadelphia Museum of Art, *Philadelphia: Three Centuries of American Art* (Philadelphia, 1976), 56.

22. *Paul Revere's Boston, 1735–1818*, illustrated 30, discussed 31.

23. Poesch, *Art of the Old South*, 81.

24. Earl G. Swem, "Views of Yorktown and Gloucester Town, 1755," *VMHB* 54 (1946): 99–102.

25. Edward J. Nygren et al., *Views and Visions: American Landscape before 1830* (Washington, 1986), 87–91, 249–51.

26. "Observations in several voyages and travels in America in the year 1736," *London Magazine* (July 1746), quoted in Swem, "Views of Yorktown and Gloucester Town," 101.

27. Quoted in Nicholas Penny, ed., *Reynolds* (London, 1986), 30. Reynolds's *Discourses* were published in London in 1779.

28. David Hackett Fischer and James C. Kelly, *Away, I'm Bound Away: Virginia and the Westward Movement* (Richmond, Va., 1993), 65.

29. Clipping in Valentine Museum files.

30. Postcard "Published for J. S. De Neufville, Yorktown, Va. by C. R. Brown, Pearl River, N.Y." We are obliged to Professor Stephen Adams of the University of Minnesota for drawing our attention to this.

Chapter II

1. George B. Tatum, "Nature's Gardener," in Tatum and Elisabeth Blair MacDougall, eds., *Prophet with Honor: The Career of Andrew Jackson Downing, 1815–1852* (Washington, 1989), 57–58.

2. Edmund Burke, *A Philosophical Inquiry into the Origin of Our Ideas of the Sublime and Beautiful* (Philadelphia, 1806), 68–69, 131, 137; Tatum, "Nature's Gardener," 58.

3. This was A. J. Downing's explanation of the Beautiful in garden design; see Tatum, "Nature's Gardener," 46.

4. Kenneth Clark, *Civilisation, A Personal View* (New York and Evanston, Ill., 1969), 307–8.

5. C. P. Barbier, *William Gilpin: His Drawings, Teaching, and Theory of the Picturesque* (Oxford, 1963), 98–147; U. Price, *Essays on the Picturesque* (London, 1820), 10, both cited in Tatum, "Nature's Gardener," 59–60.

6. Kenneth Clark, *Landscape into Art* (New York, 1976), 109.

7. Tatum, "Nature's Gardener," 59, n. 19.

8. Clark, *Landscape into Art*, 128.

9. Thomas Jefferson, *Notes on the State of Virginia*, ed. William Peden (Chapel Hill, N.C., 1955), 24–25 and 263–64, n. 5.

10. Quoted in William Cullen Bryant, ed., *Picturesque America* (New York, 1872), 1: 82–88. Chastellux had access to Jefferson's *Notes* before they were published; see *Notes*, xv, n. 12.

11. Roberts to Jefferson, 26 Feb. 1808; quoted in Barbara C. Batson, "Virginia Landscapes by William Roberts," *Journal of Early Southern Decorative Arts* 10 (Nov. 1984): 35–49. Roberts gave Jefferson an aquatint of the bridge.

12. Constance D. Sherman, "A French Artist Portrays the Natural Bridge," *VMHB* 68 (1960): 164–70.

13. [James Kirke Paulding], *Letters from the South Written During an Excursion in the Summer of 1816* (New York, 1817), 2: 65–66.

14. Quoted in James W. Alexander, *The Life of Archibald Alexander, D.D.* (New York, 1854), cited in Michael P. Branch and Daniel J. Philippon, eds., *The Height of Our Mountains: Nature Writing from Virginia's Blue Ridge Mountains and Shenandoah Valley* (Baltimore and London, 1998), 169.

15. An account of 1886, signed E. L. B., reads, "As much as one is delighted with loveliness of the region, he is impressed with the peace and calm that pervade it. It is one of those spots of earth that seem made for rest" (*A Description of The Natural Bridge of Virginia and Its History* [Philadelphia, 1887], 57).

16. Edward A. Pollard, *The Virginia Tourist* (Philadelphia, 1870), 55.

17. Andrew Buni, ed., "Rambles among the Virginia Mountains: The Journal of Mary Jane Boggs, June 1851," *VMHB* 77 (1969): 98–99.

18. Burke, *The Sublime and the Beautiful*, 95–100.

19. [Paulding], *Letters from the South*, 2: 251.

20. *Notes on the State of Virginia*, 19–20.

21. Elizabeth Cometti and Valeria Gennaro-Lerda, eds., "The Presidential Tour of Count Carlo Vidua with Letters on Virginia," *VMHB* 77 (1969), 394.

22. William Gilmore Simms, *Southward Ho! A Spell of Sunshine* (New York, 1854), cited in Branch and Philippon, eds., *Height of Our Mountains*, 174–75.

23. Isaac Weld, *Travels Through the States of North America . . . During the Years 1795, 1796, and 1797* (3rd ed., London, 1800), 1: 242–45.

24. [Paulding], *Letters from the South*, 2: 252.

25. Ralph D. Gray, ed., "A Tour in Virginia in 1827: Letters from Henry P. Gilpin to his Father," *VMHB* 76 (1968): 449.

26. Quoted in Branch and Philippon, eds., *Height of Our Mountains*, 299.

27. Jefferson, *Notes on the State of Virginia*, 7.

28. Sherman, "A French Artist Portrays the Natural Bridge," 166–70.

29. Edward King, *The Great South* (Baton Rouge, La., 1972 repr. of 1875 ed. by W. Magruder Drake and Robert R. Jones), 564.

30. Pollard, *Virginia Tourist*, 66.

31. Buni, ed., "Journal of Mary Jane Boggs," 102.

32. [Samuel Mordecai], *Description of the Album of Virginia: or The Old Dominion, Illustrated* (Richmond, 1980 reprint of 1857 ed.), 14–15. For the *Album* Edward Beyer produced two lithographs with the title "View from the Peak of Otter" with the hope that multiple views might replicate the sensation experienced there; they failed to match the written accounts.

33. Quoted in Will Sarvos, "Turnpike Tourism in Western Virginia, 1830–1860," *Virginia Cavalcade* 48 (Winter 1999): 19.

34. A description that appeared in the *Southern Literary Messenger*, quoted in Ele Bowen, *Rambles in the Path of the Steam-Horse* (Philadelphia, 1855), 198–99.

35. *Virginia Illustrated*, quoted in Branch and Philippon, eds., *Height of Our Mountains*, 176–81.

36. Bryant, ed., *Picturesque America*, 1: 212–19.

37. *The Poetry of Travelling in the United States* (New York, 1838), quoted in Branch and Philippon, eds., *Height of Our Mountains*, 164.

38. [Mordecai], *Description of the Album of Virginia*, 12. The last sentence that is quoted here so effectively suggests the experience at Weyer's Cave that it was used repeatedly by any number of the travel writers; it did not originate with Mordecai but can be traced back at least to the 1855 publication by John Disturnell, *Springs, Water-Falls, Sea-Bathing Resorts, and Mountain Scenery in the United States and Canada* (New York, 1855), 135.

39. William Burke, M.D., *The Virginia Mineral Springs, with Remarks on Their Use* (Richmond, 1853), 18–23.

40. Amos H. Gottschall, *Travels From Ocean to Ocean* (Harrisburg, Pa., 1894), 167–68.

41. Burke, *The Sublime and The Beautiful*, 48.

42. Gardner may have composed this scene; he is known to have rearranged bodies on the battlefield for effect.

43. Charles Joseph Latrobe, *The Rambler in North America* (London, 1835), 37–39.

44. [Paulding], *Letters from the South*, 2: 42–44.

45. Godfrey T. Vigne, *Six Months in America* (London, 1832), 1.

46. [Mordecai], *Description of the Album of Virginia*, 5.

47. *Resorts and Resources of the Chesapeake & Ohio Railway* (Richmond, 1879), 10.

48. Joseph Martin, *A New and Comprehensive Gazetteer of Virginia, and the District of Columbia* (Charlottesville, Va., 1836), 425.

49. *Resorts and Resources of the Chesapeake & Ohio Railway*, 46.

50. Jefferson, *Notes on the State of Virginia*, 19.

51. [Mordecai], *Description of the Album of Virginia*, 7.

52. Quoted in Branch and Philippon, eds., *Height of Our Mountains*, 174.

53. *M. & M. Karolik Collection of American Watercolors and Drawings, 1800–75* (Boston, 1962), 1: 79–80.

54. *Diary of My Travels in America*, trans. Stephen Becker (New York, 1977), quoted in Branch and Philippon, eds., *Height of Our Mountains*, 132–33. Harpers Ferry failed to impress Louis Philippe because he had seen "a score of places in Switzerland where rushing waters have carved out infinitely more striking gaps"; "the scene did not strike me as very remarkable."

55. Latrobe, "Essay on Landscape," and Edward C. Carter II, John C. Van Horne, and Charles E. Brownell, eds., *Latrobe's View of America, 1795–1820: Selections from the Watercolors and Sketches* (New Haven, Conn., and London, 1985), 18, 20–21, 64.

56. Joshua Shaw, *Picturesque Views of American Scenery* (Philadelphia, 1820), introduction.

57. Bryant, ed., *Picturesque America*, 1: 73.

58. Pollard, *The Virginia Tourist*, 14.

59. Carter, Van Horne, and Brownell, eds., *Latrobe's View of America*, 18.

60. Quoted in Cora S. Dobson, "More Than Land or Sky," *Country Magazine* (Jan. 1982): 29.

61. Clark, *Landscape into Art*, 33, 49.

62. Ibid., 35.

63. Other artists in Virginia who have worked in a style like Grandma Moses include Eldridge Bagley (see *Richmond News-Leader*, 1 July 1982); Marie-Thérèse Favreau Doyon (see *Lexington News-Gazette*, 1 Dec. 1982); and Emma Serena Dillard "Queenie" Stovall (see obituary, *Richmond News-Leader*, 28 June 1980, and an article in the *Richmond Times-Dispatch*, 27 June 1982). Stovall took up painting in 1949, at age 61.

64. Dommisse, quoted in Roy Proctor, "Great Outdoors Steals Artist's Heart," *Richmond News-Leader*, 12 Sept. 1991, A-3.

65. Mary Lynn Bayliss, "Exhibitions of Talents; Adele Williams and the Richmond Art Scene," *Virginia Cavalcade* 41 (Spring 1992):

166–77 and 42 (Summer 1992): 36–46.

66. Niewald, letters to the authors.

67. White, statement to the authors.

68. Gorky's painting is illustrated in Ella-Prince Knox et al., *Painting in the South: 1564–1980* (Richmond, 1983), 312.

69. Greenberg, 1990, quoted in (Ulysses Gallery), *Maryann Harman* (New York, 1990), 2.

70. Noland's painting is illustrated in Knox et al., *Painting in the South*, 144.

71. Clark, *Landscape into Art*, 237.

72. Kass assembles the panels of his polyptychs in part by the same element of chance that he sees as governing the workings of nature, but the artist ends up with a structured and well-thought-out product. See pp. 192–3 for a discussion of the element of chance as used by John Cage.

73. Branch and Philippon, eds., *Height of Our Mountains*, 302–5.

74. Duesberry's study with the abstract painter Richard Diebenkorn more than a decade ago no doubt served to refine her abilities as a colorist.

Chapter III

1. W. S. B., "Southern Scenery," *Southern Literary Messenger* 33, no. 2 (Aug. 1861): 115.

2. The Reverend Andrew Burnaby, *Travels through the Middle Settlements in North-America* (London, 1775), 33–34.

3. "Letters from Lawrence Butler, of Westmoreland County, Virginia," *VMHB* 41 (1933): 32.

4. Charles Cramer, *Etwas Über Die Natür Wünder in Nord Amerika* (St. Petersburg, Russia, 1837).

5. Edward Pollard, *The Virginia Tourist* (Philadelphia, 1870), 18.

6. Isaac Weld, *Travels Through the States of North America . . . During the Years 1795, 1796, and 1797* (3rd ed., London, 1800), 1: 231.

7. Emory A. Allen, *A Jolly Trip, or, where we went and what we saw last summer* (Cincinnati, 1891), 67.

8. Pollard, *The Virginia Tourist*, 14.

9. George W. Bagby, "Scenes in Virginia," in William Cullen Bryant, ed., *Picturesque America* (New York, 1872), 1: 337.

10. Washington wrote in his diary on 4 Oct. 1784, "The Western Settlers—from my own observation—stand as it were in a pivet—the touch of a feather would almost incline them any way." The manner for Virginia to embrace these people "is to open a wide door, and make a smooth way for the produce of that Country to pass to our Markets before the trade may get into another channel." Donald Jackson and Dorothy Twohig, eds., *The Diaries of George Washington* (Charlottesville, Va., 1978), 4: 66.

11. The letter to the London merchant Richard Washington, 15 April 1757, is in W. W. Abbot, ed., *The Papers of George Washington, Colonial Series* (Charlottesville, Va., 1984), 4: 134. Washington's comments about the artist are in his letter of 5 Sept. 1793 to the commissioners of the District of Columbia in John C. Fitzpatrick, ed., *The Writings of George Washington* (Washington, D.C., 1940), 33: 83.

12. William M. S. Rasmussen and Robert S. Tilton, *George Washington: The Man Behind the Myths* (Charlottesville, Va., and London, 1999), 102–3; Jessie Poesch, *The Art of the Old South: Painting, Sculpture, Architecture & the Products of Craftsmen, 1560–1860* (New York, 1983), 179–80. Winstanley did paint "View on the Shenandoah in Virginia" and "View from a Sketch Taken on the Potomac in Virginia, North America." Both are unlocated. Beck also painted "The Potomac River Breaking Through the Blue Ridge."

13. The painting was engraved by T. Cartwright and published 1 Jan. 1802 by Atkins & Nightingale, London and Philadelphia. An example is at the Library of Congress. It is no. 22 in Gloria Déak, *Picturing America, 1497–1899* (Princeton, N.J., 1988), 146. The original oil is in a private collection.

14. J. E. Strickland, ed., *Journal of a Tour in the United States of America, 1794–1795, by William Strickland* (New York, 1971), between 224–5, figure 13.

15. "Great Falls of the Patowmac, one mile distant, from the road South of the river" is no. 111 in Edward C. Carter II, John C. Van Horne, and Charles E. Brownell, *Latrobe's View of America, 1795–1820: Selections from the Watercolors and Sketches* (New Haven, Conn., and London, 1985), discussed 280, illustrated 281. The close-up, "great Falls of the Potowmac taken from a Rock on the South Side," is no. 112, discussed 282, illustrated 283.

16. Quoted in Priscilla Wakefield, *Excursions in North America* (London, 1810), 35.

17. Alice E. Smith, ed., *The Journals of Welcome Arnold Greene* (Madison, Wis., 1957), 73. Greene's journal covers the years 1822–24.

18. Weld, *Travels*, 1: 135.

19. William Faux, *Memorable Days in America* (London, 1823), 135.

20. Elizabeth Cometti and Valeria Gennaro-Lerda, eds., "The Presidential Tour of Carlo Vidua with Letters on Virginia," *VMHB* 77 (1969): 395.

21. Quoted in Wakefield, *Excursions*, 136.

22. Godfrey T. Vigne, *Six Months in America* (London, 1832), 2.

23. Thomas Jefferson, *Notes on the State of Virginia*, ed. William Peden (Chapel Hill, N.C., 1955), 19.

24. Weld, *Travels*, 1: 239–41, 244–45.

25. Ralph D. Gray, ed., "A Tour in Virginia in 1827: Letters from Henry P. Gilpin to his Father," *VMHB* 76 (1968): 449.

26. William D. Hoyt, Jr., ed., "Jerome Napoleon Bonaparte: Journey to the Springs, 1846," *VMHB* 54 (1946): 134.

27. Vigne, *Six Months in America*, 3.

28. Cometti and Gennaro-Lerda, eds., "Presidential Tour of Count Carlo Vidua," 394.

29. St. Leger Landon Carter, *Nugae; or, Pieces in Prose and Verse* (Baltimore, 1844), quoted in Daniel J. Philippon, *Landmarks of American Nature Writing from Virginia's Blue Ridge Mountains and Shenandoah Valley* (Charlottesville, Va., 1997), 21–22.

30. Gray, ed., "Letters from Henry P. Gilpin," 449.

31. John Edwards Caldwell, *A Tour through Part of Virginia, in the Summer of 1808* (New York, 1809), 11.

32. Faux, *Memorable Days in America*, 141.

33. Thomas Yoseloff, ed., *Voyage to America: The Journals of Thomas Cather* (New York and London, 1961), 27–28.

34. Barbara C. Batson, "Virginia Landscapes by William Roberts," *Journal of Early Southern Decorative Arts* 10 (Nov. 1984): 36–45.

35. Quoted in William Howard Adams, ed., *The Eye of Thomas Jefferson* (Columbia, Mo., 1976), 338.

36. George Washington to commissioners of the District of Columbia, 5 Sept. 1793, in Fitzpatrick, ed., *Writings of George Washington*, 33: 83.

37. Nathaniel P. Willis, *American Scenery; or, Land, Lake, and River Illustrations of Transatlantic Nature* (London, 1840), 1, quoted in Philippon, *Landmarks of American Nature Writing*, 22–23.

38. Ele Bowen, *Rambles in the Path of the Steam-Horse*

(Philadelphia, 1855), 178.

39. [James Kirke Paulding], *Letters from the South Written During an Excursion in the Summer of 1816* (New York, 1817), 2: 255.

40. Adams, ed., *The Eye of Jefferson*, 338.

41. Bowen, *Rambles in the Path of the Steam-Horse*, 180–81.

42. Yoseloff, ed., *Voyage to America: The Journals of Thomas Cather*, 28.

43. Peyton H. Hoge and Howard R. Bayne, *The Travels of Alter and Ego* (Richmond, 1879), 18.

44. *Raymond's Vacation Excursions* (privately printed, 1887), 118–19.

45. Quoted in Constance D. Sherman, "A French Artist Portrays the Natural Bridge," *VMHB* 68 (1960): 167.

46. Gray, ed., "Letters of Henry P. Gilpin," 458. Thomas Jefferson's description of Madison's Cave appears in *Notes on the State of Virginia* (Paris, 1784–5), 34, 36, with page 35 being a map of the cave.

47. [Samuel Mordecai], *Description of the Album of Virginia; or The Old Dominion, Illustrated* (Richmond, 1980 repr. of 1857 ed.), 11.

48. Quoted in John A. Cuthbert and Jessie Poesch, *David Hunter Strother: "One of the Best Draughtsmen the Country Possesses"* (Morgantown, W.Va., 1997), 31–32.

49. Andrew Buni, ed., "Rambles among the Virginia Mountains: The Journal of Mary Jane Boggs, June 1851," *VMHB* 77 (1969): 109.

50. Gray, ed., "Letters of Henry Gilpin," 455.

51. [Mordecai], *Description of the Album of Virginia*, 11.

52. Quoted in *Resorts and Resources of the Chesapeake & Ohio Railway* (Richmond, 1879), 37.

53. Buni, ed., "The Journal of Mary Jane Boggs," 109.

54. *American Farmer* (23 Nov. 1821): 273–4, quoted in Philippon, *Landmarks of American Nature Writing*, 39.

55. Cramer, *Etwas Über Die Natür Wünder*, 6.

56. "Southern Scenery," *De Bow's Review* 6: 174.

57. George M. Neese, *Three Years in the Confederate Horse Artillery* (New York, 1911), quoted in Philippon, *Landmarks of American Nature Writing*, 46.

58. Pollard, *The Virginia Tourist*, 271.

59. Quoted in *Resorts and Resources of the Chesapeake & Ohio Railway*, 37.

60. William Cullen Bryant, ed., *Picturesque America* (New York, 1872), 1: 212–19 gives a room-by-room account of Weyer's Cave. So does Robert L. Cooke, *Description of Weyer's Cave* (Staunton, Va., 1834). Another account appears in Joseph Martin, *A New and Comprehensive Gazetteer of Virginia, and the District of Columbia* (Charlottesville, Va., 1836), 311–17.

61. Quoted in *Luray Caverns*, an undated, unpaginated company publication at the Virginia Historical Society.

62. Ernest Ingersoll, *To the Shenandoah and Beyond* (New York, 1885), 39.

63. Winefred, Lady Howard of Glossop, *Journal of a Tour in the United States, Canada, and Mexico* (London, 1897), 306; Hoge and Bayne, *Alter and Ego*, 35.

64. J. G. Panghorn, *Mountain and Valley Resorts on Picturesque B & O* (Chicago, 1884), 18.

65. Thomas Jefferson, *Notes on the State of Virginia* (Paris, 1784–5), 56.

66. Capt. Frederick Marryat, *A Diary in America, with Remarks on Its Institutions* (New York, 1839), quoted in Philippon, *Landmarks of American Nature Writing*, 35.

67. Quoted in Pollard, *The Virginia Tourist*, 16.

68. Ibid., 18.

69. Anne Royall, *Sketches of History, Life, and Manners, in the United States* (New Haven, Conn., 1826), 32.

70. [Mordecai], *Description of the Album of Virginia*, 29.

71. A Visitor, *Six Weeks in Fauquier; Being the Substance of a Series of Familiar Letters, Illustrating the Scenery, Localities, Medicinal Virtues, and General Characteristics of the White Sulphur Springs, at Warrenton, Fauquier County, Virginia. Written in 1838, to a Gentleman in New England* (New York, 1839), quoted in Philippon, *Landmarks of American Nature Writing*, 34–35.

72. Joseph M. Toner, ed., *Journal of My Journey over the Mountains by George Washington* (Albany, N.Y., 1892), 29–30.

73. William Burke, *The Virginia Mineral Springs, with remarks on their use, the diseases to which they are applicable, and in which they are contra-in-dicted, accompanied by a map of routes and distances* (Richmond, 1853), 322–23.

74. Hoyt, ed., "Jerome Napoleon Bonaparte," 128.

75. Quoted in Michael P. Branch and Daniel J. Philippon, eds., *The Height of Our Mountains: Nature Writing from Virginia's Blue Ridge Mountains and Shenandoah Valley* (Baltimore and London, 1998), 152. In *Album of Virginia* Edward Beyer pictures Sweet Springs a quarter century later, after the accommodations known by Henry Tudor had been improved considerably.

76. Quoted in *Resorts and Resources of the Chesapeake & Ohio Railway* (Richmond, 1879), 46.

77. [Mordecai], *Description of the Album of Virginia*, 23.

78. Quoted in *Resorts and Resources of the Chesapeake & Ohio Railway*, 42.

79. [Mordecai], *Description of the Album of Virginia*, 30.

80. [Paulding], *Letters from the South*, 2: 236.

81. John Disturnell, *Springs, Water-Falls, Sea-Bathing Resorts, and Mountain Scenery in the United States and Canada* (New York, 1855), 124.

82. Ibid., 125.

83. Martin, *A New and Comprehensive Gazetteer of Virginia*, 398.

84. Burke, *The Virginia Mineral Springs*, 190.

85. Martin, *A New and Comprehensive Gazetteer of Virginia*, 352.

86. Quoted in Pollard, *The Virginia Tourist*, 15.

87. Hoyt, ed., "Jerome Napoleon Bonaparte," 127.

88. Marianne Finch, *An Englishwoman's Experience in America* (New York, 1969 repr. of 1853), 326.

89. [Mordecai], *Description of the Album of Virginia*, 28–29.

90. Ibid.

91. R. Lewis Wright, "Edward Beyer and the ALBUM OF VIRGINIA," *Virginia Cavalcade* 22 (Spring 1973): 38.

92. Martin, *A New and Comprehensive Gazetteer of Virginia*, 374.

93. Harriet Martineau, *Society in America* (London, 1837), 2: 241.

94. William H. Gerdts, *The South and The Midwest in Art Across America: Two Centuries of Regional Painting 1710–1920* (New York, London, and Paris, 1990), 189.

95. Whittredge exhibited the canvases "View on the Kanawha, Morning" and "Kanawha Scenery" in 1846 and 1847.

96. Martin, *A New and Comprehensive Gazetteer of Virginia*, 39, 374.

97. Martineau, *Society in America*, 1: 243.

98. [Mordecai], *Description of the Album of Virginia*, 15.

99. Beyer, *Album of Virginia*, 20.

100. Jefferson, *Notes on Virginia* (Paris, 1784–5), 33–34.

101. George W. Knepper, ed., *Travels in the Southland, 1822–*

1823: The Journal of Lucius Verus Bierce (Columbus, Ohio, 1966), 58.

102. *The Illustrated London News*, 10 Dec. 1864, 575.

103. David Hunter Strother [Porte Crayon], "Virginia Illustrated," *Harper's New Monthly Magazine* 10 (Feb. 1855): 297.

104. In "The Mountains III," *Harper's New Monthly Magazine* 45 (June 1872): 30. Seneca Rocks were visited and painted by Russell Smith prior to the Civil War, but the painting was not published and so was little known.

105. David Hunter Strother, "West Virginia," in Bryant, ed., *Picturesque America*, 1: 387.

106. Burnaby, *Travels*, 35.

107. Joseph Lee Davis, *Bits of History and Legends Around and About Natural Bridge, 1730–1950* (Natural Bridge, c. 1949), 31–32.

108. Quoted in Adams, ed., *The Eye of Jefferson*, 338.

109. Thomas Jefferson to William Jenkings, 1 July 1809, quoted in Philippon, *Landmarks of American Nature Writing*, 26.

110. Marquis de Chastellux quoted in *A Description of the Natural Bridge of Virginia and Its History* (Philadelphia, 1887), 23–24.

111. Buni, ed., "Journal of Mary Jane Boggs," 99.

112. Disturnell, *Springs, Water-Falls*, 134.

113. Andrew Reed and James Matheson, *A Narrative of the Visit to the American Churches* (New York, 1835), 1: 167–69.

114. "Journal of a Journey Through the United States, 1795–96, by Thomas Chapman, Esq.," *The Historical Magazine*, 2nd ser., 5 (1869): 365; William M. E. Rachal, ed., *A Tour Through Part of Virginia, in the Summer of 1808*, by John Edwards Caldwell (Richmond, 1951), 23.

115. [Paulding], *Letters from the South*, 2: 65.

116. Henry Clay quoted in *A Description of the Natural Bridge of Virginia and Its History 1887*, 15.

117. Anne Henry Ehrenpreis, ed., "A Victorian Englishman on Tour: Henry Arthur Bright's Southern Journal, 1852," *VMHB* 84 (1976): 355.

118. Ingersoll, *To the Shenandoah and Beyond*, 51.

119. David Hunter Strother, "Virginia Illustrated. Third Paper," *Harper's Monthly* 11 (Aug. 1855): 289–311.

120. Gray, ed., "Letters from Henry P. Gilpin," 463.

121. Elias Cornelius, *Tour in Virginia, Tennessee, &c.&c.&c.* (London, 1820), quoted in Philippon, *Landmarks of American Nature Writing*, 29.

122. Cramer, *Etwas Über Die Natür Wünder*, 38.

123. Wakefield, *Excursions*, 44.

124. Strother, "Virginia Illustrated," 303.

125. Wakefield, *Excursions*, 43.

126. [Mordecai], *Description of the Album of Virginia*, 5.

127. William E. Wight, ed., "The Journals of The Reverend Robert J. Miller, Lutheran Missionary in Virginia, 1811 and 1813," *VMHB* 61 (1953): 145.

128. Francis William Gilmer, "On the Geological Formation of the Natural Bridge of Virginia," *Transactions of the American Philosophical Society* 1 (1818): 187–92.

129. Louis Philippe, "Seeing Virginia in 1797," *Journal of the Roanoke Valley Historical Society* 10 (1978): 2.

130. Lady Howard of Glossop, *Journal of a Tour*, 299.

131. Adams, ed., *The Eye of Jefferson*, 338.

132. The original oil is at the Nelson-Atkins Museum of Art in Kansas City, Missouri. Bartlett's print appeared in Nathaniel Willis's *American Scenery* and is discussed as no. 441 in Déak, *Picturing America*, 296.

133. Pamela H. Simpson, *So Beautiful an Arch: Images of the Natural Bridge, 1787–1890* (catalog of an exhibition at the duPont Gallery, Washington and Lee University, Lexington, Va., 4–19 Jan. 1982), 20. The Church image was unavailable for this exhibition, having previously been promised to another.

134. Johnson's paintings of rocks and waterfalls are discussed and illustrated in John K. Howat et al., *American Paradise: The World of the Hudson River School* (New York, 1987), 270–71.

135. Ibid.; Simpson, *So Beautiful an Arch*, 38–39.

136. Disturnell, *Springs, Water-Falls*, 134.

137. Carolyn J. Weekley, *The Kingdoms of Edward Hicks* (Williamsburg, Va., 1999), 94, 190. Each of the six paintings is illustrated. They are owned by Yale University (2), Mead Art Museum at Amherst College, Denver Art Museum, Reynolda House in Winston-Salem, and Abby Aldrich Rockefeller Folk Art Center, Williamsburg. Because of the current Edward Hicks retrospective, the paintings featuring Natural Bridge were not available for this exhibition.

138. Bryant, ed., *Picturesque America*, 1: 82.

139. Irene J. Murray, "Mrs. Liston Returns to Virginia," *Virginia Cavalcade* 15 (Summer 1965): 44.

140. Quoted in William E. Carson, *The Natural Wonders of Virginia* (Richmond, 1932), 10.

141. Gray, ed., "Letters from Henry P. Gilpin," 463.

142. *A Description of the Natural Bridge of Virginia and Its History 1887* (Philadelphia, 1887), 3.

143. Bowen, *Rambles in the Path of the Steam-Horse*, 198.

144. William Dickey Ogelsby, *Dick's Trip Through Virginia on Horseback* (Dayton, Ohio, 1899), 35.

145. Mary Allan-Olney, *The New Virginians* (Edinburgh and London, 1880), 2: 201.

146. Louise Closser Hale, *We Discover the Old Dominion* (New York, 1916), 220, 222.

147. Pollard, *The Virginia Tourist*, 48.

148. *Raymond's Vacation Excursions* (privately printed, 1887), 43.

149. Cramer, *Etwas Über Die Natür Wünder*, 40.

150. William W. Valentine letter from Berlin, 8 April 1863, Valentine Museum.

151. A. B. K. to editor of Richmond *Whig*, 10 May 1867, Valentine Museum artist's file. The same file includes a copy of an undated letter from Thomas Ellis to Edward Virginius Valentine stating that one Rev. Munford went to Montgomery County. "The locality was romantic, Fisher was one of his friends, and from personal regard painted him a good size picture of the log schoolhouse and its surroundings, with such success that almost anybody must look at it with pleasure."

152. *Raymond's Vacation Excursions*, 43.

153. "Journal of a Journey Through the United States, 1795–96, by Thomas Chapman, Esq.," *The Historical Magazine*, 2nd ser., 5 (1869): 365; Marianne Finch, *An Englishwoman's Experience in America* (New York, 1969 repr. of 1853), 315.

154. Herman Melville, *Moby Dick* (New York, 1851), 604–5. In fairness, it should be pointed out that Natural Bridge also has inspired much doggerel. One such poem appeared in the *Nashville* (Tenn.) *Sunday Journal*, 7 Oct. 1883, reproduced in *A Description of the Natural Bridge of Virginia and Its History 1887* (Philadelphia, n.d.), 48. Another appears in William Maxwell, *Poems* (Philadelphia, 1816).

155. Jefferson, *Notes*, 32.

156. Ibid.; Mount Rogers in Tazewell County is the highest in Virginia at 5,729 feet.

157. Weld, *Travels*, 1: 213. Mount Snowden is 3,560 feet. At the Peaks, Sharp Top is 3,875 feet and Flat Top 4,001 feet high.

158. Charles Lanman, *Letters from the Allegheny Mountains* (New York, 1849), Letter XXI, quoted in Philippon, *Landmarks of American Nature Writing*, 23.

159. [Paulding], *Letters from the South*, 2: 40.

160. Gray, ed., "Letters from Henry P. Gilpin," 461; Richard Beeman, ed., "Trade and Travel in Post-Revolutionary Virginia: A Diary of an Itinerant Peddler, 1807–1808," *VMHB* 84 (1976): 180.

161. Ingersoll, *To the Shenandoah and Beyond*, 87.

162. Marquis de Chastellux, *Travels in North America in the Years 1780, 1781, and 1782* (London, 1787), 2: 111.

163. Anne Royall, *Mrs. Royall's Southern Tour* (Washington, D.C., 1830), 99.

164. The original, in charcoal, is at the Virginia Historical Society.

165. Henry Clay Pate, *The American Vade Mecum; or, The Companion of Youth, and Guide to College* (Cincinnati, 1852), quoted in Philippon, *Landmarks of American Nature Writing*, 24.

166. Bryant, ed., *Picturesque America*, 563.

167. [Mordecai], *Description of the Album of Virginia*, 14.

168. Ingersoll, *To the Shenandoah and Beyond*, 87.

169. Quoted in Bowen, *Rambles*, 198.

170. Samuel M. Janney, *The Last of the Lenape, and Other Poems* (Philadelphia, 1839), quoted in *Landmarks of American Nature Writing*, 25.

171. John Goode, "Recollections of a Lifetime," 1906, quoted in Joseph Lee Davis, *Bits of History and Legends around and about the Natural Bridge of Virginia* (Lynchburg, Va., c. 1949), 59.

172. John Boyle O'Reilly, cited in David C. Miller, *Dark Eden: The Swamp in Nineteenth-Century American Culture* (Cambridge, England, 1989), 30.

173. See Hubert J. Davis, *The Great Dismal Swamp: Its History, Folklore and Science* (Murfreesboro, N.C., 1971).

174. Republished in J. O. Kerbey, *On the War Path: A Journey over the Historic Grounds of the Late Civil War* (Chicago, 1890), 80.

175. Cited in Miller, *Dark Eden*, 37.

176. Miller, *Dark Eden*, 207.

177. Quoted in Poesch, *Art of the Old South*, 185.

178. Chapman listed the painting in his date book for 1824–48, p. 34; it measured 36 by 48 inches and was sold for two hundred dollars to William Bancroft for use in *The Magnolia* of 1837. It also appeared in *The Ladies' Repository* in 1850. Chapman's unpublished record books are owned by Robert Mayo, Gloucester, Virginia.

179. Mark Van Doren, ed., *Travels of William Bartram* (New York, 1955, 138), cited in Miller, *Dark Eden*, 6.

180. Miller, *Dark Eden*, 30.

181. William H. Gerdts and Carrie Rebora, *The Art of Henry Inman* (Washington, D.C., 1987), 172.

182. Wakefield, *Excursions*, 60.

183. William S. Forest, *Historical and Descriptive Sketch of Norfolk and Vicinity* (Philadelphia, 1853), 99.

184. Published in William Gilmore Simms, *Poems, Descriptive, Dramatic, Legendary and Contemplative* (New York, 1853), cited in Miller, *Dark Eden*, 80.

185. See Miller, *Dark Eden*, for a discussion of these ideas.

186. Fisher's "The Dismal Swamp" (c. 1858, 30 x 50 inches) is at the Maier Museum of Art, Randolph-Macon Woman's College.

187. Gignoux exhibited at the National Academy of Design in New York canvases entitled "Dismal Swamp, North Carolina" and "The Dismal Swamp" in 1850 and 1858.

188. *Harper's New Monthly Magazine* (Sept. 1856): 441–55, cited in Miller, *Dark Eden*, 23–29.

189. Longfellow and Stowe are cited in Miller, *Dark Eden*, 90,

92. Higginson's essay "Barbarism and Civilization" appeared in *Out-Door Papers* (Boston, 1863); it is cited in Miller, *Dark Eden*, 56.

190. "The Dismal Swamp," *Chamber's Edinburgh Journal* (14 Dec. 1850): 373–75, cited in Miller, *Dark Eden*, 37.

191. Edward King, *The Great South* (Baton Rouge, La., 1972 reprint of 1875 ed. by W. Magruder Drake and Robert R. Jones), 589.

192. Burnaby, *Travels*, 28.

193. Quoted in Richard M. Ketchum, *The World of George Washington* (New York, 1974), 34.

194. Christie's catalog sale no. 8578 (18 Jan. 1997), 148.

195. Claude Aragonnès, *Prises de Vues Americaines* (Paris, 1945), 66.

196. Quoted in "The Autobiography of Peter Stephen Du Ponceau," *Pennsylvania Magazine of History and Biography* 63 (1939): 312–13.

197. Burnaby, *Travels*, 28.

198. Quoted in D. R. Preston, *The Wonders of Creation, Natural and Artificial* (Boston, 1807), 39.

199. Theodore Dwight, Jr., *Things as They Are: or, Notes of a Traveller* (New York, 1834), 11.

200. *Letters and Poems Written by Edith Mabel Porter Kimball* (n.p., 1920), 31.

201. Dwight, *Things as They Are*, 12.

202. E. Kennedy, "Mount Vernon—A Pilgrimage," *Southern Literary Messenger* 18, no. 1 (Jan. 1852): 54.

203. Ibid., 56.

204. [Earl of Carlisle], *Two Lectures . . . Travels in America by the Rt. Hon. The Earl of Carlisle* (London, 1851), 34.

205. Hon. Charles Augustus Murray, *Travels in North America During the Years 1834, 1835, & 1836* (London, 1839), 1: 140.

206. King, *The Great South*, 798.

207. Jackson's visit to Mount Vernon (handwritten by Maj. John Reid and endorsed in Jackson's hand), Nov. 1815 (John Spencer Bassett, ed., *Correspondence of Andrew Jackson* [Washington, 1929], 219–20).

208. Dwight, *Things as They Are*, 14.

209. Clayton Torrence, ed., "Arlington and Mount Vernon 1856, as Described in a Letter of Augusta Blanche Berard," *VMHB* 57 (1949): 155.

210. Rasmussen and Tilton, *George Washington*, 266.

211. *Letters and Poems Written By Edith Mabel Porter Kimball*, 33.

212. Rev. Newman Hall, *From Liverpool to St. Louis* (London and New York, 1870), xviii–xix.

213. Bryant, ed., *Picturesque America*, 2: 576.

214. Willa Cather, *Sapphira and the Slave Girl*, Book 1, Section 3, quoted in Branch and Philippon, eds., *Height of Our Mountains*, 238.

215. Published as a supplement to the *American Agriculturalist* 45 (May 1886), accompanying an article by James Parton.

216. Ernst Prossinagg, *Das Anlitz Amerikas: drei Jahre dipolmatischer Mission in den U.S.A.* (Zürich, 1931), 225–33. Prossinagg's posting was from 1926 to 1928. The larger study is Lawrence S. Thompson, "Books in Foreign Languages About Travel in Virginia, 1900–1950," *VMHB* 61 (1953): 167–78. The comparison of Mount Vernon to Monticello is on page 167.

217. Chastellux, *Travels*, 2: 41.

218. *Luigi Castiglioni's Viaggio: Travels in the United States of North America, 1785–1787*, trans. Antonio Pace (Syracuse, N.Y., 1983), 119.

219. Weld, *Travels*, 1: 208.

220. Gray, ed., "Letters from Henry P. Gilpin," 467.

221. Christie's catalog sale no. 8490 (16 Oct. 1996), lot 1, p. 18.

222. Quoted in Wakefield, *Excursions*, 42.

223. King, *The Great South*, 651.

224. John Robert Godley, *Letters from America* (London, 1844), 2: 201.

225. Gherardi Davis, *How I Spent a Few Days in Virginia in April 1939* (n.p., 1939), 16.

226. Frank Edgar Grizzard, Jr., ed., "Three 'Grand and Interesting Objects': an 1828 Visit to Monticello, the University, and Montpelier," *Magazine of Albemarle County History* 51 (1993): 116.

227. Ibid., 123–24.

228. Cooke's "View of Monticello" was engraved and published in *Family Magazine* 4 (1837); Henry Howe's *Historical Collection of Virginia* (1848), 168; and *Sears' Pictorial Description of the United States* (1853).

229. Grizzard, ed., "Three 'Grand and Interesting Objects,'" 124–25.

230. Quoted in "Southern Scenery," *DeBow's Review* 6, no. 2 (1861): 171.

231. Introduction to William Wirt, *Letters of a British Spy* (10th ed., New York, 1848), 75.

232. William J. Hinkle, ed., "Report of the Journey of Francis Louis Michel From Basel, Switzerland, to Virginia, October 2, 1701–December 1, 1702," *VMHB* 24 (1916): 25.

233. Gregory A. Stiverson and Patrick H. Butler III, eds., "The Travel Journal of William Hugh Grove," *VMHB* 85 (1977): 26.

234. "The Autobiography of Peter Stephen Du Ponceau," *Pennsylvania Magazine of History and Biography* 63 (July 1939): 318.

235. Wirt, *Letters of a British Spy*, 186. For notice of the "Jubilee at Jamestown" see *The Enquirer* (Richmond), 1 May 1807.

236. Ibid., 188.

237. Formerly in the collection of Dr. R. Lewis Wright of Richmond.

238. At the Virginia Historical Society, Lora Robins Collection of Virginia Art.

239. Bishop [William] Meade, *Old Churches, Ministers and Families of Virginia* (Philadelphia, 1857), 1: 111–14.

240. Dwight, *Things as They Are*, 11.

241. Joan E. Cashin, "Landscape and Memory in Antebellum Virginia," *VMHB* 102 (1994): 477–500.

242. Frederic Edwin Church's landscapes of "Hooker and Company Journeying through the Wilderness from Plymouth to Hartford in 1636" (1846, Wadsworth Atheneum) and "West Rock, New Haven" (1849, New Britain Museum of American Art) are Connecticut examples of the historical landscapes of this period.

243. Wirt, *Letters of a British Spy*, 191.

244. [Paulding], *Letters from the South*, 1: 95–96.

245. George W. Knepper, ed., *Travels in the Southland, 1822–1823: The Journal of Lucius Verus Bierce* (Columbus, Ohio, 1966), 64.

246. "Journal of a Trip to the Mountains, Caves, and Springs of Virginia, by a New Englander," *Southern Literary Messenger* 4 (Jan. 1838): 92.

247. Kerbey, *On the War Path*, 81–82.

248. "Loungings in the Footprints of Pioneers," *Harper's New Monthly Magazine* (May 1859): 747.

249. Hale, *We Discover the Old Dominion*, 305.

250. Burnaby, *Travels*, 4.

251. "The Autobiography of Peter Stephen Du Ponceau," 316.

252. Wakefield, *Excursions*, 53.

253. Quoted in Parke Rouse, Jr., *Cows on the Campus, Williamsburg in Bygone Days* (Richmond, 1973), 23.

254. King, *The Great South*, 623.

255. Kerbey, *On the War Path*, 88–89.

256. John Sergeant Wise, *Diomed, The Life, Travels, and Observations of a Dog* (Boston, London, and New York, 1897), 307, 311.

257. Hale, *We Discover the Old Dominion*, 293.

258. Wilkinson's watercolors are at the Virginia Historical Society, Richmond. Chadwick's are in the property of R. Lewis Wright, who wrote "A Portfolio from the Virginia Sketchbook of Edith Clark Chadwick," *Virginia Cavalcade* 29 (1980): 150–55.

259. Rouse, *Cows on the Campus*, 125.

260. Stiverson and Butler, eds., "Travel Journal of William Hugh Grove," 26.

261. Weld, *Travels*, 1: 169.

262. Natalie Spassky et al., *American Paintings in the Metropolitan Museum of Art* (New York, 1985), 2: 546.

263. The interior was restored to its original condition partially in 1905 and fully in 1938.

264. Among other artists working in Williamsburg in the 1930s was Tom Brown, whose "From My Window in Williamsburg," "Bruton Church Tower," "Tucker Coleman House Kitchen," and "Bassett Hall" were featured in an exhibition at the Williamsburg-Jamestown-Yorktown Association. See *Richmond News-Leader*, 16 March 1935. Edmund S. Campbell's "A Shop in Williamsburg" and "The Boxwood Garden, Williamsburg" were in an exhibition at the Richmond Academy of Sciences and Fine Arts (*Richmond News-Leader*, 9 Feb. 1939), and his "Bruton Church Tower" was in an exhibition at the Virginia Museum of Fine Arts, 6 March–6 April 1938. Valentine Museum files.

265. "J. J. Lankes" artist file, Valentine Museum.

266. Harold Dunn, ". . . when it isn't a girl. Missouri schoolchildren give their views on a bewildering place called Virginia," *The Commonwealth* (March 1964): 31.

267. *Virginia Historical Society Acquisitions, 1948–1977* (Richmond, 1978), no. 64.

268. Carter, Van Horne, and Brownell, eds., *Latrobe's View of America*, 158.

269. Weld, *Travels*, 1: 165.

270. W. S. B., "Historic Landmarks in Lower Virginia," *Southern Literary Messenger* 33 (August 1861), 122.

271. Poesch, *Art of the Old South*, 280. Chapman's paintings are reproduced in Rasmussen and Tilton, *George Washington*, 145–7.

272. [Paulding], *Letters from the South*, 1: 61; E. A. Allen, *A Jolly Trip* (Cincinnati, 1891), 108–109.

273. Communication with the authors, 28 Dec. 1999.

274. [Paulding], *Letters from the South*, 1: 59–60.

Chapter IV

1. Gregory A. Stiverson and Patrick H. Butler III, eds., "The Travel Journal of William Hugh Grove," *VMHB* 85 (1977): 26.

2. Marquis de Chastellux, *Travels in North America in the Years 1780, 1781, and 1782* (London, 1787) 2: 163.

3. Marion Rose Tinling, ed., *The Correspondence of the Three William Byrds of Westover, Virginia, 1684–1776* (Charlottesville, Va., 1977), 2: 603.

4. Edward C. Carter II, John C. Van Horne, and Charles E. Brownell, *Latrobe's Views of America, 1795–1820: Selections from the Watercolors and Sketches* (New Haven, Conn., and London,

1985), 120.

5. Arthur Singleton, *Letters from the South and West* (Boston, 1824), 61.

6. W. L. Whitwell, "Edward Beyer (1820–1865)," in Sotheby's sale catalog 6716, The Collection of Dr. and Mrs. Henry P. Deyerle, 26–27 May 1995, following lot 802.

7. *Edward Beyer's CYCLORAMA, Pictorial Journey from Bremen to New York and through the United States of North America and back to Hamburg* (2nd ed., Dresden, 1860–63, translated by Holle Schneider, 1993), no. 17, p. 94, provided courtesy of Professor W. L. Tony Whitwell.

8. Singleton, *Letters from the South and West*, 60.

9. Ernest Ingersoll, *To the Shenandoah and Beyond* (New York, 1885), 88.

10. M. H. Harris, ed., "Diary of Travels from Virginia to Tennessee 1832," *WMQ*, 2nd series, 13 (1933): 164.

11. Quoted in Royster Lyle, Jr., and Matthew W. Paxton, Jr., "The VMI Barracks," *Virginia Cavalcade* 23 (1974): 19.

12. Andrew Buni, ed., "Rambles Among the Virginia Mountains: The Journal of Mary Jane Boggs, June 1851," *VMHB* 77 (1969): 95.

13. Buni, ed., "The Journal of Mary Jane Boggs," 86.

14. John Robert Godley, *Letters from America* (London, 1844), 2: 198.

15. Frank Edgar Grizzard, Jr., ed., "Three 'Grand and Interesting Objects': An 1828 Visit to Monticello, the University, and Montpelier," *Magazine of Albemarle County History* 51 (1993): 119–20, 122.

16. Anne Royall, *Mrs. Royall's Southern Tour* (Washington, D.C., 1830), 100–101.

17. Mary Frances Williams, *Catalogue of the Collection of American Art at Randolph-Macon Woman's College* (Charlottesville, Va., 1977), 115. The originals of the Richmond and Jamestown views are in the New York Public Library and appear in Gloria Déak, *Picturing America, 1497–1899* (Princeton, N.J., 1988), nos. 534, 538.

18. Ingersoll, *To the Shenandoah and Beyond*, 83.

19. Louise Closser Hale, *We Discover the Old Dominion* (New York, 1916), 229.

20. Quoted in Helen Covey Milius, "Gari Melchers," *The Commonwealth* (April 1959): 26–32.

21. The oil painting is reproduced in *Presidents Collection, Virginia State Bar* (Richmond, Va., 1993), 23.

22. "Art and Artists," *New-York Home Journal* (5 June 1851): 3, quoted in Angela Miller, *The Empire of the Eye, Landscape Representation and American Cultural Politics, 1825–1875* (Ithaca, N.Y., and London, 1993), 12.

23. Estill Curtis Pennington, *A Southern Collection: Select works from a permanent collection of painting in the South prepared for the opening of the Morris Museum of Art, September 24, 1992* (Augusta, Ga., 1992), 82.

24. Kenneth Clark, *Landscape into Art* (London, 1953), 22.

25. *Luigi Castiglioni's Viaggio: Travels in the United States of North America, 1785–1787*, trans. Antonio Pace (Syracuse, N.Y., 1983), 196.

26. Quoted in James C. Kelly, *The Horse in Virginia* (Richmond, 1999), 7.

27. Quoted in a letter from Nannie Francisco Porter to the editor of the *Richmond News-Leader*, 12 Dec. 1949, Valentine Museum artists' files.

28. *Antiquarian Pursuits, Southern Art from the Holdings of Robert M. Hicklin, Jr., Inc.* (Spartanburg, S.C., 1992), 42.

29. At the Virginia Historical Society.

30. An article in the *Richmond Times-Dispatch* of 28 Oct. 1907 reads on p. 5, "Virginia, which is the home of fox hunting in America, . . . claims more clubs than all the rest of the country together." We thank Jane Reid for calling our attention to this article.

31. Alexander Mackay-Smith, *The Race Horses of America 1832–1872: Portraits and Other Paintings by Edward Troye* (Saratoga Springs, N.Y., 1981), 29, 31. The painting of Argyle is at the Virginia Historical Society.

32. Ingersoll, *To the Shenandoah and Beyond*, 77.

33. Hale, *We Discover the Old Dominion*, 254.

34. Quoted in Michael P. Branch and Daniel J. Philippon, eds., *The Height of Our Mountains: Nature Writing from Virginia's Blue Ridge Mountains and Shenandoah Valley* (Baltimore and London, 1998), 195–200.

35. J. P. Brissot de Warville, *New Travels in the United States of America. Performed in 1788* (London, 1792), 434.

36. [James Kirke Paulding], *Letters from the South Written During an Excursion in the Summer of 1816* (New York, 1817), 1: 50; Godley, *Letters from America*, 2: 194; [Earl of Carlisle], *Two Lectures . . . Travels in America by the Rt. Hon. The Earl of Carlisle* (London, 1851), 34.

37. Quoted in Déak, *Picturing America*, 359.

38. William Wirt, *Letters of a British Spy* (10th ed., New York, 1848), 106–107.

39. Déak, *Picturing America*, no. 251.

40. Linda Crocker Simmons, "The Emerging Nation, 1790 to 1830," in Ella-Prince Knox et al., *Painting in the South: 1564–1980* (Richmond, Va., 1983), 60.

41. James C. Kelly, *The South on Paper: Light, Line, and Color* (Spartanburg, S.C., 1985), 42.

42. J. R. Thompson in Bryant, ed., *Picturesque America*, 1: 73.

43. Virginia Historical Society, Adèle Clark file. The booklet is undated but probably is from the 1920s.

44. Richmond *Enquirer*, 21 May 1814, Valentine Museum files.

45. Richmond *Compiler*, 28 June 1821, Valentine Museum files.

46. Richmond *Whig*, 9 Oct. 1846, Valentine Museum files.

47. Richmond *Semi-Weekly Examiner*, 18 Jan. 1850, Valentine Museum files.

48. Richmond *Dispatch*, 14 April 1859, Valentine Museum files.

49. Ibid., 22 Aug. 1857, 1 Jan. 1859, Valentine Museum files.

50. Richmond *Daily Examiner*, 16 Dec. 1865, Valentine Museum files.

51. "Carter Nelson Berkeley" artist's file, Valentine Museum, which owns an 1881 Richmond armory scene by him and an 1894 view of Richmond.

52. Thomas Ellis, "Art in Richmond and Virginia in the Past," newspaper reprinting of a letter from Thomas H. Ellis to Miss Zitella Cocke, 1881, Virginia Historical Society Mss 5: 7 B8122:1, ff. 84–7.

53. William H. Gerdts, *The South and The Midwest* in *Art Across America: Two Centuries of Regional Painting, 1710–1920* (New York, London, and Paris, 1990), 27–28.

54. [Paulding], *Letters from the South*, 1: 90.

55. H. S. Parsons, "Contemporary English Accounts of the Destruction of Norfolk in 1776," *WMQ*, 2nd ser., 13 (1933): 220.

56. Francis Baily, *Journal of a Tour in Unsettled Parts of North America in 1796 and 1797*, ed. by Jack D. L. Holmes (London and Amsterdam, 1969), 21.

57. Priscilla Wakefield, *Excursions in North America* (London, 1810), 52, 60.

58. The sketches of Tidewater by Auguste Plée (1787–1825) are in the Museum of Natural History, Paris. See Parke Rouse, Jr., "The American Travels of a French Botanist," *Antiques* 96 (1969): 764–67.

59. "Diary of John Harvey Darrell," *Bermuda Historical Quarterly* 5 (1948): 143.

60. Emory A. Allen, *A Jolly Trip* (Cincinnati, 1891), 109–10.

61. Quoted in Carl Abbott, "Norfolk in the New Century: The Jamestown Exposition and Urban Boosterism," *VMHB* 85 (1977): 86–87.

62. Julian Street, *American Adventures* (New York, 1917), 254.

63. Kenneth Harris's obituary in the *Virginian-Pilot*, 15 May 1983. The *Richmond Times-Dispatch* of 10 March 1962 reported an exhibition of thirty-five of Harris's watercolors of Richmond.

64. Allen, *A Jolly Trip*, 86–87.

65. Ingersoll, *To the Shenandoah and Beyond*, 61.

66. Clayton Torrence, ed., "Arlington and Mount Vernon 1856, as Described in a Letter of Augusta Blanche Berard," *VMHB* 57 (1949): 155.

67. Quoted in Alistair Howe, *How Far from Austerlitz? Napoleon, 1805–1815* (New York, 1996), 384.

68. Isaac Weld, *Travels through the States of North America* (3rd ed., London, 1800), 1: 90.

69. Rev. S. L. M. Conser, *Virginia After the War* (Indianapolis, 1891), 9.

70. Mary Elizabeth Banner and Barbara Ellen Moore, "The Federal Government and the Changing Landscapes of Northeastern Virginia," *Bulletin of the Virginia Geographical Society* (April 1961): 16–19; "Glimpses of the Route from Alexandria to the Blue Ridge," *Southern Literary Messenger* 18 (Jan. 1852): 52.

71. Ingersoll, *To the Shenandoah and Beyond*, 56.

72. The drawings are at the Virginia Historical Society.

73. Rupert Martin, *Night Trick by O. Winston Link: Photographs of the Norfolk and Western Railway, 1955–1960* (London, 1983), 3.

74. Quoted in Simon Schama, *Landscape and Memory* (New York, 1995), 7; [Paulding], *Letters from the South*, 1: 102.

75. David Hunter Strother in Bryant, ed., *Picturesque America*, 1: 377–78.

76. John A. Cuthbert and Jessie Poesch, *David Hunter Strother: "One of the Best Draughtsmen the Country Possesses"* (Morgantown, W.Va., 1997), 94–95.

77. There are many early instances of such fears. An example is John Edwards Caldwell, who in 1808 wrote that "Timber is wasting rapidly throughout the state of Virginia." William M. E. Rachal, ed., *A Tour Through Part of Virginia, in the Summer of 1808*, by John Edwards Caldwell (Richmond, 1951), 13.

78. Bruce W. Chambers, *Art and Artists of the South: The Robert P. Coggins Collection* (Columbia, S.C., 1984), 17–18.

79. Clement Conger et al., *Treasures of State: Fine and Decorative Arts in the Diplomatic Reception Rooms of the U.S. Department of State* (New York, 1991), 437.

80. "William Louis Sonntag," *Cosmopolitan Art Journal* (3 Dec. 1858): 27; *History of the Great Western Sanitary Fair* (Cincinnati, 1864), both cited in Miller, *Empire of the Eye*, 138–42.

81. Quoted in Branch and Philippon, eds., *Height of Our Mountains*, 140.

82. Quoted in ibid., 156.

83. "Williamsburg and William and Mary College after the Battle of Williamsburg, May 5, 1862, as Seen by a Confederate Soldier," *WMQ*, 2nd ser., 13 (1933): 27.

84. Related sketches are in the Valentine Museum.

85. A painting of Drewry's Bluff by John Ross Key is in the Museum of the Confederacy.

86. Henry Chester Parry to his parents, 29 Dec. 1864, Virginia Historical Society.

87. *The Civil War: A Centennial Exhibition of Eyewitness Drawings* (Washington, D.C., 1961), 11–12, 136.

88. Quoted in Branch and Philippon, eds., *Height of Our Mountains*, 189.

89. E. L. Henry to Edward V. Valentine, 21 Sept. 1870, Valentine Museum. One of Henry's oil paintings of Westover was given to the Century Club in New York in lieu of the usual initiation fee. Another version dated 1869 is in the Corcoran Gallery, Washington, D.C.

90. Harold Holzer and Mark E. Nelly, Jr., *Mine Eyes Have Seen the Glory: The Civil War in Art* (New York, 1993), 26–27. The bustle at City Point did not last. In 1869 a visitor wrote, "But it is a shabby place now. Only one old wharf for the steamers to make a landing and no warehouses of any kind." Russell H. Conwell, *Magnolia Journey: A Union Veteran Revisits the Former Confederate States* (Tuscaloosa, Ala., 1974 repr. of 1869), 33.

91. James I. Robertson, Jr., ed., "English Views of the Civil War, a Unique Excursion to Virginia, April 2–8, 1865," *VMHB* 77 (1969): 209.

92. Richmond *Daily Examiner*, 30 July 1862; Richmond *Examiner* 5 and 27 Jan. 1864. Valentine Museum files.

93. Branch T. Archer to Frances Archer and Jane Segar Archer, 19 Dec. 1848, Archer Papers, Virginia Historical Society.

94. Nathaniel Beverly Tucker, *George Balcombe: A Novel* (2 vols., New York, 1836); George Tucker, *Valley of the Shenandoah, or, Memoirs of the Graysons* (2 vols., New York, 1824), 2: 31.

95. One visitor who would have thought a "retro" picture of Richmond unnecessary was Henry Latham, who in 1867 expressed the view that "it looks nearly a century older." Henry Latham, *Black and White: A Journal of Three Months' Tour in the United States* (Philadelphia, 1867), 100.

96. "Loungings in the Footprints of the Pioneers," *Harper's New Monthly Magazine* (May 1859): 743; W. S. B., "Landmarks in Lower Virginia," *Southern Literary Messenger* 33 (August 1861): 124. The wealth of antiquarian sites around Gloucester attracted the attention of several local artists in the twentieth century, among them Elizabeth Harwood ("Rosewell," "Higate," "Powhatan's Chimney"), Wing Jackson ("Rosewell," "Slave House at Fairfield"), and Nellie Coleman Turner Gray ("Marlfield," "Marlfield Graveyard," "Lawyer's Row at Gloucester"). Valentine Museum files.

97. "The Virginia Battlefields," in *As We Speed*, a railroad brochure at the Virginia Historical Society.

98. Conwell, *Magnolia Journey*, 7.

99. Henry Latham, *Black and White*, 105. A famous painting of the battle of the Crater by John A. Elder is at the Commonwealth Club in Richmond. Elder was an eyewitness to the explosion and sketched it immediately afterward.

100. Louise Smith Squier, *Sketches of Southern Scenes* (New York, 1885), 53; Hale, *We Discover the Old Dominion*, 253.

101. Latham, *Black and White*, 95.

102. Conwell, *Magnolia Journey*, 19, 23.

103. Conser, *Virginia After the War*, 11; Conwell, *Magnolia Journey*, 7; Latham, *Black and White*, 96, 105.

104. Sir George Campbell, *White and Black: The Outcome of a Visit to the United States* (New York, 1879), 281; Hale, *We Discover the Old Dominion*, 251.

105. Conwell, *Magnolia Journey*, 27.

106. "Virginia Art Spouts at Richmond's Spring Show," *Life* (1940): 67.

107. David Levi Strauss, "Sally Mann," *Artforum* (Feb. 1998): 16.

108. Sally Mann, *Mother Land* (New York, 1997), 5.

109. *Gone with the Wind*, technical shooting script of Wilbur Kurtz, 27 Feb. 1939, Atlanta History Center.

110. Thomas Nelson Page, "The Old Dominion," *Harper's New Monthly Magazine* (Christmas 1893): 20.

111. Sir George Campbell, *White and Black*, 280. Campbell based his observation on a train ride from Norfolk to Petersburg.

112. *The State*, 6 Oct. 1880, quoting the *New York Herald*. Valentine Museum files.

113. Judith Kahn, "Christmas with Eagles, Mason Neck," in *Uncommon Wealth: Essays on Virginia's Wild Places*, ed. Robert M. Riordan (Helena, Mont., 1999), 42–44.

114. Bryant, ed., *Picturesque America*, 1: preface and 75.

115. Ingersoll, *To the Shenandoah and Beyond*, 61.

116. "Character in Scenery: Its Relation to the National Mind," *Cosmopolitan Art Journal* 3 (Dec. 1858): 9, quoted in Miller, *Empire of the Eye*, 235.

117. Thomas Richards, *The Romance of the American Landscape* (New York, 1854), 48–49, 113–14, quoted in ibid., 238–40.

118. See the chapter "The Hudson River School in Eclipse" in John K. Howat et al., *American Paradise: The World of the Hudson River School* (New York, 1987), 71–90.

119. For a thorough and thoughtful analysis of the encyclopedic publication *Picturesque America*, see Sue Rainey, *Creating Picturesque America: Monument to the Natural and Cultural Landscape* (Nashville, 1995).

120. Bryant, ed., *Picturesque America*, 1: 337.

121. The Cumberland Gap lies at the juncture of the present state boundaries of Virginia, Tennessee, and Kentucky; today the town of Cumberland Gap lies just beyond the Virginia state line in Tennessee.

122. There is a sense of drama and an exaggeration of both terrain and atmospheric effects in the imagery in *Picturesque America* that served to keep alive the idea that the American landscape offered renewal. William Cullen Bryant, in the unpaginated preface, introduced these prints with the explanation that they "possess spirit, animation, and beauty, which give to the work of the artist a value higher than could be derived from mere topographical accuracy."

123. Ibid., 1: 232–35.

124. Ibid., 1: 338.

125. The artist of the 1830 engraving is unidentified; the work is titled "Natural Tunnel, Scott County, Virginia" and measures 5 x 4 inches.

126. Bryant, ed., *Picturesque America*, 1: 342.

127. Bruce Stutz, "Ridge, Valley, and River: A Journey to the New," quoted in Branch and Philippon, eds., *Height of Our Mountains*, 332–33.

128. Constable's drawing is owned by the Virginia Historical Society; he pictures the landscape straight on, with no figures included.

129. Bryant, ed., *Picturesque America*, 1: 356.

130. Ibid., 1: 352–54.

131. For a study of Woodward's fifty-year career in art, which carried him to many parts of the United States and to Europe and the Holy Land, see Sue Rainey and Roger Stein, *John Douglas Woodward: Shaping the Landscape Image, 1865–1910* (Charlottesville, Va., 1997).

132. Of course the Balcony Falls region had changed at least a little by the 1870s. The tourist Edward Pollard was able to visit; he called the falls "surpassingly picturesque" (Pollard, *The Virginia Tourist* [Philadelphia, 1870], 49).

133. Nicholas B. Wainwright, "Augustus Köllner, Artist," *Pennsylvania Magazine of History and Biography* 84 (1960): 346.

134. Like Sonntag, Johnston produced a now lost series of four paintings entitled "Progress," in 1859; the first image depicted wilderness and the final canvas was a scene of civilization. As with Sonntag, this shows that after mid-century artists viewed progress through the wilderness only in positive terms, a change from earlier, and that Johnston's Blue Ridge scene was meant to signal a beginning. See "John R. Johnston," *Cosmopolitan Art Journal* 3 (Sept. 1859): 178, cited in Miller, *Empire of the Eye*, 144–45.

135. *Letters from the South*, 1: 108.

136. Andrew Burnaby, *Travels through the Middle Settlements in North-America*, quoted in Branch and Philippon, eds., *Height of Our Mountains*, 98.

137. Kenneth Clark, *Landscape into Art* (New York, 1976), 53.

138. William Gilmore Simms, *Southward Ho! A Spell of Sunshine* (New York, 1854), quoted in Branch and Philippon, eds., *Height of Our Mountains*, 175.

139. The term "visions of order" is borrowed from Richard Weaver's book *Visions of Order: The Cultural Crisis of Our Time* (Baton Rouge, La., 1964), where the southern landscape is discussed as a "refuge of sentiments and values." Rick Stewart, in *Painting in the South*, 106, was the first to apply Weaver's concepts about postbellum thought to southern landscape painting.

140. Inness was in Goochland in 1884 and possibly later as well; among the half-dozen works by him that are Virginia scenes, at least one is dated 1889. Another landscape with "West Virginia" in its title suggests that he may have moved through different parts of the commonwealth. See Leroy Ireland, *The Works of George Inness: An Illustrated Catalogue Raisonné* (Austin, Tex., 1965), 277–84.

141. George Inness, "A Painter on Painting," *Harper's New Monthly Magazine* 56 (Feb. 1878): 461, quoted in Howat et al., *Hudson River School*, 236.

142. See John I. H. Baur, *Theodore Robinson, 1852–1896* (New York, 1946), 91. Robinson's "House in Virginia" of 1893 is pictured in Sotheby's *American Paintings, Drawings and Sculpture*, sale 7320, 27 May 1999, lot 77-A, p. 55.

143. Eileen Lambert, "A Walk in the Forest Primeval," quoted in Branch and Philippon, eds., *Height of Our Mountains*, 307.

144. Napier Shelton, *The Nature of the Shenandoah*, quoted in ibid., 294.

145. Franklin D. Roosevelt, "Address at the Dedication of Shenandoah National Park," quoted in ibid., 237.

146. William Carlos Williams, "An Essay on Virginia," quoted in ibid., 230.

147. See the *New York Times* Book Review of 4 May 1930, which pictures two of Lankes's Virginia woodcuts.

148. *Letters and Poems Written by Edith Mabel Porter Kimball* (n.p., 1920), 19.

149. *Richmond News-Leader*, 2 March 1938. The trustee was a former Richmonder living in New York, Mrs. Thelma Wheaton.

150. Hamner, quoted in Branch and Philippon, eds., *Height of Our Mountains*, 268.

151. Adèle Clark, quoted in the *Richmond News-Leader*, 24 Sept. 1982.

152. Ellen Glasgow, quoted in Branch and Philippon, eds., *Height of Our Mountains*, 231.

153. Franklin D. Roosevelt, "Address at the Dedication of Shenandoah National Park," quoted in Branch and Philippon, eds., *Height of Our Mountains*, 237.

154. Robert Gwathmey, quoted in *Painting in the South*, 129.

155. Gwathmey's vocabulary, which includes elements seen here like the tombstones and church, is fully discussed in Michael Kammen and Robert Gwathmey, *The Life and Art of a Passionate Observer* (Chapel Hill, N.C., and London, 1999), where the artist's entire career is analyzed and put into context.

156. Roy Proctor, "A Portrait of Theresa Pollak," *Richmond Times-Dispatch*, 18 Oct. 1998.

157. Colt, quoted in "Retrospective Honors Retiring Art

Professor Jeanne Campbell," *University of Richmond Magazine* (Summer 1983): 21–22.

158. Pamela Hemenway Simpson, *Marion Montague Junkin, 1905–1977* (Lexington, Va., 1977), 5–7.

159. Katie Letcher Lyle, "Only in the Land of Goshen; Goshen Pass," in Riordan, ed., *Uncommon Wealth*, 166–76.

160. Janet Lembke, "And This Way the Water Comes Down at the Gorge," in ibid., 212.

161. *The Journal of Philip Vickers Fithian*, quoted in Branch and Philippon, eds., *Height of Our Mountains*, 101.

162. Cited in ibid., 249.

163. Murray, from *Wild Wings*, 1947, a collection of children's nature essays, quoted in ibid., 248.

164. Teale, in *North with the Spring* (1951), quoted in ibid., 255.

165. Two examples of conservation activities in the West cited to the authors by landscapist Marjorie Portnow are those by artists in Santa Barbara and Boulder, beginning in the mid-1980s. For the former, see Thomas Bolt, "Painters as Preservationists: Members of the Open Airing Klub of Santa Barbara, California, organize exhibitions of their paintings in order to raise money and increase public awareness of the endangered land that they depict in their pictures," *American Artist* (Oct. 1988): 72–77. In Virginia, Guy Crittenden, both a landscapist and a hunter, is a member of Ducks Unlimited, which saves land. John Barber writes that his "intent is to capture all threatened and vanishing aspects of the [Chesapeake] Bay. . . . I strive to bring attention to the need for protecting this great natural resource" (artist's statement quoted in *Presidents Collection, Virginia State Bar* [Richmond, Va., 1993], 16). Sharon Yates, a New England painter, accepted a fellowship to paint at Roland Farm, a nature conservancy in Fauquier County.

166. Portnow, conversation with the authors.

167. Philip Geiger, artist's statement, quoted in *Presidents Collection, Virginia State Bar* (1993), 38. The full statement is, "In painting, I want to yield to something outside of myself. I am most challenged to move beyond my habits of perception by pursuing the specific vanishing visual event. Really seeing the actual unique strangeness of nature is a never-achieved goal that gives me the best chance of recovering and transmitting real emotion through pictorial means."

168. David Summers, "Philip Geiger," *Arts Magazine* 60 (March 1986): 106.

169. Geiger, letter to the authors.

170. Portnow, conversation with the authors.

171. Richard Crozier, statement provided by the artist, as quoted in John Arthur, *Spirit of Place: Contemporary Landscape Painting and the American Tradition* (Boston, 1989).

172. Richard Crozier, statement provided by the artist, as quoted in Richard Crozier with Thomas Bolt, *Inventing the Landscape* (Bolt, Watson-Guptill Press, 1989), 8–9.

173. Robert Rosenblum, "Art: Contemporary Romantic Landscapes," *Architectural Digest* (May 1993): 193–95, 230.

174. Richard Waller and Ephraim Rubenstein, *Ephraim Rubenstein: The Rilke Series* (Richmond and New York, 1994), an exhibition catalogue, n.p.

175. Rosenblum, "Romantic Landscapes," 230.

176. Waller and Rubenstein, *The Rilke Series*, n.p.

177. Elliott, letter to the authors.

178. Margo Crutchfield, *Un/Common Ground: Virginia Artists 1990* (Richmond, 1990), n.p.

179. Shatter, statement provided for the authors.

180. For the new Hudson River painters, see Doug Alderfer-Abbott and Judy Alderfer-Abbott, *Enduring Vision: Contemporary Painters in the Tradition of the Hudson River School* (Schenectady, N.Y., 1999), n.p., a brochure for an exhibition at Union College. The curators write, "This continuum remains unbroken today. Many artists still derive their inspiration from the landscape, altered by man as it might be." For the national scene, see John Arthur, *Green Woods & Crystal Waters: The American Landscape Tradition* (Tulsa, Okla., 1999), a 175-page catalogue for an exhibition at the Philbrook Museum of Art. Arthur presents the work of eighty-nine contemporary landscapists who paint in a variety of traditional styles and who all approach the landscape with reverence akin to that of their nineteenth-century predecessors; he states that "for every painter or graphic artist included, three or four others of equal merit have been omitted" (p. 11).

181. Kenneth Clark, *Civilisation, A Personal View* (New York and Evanston, Ill., 1969), 269–91. See also Kenneth Clark, *The Romantic Rebellion, Romantic versus Classic Art* (New York, Evanston, Ill., San Francisco, and London, 1973), 280–82.

182. Quoted in Clark, *Romantic Rebellion*, 282, and Clark, *Civilisation*, 279.

183. Annie Dillard, *Pilgrim at Tinker Creek*, quoted in Branch and Philippon, eds., *Height of Our Mountains*, 281–90.

184. Dillard, *Pilgrim at Tinker Creek*, quoted in ibid., 281–90.

185. Yates, quoted in Alan Gussow, *A Sense of Place: The Artist and the American Land* (Washington, D.C., 1997), 50.

186. Frank Levering and Wanda Urbanska, *Simple Living: One Couple's Search for a Better Life*, quoted in Branch and Philippon, eds., *Height of Our Mountains*, 321.

187. Clark, *Romantic Rebellion*, 147, 153.

188. Cited in Clark, *Landscape into Art*, 61–64.

189. Dommisse, quoted in Roy Proctor, "Great Outdoors Steals Artist's Heart," *Richmond News-Leader*, 12 Sept. 1991, A-3.

190. Berry, Racenis, letters to the authors.

191. Berry, letter to the authors.

192. Freed, letter to the authors.

193. Elizabeth Seydel Morgan, "Wild in the City: The Urban James River," in Riordan, ed., *Uncommon Wealth*, 177–85.

194. Christopher Camuto, in *A Fly Fisherman's Blue Ridge*, quoted in Branch and Philippon, eds., *Height of Our Mountains*, 312.

195. Donald Culross Peattie, *The Great Smokies and the Blue Ridge*, quoted in ibid., 245.

196. When Beyer devoted two of the lithographs in his *Album of Virginia* to views *from* the Peaks of Otter, the wilderness scenery that he depicted seems only monotonous to our eyes, so empty is it of interesting visual elements. Beyer's purpose with these views was to suggest the sublimity that is experienced there, but as we saw earlier, that feeling does not transfer easily to art.

197. Henry Ruffner, *Judith Bensaddi*, quoted in Branch and Philippon, eds., *Height of Our Mountains*, 166–68. Washington College is now Washington and Lee University. Students there would hike nearby House Mountain (shown by Seth Eastman in fig. 4.6) and camp overnight there in order to enjoy "the morning beauties of the scene, which are by far the most interesting."

198. Arthur, *Green Woods & Crystal Waters*, 103–104, 114.

199. These ideas are discussed in Howard Risatti, *The Mountain Lake Workshop: Artists in Locale* (Richmond, Va., 1996), 2–8, 11–18.

200. Peirce F. Lewis, "Axioms for Reading the Landscape," in Donald W. Meinig, ed., *The Interpretation of Ordinary Landscapes: Geographical Essays* (New York, 1979), 12.

201. James Tice Moore to James C. Kelly, 2 April 1999, Virginia Historical Society.

INDEX